God Loves You:
Some Restrictions May Apply

(And Many Other Christian Dilemmas)

T O N Y   D A V I S

PAGE PUBLISHING, INC.
New York, NY

First originally published by Page Publishing, Inc. 2019

ISBN 978-1-64462-186-8 (Paperback)
ISBN 978-1-64462-187-5 (Digital)

Printed in the United States of America

To the theists: I began writing this not in hopes of proving you wrong but in hopes that I was wrong and you could show me how… I'm still waiting.

CONTENTS

Part I—The Genesis of Doubt

Introduction..9

Chapter 1: Devolution of Faith..............................29

Chapter 2: Epistemology: How We Know What We
            Know (and How We Know You Can't Really
            Know What You Claim to Know) 68

Part II—Failure of Reason and Lack of Evidence

Chapter 3: Cognitive Dissonance: The True Nature of
            the Good Book..89

Chapter 4: Refutations of Christian Apologetics (and
            Other Good Reasons for Rejecting Bad Ideas)........174

Part III—Why Preach about Unbelief?

Chapter 5: Okay, so If You Don't Believe in God, Why
            Preach about It? (The Intrinsic Value of Truth).......229

Chapter 6: "Harmless Beliefs" Aren't Necessarily Harmless 277

Chapter 7: Conclusion: Significance Redux 298

Appendices

Appendix A: Comparison of Gospel Accounts of the Trial,
            Crucifixion, and Resurrection Stories of Jesus.........307

Appendix B: Comparison of Gospel Genealogies.......................309

Appendix C: Data Comparing Religiosity with Human
            Well-Being 310

References 313

PART I

The Genesis of Doubt

INTRODUCTION

Beloved, let us love one another: for love is of
God; and every one that loveth is born of God,
and knoweth God.

—1 John 4:7, King James Version

I have cut off the nations: their towers are deso-
late; I made their streets waste, that none passeth
by: their cities are destroyed, so that there is no
man, that there is none inhabitant.

I said, Surely thou wilt fear me, thou wilt
receive instruction; so their dwelling should not
be cut off, howsoever I punished them: but they
rose early, and corrupted all their doings.

Therefore wait ye upon me, saith the LORD,
until the day that I rise up to the prey: for my
determination is to gather the nations, that I
may assemble the kingdoms, to pour upon them
mine indignation, even all my fierce anger: for all
the earth shall be devoured with the fire of my
jealousy.

—Zephaniah 3:6–8, King James Version

God loves you. He loves me too. He loves all of us. In fact, one
of the very few perfect, unconditional, and infinite things
in the universe is the love God has for us. I was taught in
Sunday school that God's infinite, perfect love was not just for you
and me but for every one of us—living, dead, and yet to be born.
But there is a catch—a very big catch, in fact. According to Christian
doctrine, if the world were to end right now, well over five billion
of the people alive today would go to hell, where they would suf-

fer unimaginable torture for all eternity—and this is in accordance with God's perfect plan. Realizing this logical outcome of Christian dogma was one of the very first steps to my path away from religion. There is, of course, very much more to the story.

This is a book about three overarching themes. First, a personal journey from faith to reason—basically, how I went from Christian to nonbeliever and why. Second, it is about how so much of what so many (especially true believers) think about religion simply is not supported by facts, evidence, reason, or logic. Third and finally, this is a book about why this is such a profoundly important subject that we should all care about deeply. These three themes will, of necessity, not necessarily flow one from the other as day follows night but will often be intertwined, backtracked, revisited, and overlap. One tactic I will use to illustrate these themes is to point out key dilemmas inherent in religious belief generally and in Christian belief specifically. We have already begun delving into one of these dilemmas, as you will see.

For now, back to the opening thought two paragraphs previous, that most of those alive today would suffer unimaginable torture, by God's own design, if the world ended today. Actually, there is an easy case to make that far more than five billion people would actually go to hell to suffer this torture. Of the roughly seven and a half billion people alive today, just barely over two billion *claim* to be Christian. If Christianity is the "right" religion, that means almost five and a half billion people are going to hell because they have not accepted Christ as their personal savior. Christianity is the most widely accepted religion in the world—for now anyway. Islam is growing at a rate faster than that of Christianity, and according to Samuel Huntington, Islam will have 5 percent more adherents that Christianity by 2025 (Huntington 1996). If another less popular religion proved to be right, then the number of those going to hell (or whatever that religion's version of hell might be) could be much higher. That is, unless of course, the one religion that happened to be right one turned out to not have a hell.

Clearly, this is far from a happy idea one might expect from a perfect, loving god. Later I will address an idea espoused by some that all the bad parts of the Bible, primarily in the Old Testament, were changed with the arrival of Jesus—Prince of Peace—but consider that even Judaism doesn't subscribe to the horrible and unjust idea of eternal, infinite, punishment for finite sins (neither does Islam by the way). Jesus, it seems, ushered in the idea of eternal punishment (see Matthew 18:8 for eternity in hell). Even in the religions for which there is no eternal hell, however, there is often some sort of extreme punishment for simple nonbelief. In any event, even if you "believe" in the world's most common religion, you hold a minority belief.

Consider also that a huge number of the 2.2 billion who *claim* to be Christians do so as a matter of social identification only. They often do not actually practice the rituals or necessarily even believe the claims of the religion they identify as their own. It may also be problematic that even within Christianity there are more denominations than there are sentences in the Bible, and surely not all of those denominations are "doing Christianity" correctly. It seems entirely likely that even large numbers of Christians may also be hellbound. As a Southern Baptist in my youth, imagine how disconcerting it was to visit a church of Christ only to hear that I was at risk of going to hell for having the wrong view of Christianity. For the sake of this discussion, however, let's be exceedingly generous and not count a single person who at least *claims* to be Christian among those who will go to hell. That still leaves most of us out in the cold—or rather in the extreme heat.

If we continue this line of reasoning, we must be concerned not only about those who are alive today but the great many who came before us. One of the first things that struck me when reading Dante Alighieri's *The Divine Comedy* was how Dante's guide and companion through hell and purgatory, Virgil (Publius Vergilius Maro, the great Roman poet who penned the *Aeneid*) (Dante, 2008 Compilation), could not lead Dante through Paradise. Due to the accident of being born in 70 BC, Virgil came before Christ and as such could not have been saved through grace. The Population Reference Bureau estimates that there have been about 108 billion humans (as of October 2011) in the history of our species (Haub 2011). If, as Christian dogma suggests, it is only through accepting

Christ that we may enter the kingdom of heaven, then hell will be a very full place indeed.

This may only be a concern if the more fundamentalist strain of Christianity is the valid belief system. By fundamentalist, I mean those who actually believe the words of the Bible, not just what they want to be true. Some Christians have told me that you don't actually go to hell just for not believing in and worshiping Jesus; you only have to live a good life. This even seems to be the position of none other than Billy Graham in his final years. I am not sure how sincere a belief this is, however. If you reverse engineer this line of thought and ask believers why you too should believe in Christ, the answer is normally because that is how you get to heaven. Some Christians may try to avoid the logical outcome of their beliefs on this matter and assert that good people won't actually go to hell, but this is not what the party line of their coreligionists has been for most of the past two thousand years, nor is it today. The Christian threat of hell has been one of the strongest sales tactics ever used in the history of religion. Anyone who doubts this need only attend a good old-fashioned Southern Baptist sermon on any given Sunday.

If it is true that some Christians sincerely believe that just being a good person is enough and it turns out God, heaven, and hell are real, then I hope they are right. There are many good people in the world that just didn't get the benefit of Christ's teachings or whose conditions were such that they couldn't readily accept the "truth" of God's message. Eternal torture is not a just result of this outcome. Only a cruel and malevolent god would allow such a situation.

As mentioned earlier, I will talk often about the dilemmas inherent in religious thinking and herein lies the first of many dilemmas faced by the true believer. You either need to believe in Christ to avoid going to hell or you do not. Most Christians seem to both believe this (that you must believe in Christ to go to heaven) and deny the consequences (don't believe and you go to hell) of this belief at the same time. Very often when I talk to Christian friends, even clergy, about the unjust nature of going to hell forever for thought crimes, they try to back away from that idea. I am talking here about clearly competing claims from theists: (1) only through belief in Christ can you achieve salvation and (2) good, innocent unbelievers don't necessarily go to hell because God is loving and just. The inescapable fact is that if the first premise is true, then you do, in fact, go to hell for not believing in Christ. Further, if God is indeed just, then you deserve that fate for not believing. God is not bad for sending you to hell. You go to hell because you are bad for not believing. After all, any truly just god would not punish the innocent. Right? No, if God is just, and you go to hell, it is because you deserve it.

This raised troubling questions for me when I was a young Christian. Among them, if you don't go to hell simply for not believing in Christ, then why is belief in Christ so important? For that matter, why was Christ even necessary in the first place? Any attempt to argue one's way out of this dilemma only leads to the theist's painting himself into an exegetical corner. For many centuries, belief in Christ was deemed so important that to admit a lack of belief could result in torture and even capital punishment in this world and not only the next. This was necessary, so went the thinking, because while torture in this world may be bad, eternity in hell is much worse, and the only way to avoid that eternity in hell was to accept Jesus Christ even if torture was required to secure this acceptance.

Well-meaning Christians have often challenged me on this point. "Where do you get the idea that you go to hell just for not accepting Jesus Christ?" they often ask, or they may say, "I don't believe that!" But consider what is perhaps the most famous Bible verse of them all—John 3:16, "For God so loved the world, that he gave his only begotten Son, that whosoever believeth in him should not perish, but have everlasting life." What are we to take from "whosoever believeth in him should not perish, but have everlasting life"? Only the most incurious person would not wonder at the fate of whoever believeth *not* in him. The Bible verse in question does not say anything about a general state of grace that was bestowed on all humankind as a result of Christ's death and resurrection; it states "that whosoever believeth in him" gets the golden ticket to heaven. Of course, there are a great many Christians who are not at all shy about saying clearly that going to hell is exactly what happens if you don't believe in Jesus.

While many Christians never put much thought into this, consider how repugnant a belief this is from the perspective of the non-Christian. If you exercise human intellect and the outcome of that exercise is that you don't see any rational reason to believe in God or even that you believe in God but not that Jesus is divine or believe in a different god altogether, then you will not only be punished but tortured for all eternity. Assume that, like me, you could no longer pretend to believe in God and professed yourself a nonbeliever at about age twenty. Further, assume you are very lucky to live to be one hundred[1] and never again change your beliefs with respect to God. Then you will have not believed in God for eighty years when you die. For this eighty years of believing what seemed logical for you to believe based on the available evidence, you get not an eighty-year sentence in a Third World country penitentiary (oh, how lucky that would be by comparison!) but an infinity of the most agonizing torture imaginable. You would be burned alive only to have your flesh grow back, only to be burned off yet again and again and again. Infinite punishment for finite crimes is not justice by any reasonable measure. It is worth remembering that if God is indeed real and in control of everything, he not only designed this unjust system of reward and punishment, he is responsible for the lack of evidence that led to your lack of belief. He is culpable in your crime of unbelief.

Among the poor unfortunates doomed to hell are the pitiable Hindus who were unlucky enough to have been born and raised in a predominantly Hindu nation. Also doomed would be most of the populations in countries like Japan, China, Thailand, and Denmark unfortunate as they all are having been born in predominantly Shinto, Buddhist, or largely atheist nations. After all, circumstance

---

[1] Michael Shermer, in his book *Why People Believe Weird Things*, shares some interesting statistics on centenarians. Among them is "only one person will live to be 115 years old for every 2,100 million (2.1 billion) people" (Shermer 1997).

of birth is the single biggest determinant of religious affiliation. And of course among the damned would be those of us who were cursed with a skeptical nature that leads us to accept most propositions only in proportion to the available evidence in spite of what your popular culture may be. A major factor in my own deconversion was that I have been fortunate enough to know a large number of wonderful people from many countries, many religions, myriad background; and so far, I've yet to meet a group of people who deserve eternal torture. I have also found no reason to believe Christians are any better or more deserving of eternal paradise than any of the non-Christians I have come to know.

It is abundantly clear that religions are not normally chosen based on any clear-thinking analysis of evidence for and against the various choices. On this, Richard Dawkins wrote, "No doubt soaring cathedrals, stirring music, moving stories and parables, help a bit. But by far the most important variable determining your religion is the accident of birth" (Dawkins, *Viruses of the Mind*, 1993). I agree with Dawkins, and a deeper discussion on the nature of belief follows in chapter 2.

As a brief aside, on the issue of soaring cathedrals, I have actually heard it argued that breathtaking architecture, such as Notre Dame or St. Peter's Basilica, is somehow evidence for the truth of theism, though I have yet to hear a good reason for just why that is specifically. Somehow, architecture of such grandeur is proof, to some, of God's divine hand at work. I have been told this personally by more than one religions friend or relative. The beauty of such structures moves me to be sure, but architecture is a science, not a religion, and there are no blueprints for beautiful buildings in the Bible. I do have Christian friends who argue that beautiful cathedrals are somehow evidence of God. I remind them that I have visited Angkor Wat, the Taj Mahal, the Tian Ten Buddha, the Sultan Ahmed Mosque, and the Great Pyramid of Giza (to name only a few examples). These are all strikingly beautiful but have nothing at all to do with Jesus. I doubt Christians would see these amazing structures as evidence for the truth of Buddhism, Islam, or Khufu.

Herein lies the second dilemma with respect to beliefs held by friends of religion. Most true believers actually can't articulate why they believe. They not only have no idea why they believe, the degree to which they claim to believe is often grossly out of proportion, inversely so, to the evidence, and they don't know why that is either. If you ever doubt this, just ask a representative sampling of theists why they believe, and the odds are you will get a gratuitous assertion that "it's just true" without any justification for why they actually believe it's true. If it is not readily apparent why this is a dilemma, consider that most religious people feel obligated to share their religious convictions with others because this is the most important set of beliefs in their lives in spite of the fact that they can rarely tell you clearly and convincingly why they believe. I grew up in Alabama, and it is not at all hard to find a die-hard Bama fan who will tell you Bear Bryant was the greatest college football coach in history and may even tell you exactly why—six national, one South Western Conference, and fourteen SEC championships, for example. But for the most important belief, that God is real and Jesus is the way to eternal salvation, you get "Well, it's just true" or "The Bible says so."

"It says so in the Bible" is often the reason first given for belief. However, when a true believer points to the Bible as their justification, just ask some of the questions raised in chapter 3 of this book. You may (or may not) be surprised that most good Christian folk have no idea at all that the "Good Book" actually sanctions rape, genocide, slavery, and a whole host of other bad behaviors. The Bible is replete with internal contradictions. It is not in accordance with the best evidence we have available for how the universe actually works; it is of questionable origin, and the scholarly consensus is that much of what is in the Bible was forged by unknown authors long after the original texts were written.

That most Christians really have little idea what is really in the Bible yet rely on it completely as the only source document for their beliefs is dilemma number 3. Granted, dilemma 3 is closely related to dilemma 2, but I treat them separately in this case primarily because there is so much to say about different aspects of these two ideas. While relying on the Bible as your excuse for belief when not knowing what is in the Bible may equate to not really knowing why you believe, I also treat this as a separate dilemma because there is a subtle difference between not knowing why you believe and believing because you think the Bible is "proof" (when really the Bible is the claim, not the evidence for a claim) while not knowing what is actually in the Bible. I will elaborate on these challenges in chapter 3.

In chapter 4, I deconstruct and refute many of the most popular arguments used by believers to justify their belief in God. It is instructive to consider that it is often only after each of these arguments have been successfully refuted that believers fall back on faith as the final argument. Often they will even proudly state that the fact that there is no evidence is one of the things that make faith so important, but this position is often only taken after the claims of proof in the Bible and apologetic arguments (again, to be mentioned in chapter 4) have been shown to be unsupportable. Faith, it is claimed, is what is most important, not evidence, reason, or logic. It is difficult to overstate the importance of this point. The very nature of the assertion that faith is what is most important, especially in light of the fact that the faith card is normally only played after all other options have been exhausted, tells us something very important about the nature of religious belief.

The dilemmas of not really knowing why you believe, coupled with an absolute reliance upon a book of striking moral ambiguity and consistent unreliability for the specifics of belief, segue nicely into the fourth Christian dilemma. God is claimed by his followers to be all-powerful, all-knowing, all-merciful, and infinitely good; but with all the evil in the world, we can't really take seriously the notion that a god could be all these things. In fact, the world works exactly as we should expect if this were in fact not true. If we accept for the sake of argument that God is real, all available information we have on the nature of this God points to a god who is not all-powerful and all-knowing or is clearly not all-merciful and infinitely good. How is it that a god who is infinitely powerful, all-knowing, and infinitely good would allow a situation in which most of his dearest creations would suffer such pain and injustice in this world only to then face unspeakably cruel torture for all eternity after this life ends? It is worth noting here that I am making a huge concession just for the sake of this discussion and not even addressing for the moment the evidence for God's existence, which is very little and very unconvincing. I am talking here about what the Bible says about the nature of God, not about the lack of evidence for God's existence in the first place.

This fourth dilemma is in no way a new idea. Like so many other concerns I have with religious faith, after learning more about what others have said throughout history, I find that I am far from alone. In fact, one of the most famous challenges to the infinitely good, powerful, and benevolent nature of God was made three centuries before Christ in the riddle posed by Epicurus: "Is God willing to prevent evil, but not able? Then he is not omnipotent. Is he able, but not willing? Then is he malevolent. Is he both able and willing? Then whence commeth evil? Is he neither able nor willing? Then why call him God?"[2]

A personal encounter with a small group in Seoul, South Korea, can (hopefully) bring these first four dilemmas into sharp focus, personalize them a bit, and introduce a fifth dilemma (the hurt feelings card). This little story will also introduce something I talk about more in chapter 1, something I call "drive-by proselytizations." I was invited to meet this group by a mutual friend who wanted to introduce me to several of his friends.

During the course of getting acquainted, one of those present asked where I go to church. I at first thought this was just "making conversation," but when I replied that I don't go to church, she was clearly bothered. Not wanting to get into a religious discussion with

---

[2] Thanks to Professor Russell Burgos for a citation on the Riddle of Epicurus. I was struggling to find a reference, and he provided the following: "The Epicurean Paradox (Riddle of Epicurus) was credited to Epicurus, though it does not appear in any of his surviving writings, by the Christian theologian Lactantius in the Treatise on the Anger of God, in which Lactantius criticizes what he *claims* was the paradox proposed by Epicurus. To this day, it remains known as the Epicurean Paradox though it is credited *via* Lactantius." See Norman Wentworth De Witt, *Epicurus and His Philosophy* (University of Minnesota Press, 1954), p. 276.

this new group of nascent friends, I quickly changed the subject. She kept bringing us back to the church discussion, however. "Why don't you go to church?" "Do you not have a church yet in Korea?" "Do you want to come to my church?"

This has often happened to me in the United States, but this was a first for me in a foreign country, so I decided to try something that had often ended similar discussions in America. I asked her, "Why is it important that I go to church?" At first, she looked at me as if I'd asked a ridiculous question. After a brief pause, she replied, "Well, you want to go to heaven, don't you?" It seemed a teachable moment had presented itself. Without letting her see what I was writing, I made a brief note on a napkin and quickly turned it over and then asked her a couple more questions. Before I asked the questions, however, I stressed to her that it was very important to remember that she was the one who initiated this conversation and that try as I might it would be very difficult to have this conversation without feelings being hurt. I asked her if she was really sure she wanted to discuss this and that I was more than happy to talk about anything else. No, this was important, she insisted. I then took a second napkin, wrote one additional note, turned it over, and continued.

"Can't I go to heaven if I am a really good person and treat others well even if I don't happen to believe in Jesus or go to church?" I asked. She replied that I couldn't. Next I asked her, "If I believe in Jesus with all my heart but in most other respects I am actually a rude and insensitive person, can I still go to heaven?" Her reply was that not all Christians are nice people necessarily, but if they have a relationship with Jesus, then they go to heaven. She also elaborated that a relationship with Jesus tends to make one a kind person (something not necessarily supported by the evidence). Being nice, she insisted, was not what gets one into heaven; it is only a personal belief in Jesus that can achieve that miracle.

My next query for her dealt with the nature of forgiveness. "So if I live a really terrible life and do lots of really horrible things but then accept Jesus before my death and ask forgiveness, can I go to heaven?" She replied that, of course, I could and that Jesus can forgive anything. I avoided the temptation here to point out that there is actually one "unforgivable" sin in the Bible that even Jesus can't absolve. According to Matthew 12:31, "Wherefore I say unto you, All manner of sin and blasphemy shall be forgiven unto men: but the blasphemy against the Holy Ghost shall not be forgiven unto men." Then in Mark 3:29: "But he that shall blaspheme against the Holy Ghost hath never forgiveness, but is in danger of eternal damnation."

I then offered a hypothetical situation. I stressed to her than I, of course, have no way at all of knowing that this actually happened and conceded that it probably didn't, but what if Adolf Hitler fell to his knees just before he died and sincerely admitted the horrible things he'd done and asked Jesus for forgiveness. Could he go to heaven? After she replied that he could, I turned over the napkin to show that I had written the names Adolf Hitler and Anne Frank, and beside Hitler's name, I had the word *heaven*. Beside Anne Frank's name, I had the word *hell*. This is because if hers was an accurate description of what Christians believe (and of course, I can only go on what Christians like her tell me they believe), then this is what would result in our hypothetical situation.

When confronted with this logical outcome of her belief system, this Christian lady tried to argue that I simply didn't understand, but it was clear that in her view of her own religion Hitler could indeed go to heaven if only he (who claimed to be a Christian by the way) asked forgiveness for his sins and Anne Frank, as a Jew who did not accept Jesus, would surely go to hell. She tried to argue that Anne Frank wouldn't have to go to hell, *necessarily*, but herein lies the first of the fatal flaws to my new friend's position. As a Jew, Anne Frank would not accept that Jesus was to be worshipped as God, and for most of our conversation to this point, this lady's position was that I should believe in Jesus specifically because that is the *only* way I can go to heaven (dilemma 1).

When I asked why she believed these things to be true, this Christian lady could offer nothing beyond "It's just true" and "The Bible says so." When I asked how she knows the Bible is true, she said, "Because it is God's word." And when I asked how she knows that, she said, "It says this in the Bible." She clearly had no sound rationale for her beliefs other than blind faith, yet she believed with all her heart (dilemma 2), and she was compelled to get me to believe it also. In stating that Jesus can forgive anything in spite of the fact that two different Gospel passages say otherwise, she demonstrated her lack of understanding of what is actually in the Bible (dilemma 3). Finally, the notion that an all-powerful, all-knowing, and all-loving god would not only create a universe knowing full well that Hitler would come to power and Anne Frank would be killed as a result but also that Hitler could possibly go to heaven and Anne Frank would surely go to hell is unthinkable (dilemma 4).

After trying to equivocate, make excuses, argue that I was simply taking things out of context or I just didn't understand, this otherwise nice lady resorted to playing the "hurt feelings" card. She asked why I felt the need to take God away from other people. Why couldn't I just leave people alone to believe and not try to force my unbelief on others? She literally said it was rude for me to do that. I then turned over the other napkin to reveal my second note, "You will almost certainly forget that it was you who insisted on this conversation and will accuse me of being rude." This is the fifth dilemma, the "hurt feelings" card. Theists are often resolute enough in their beliefs that they will approach strangers in order to proselytize, even threaten them with hell, yet are unable to not play the hurt feelings card when their evidence is effectively refuted by a nonbeliever. If you want to talk about God that is fine, but don't be offended when others don't agree with you or if you are not allowed to change the subject when things don't go your way. Religion has been given a free pass for so long and by so many that to simply ask legitimate questions and not blindly agree with religious proclamations one is labeled militant, rude, strident, or somehow evil.

An interesting thing happened while writing this book. My original intent was to understand why so many truly intelligent, genuinely kind, and sincerely decent people actually believe things on insufficient evidence but also know so little about the evidence they think they actually have. Let me be very clear on this point, most of the religious people I have personally known have been intelligent and *normally* rational individuals. I did not feel it was just a matter of me being smarter than they were (at least not all of them). What were they seeing that I was not? I actually felt, at least on a certain level, that I might find the evidence that would lead me to once again believe. I actually wanted to believe in God, at least initially. Thus far, however, no evidence has been forthcoming, and my search for that evidence has truly been sincere. At every turn, I have found the arguments lacking any persuasive power at all. I have also found that it is only by ignoring much of what is actually in the only rule book that Christians have (the Bible) that they can actually be truly kind and decent human beings, something I will explore in detail in chapter 3. This caused me to modify one aspect of my search. I would still like there to be a god and an afterlife—I love life and would, of course, like to live forever. If, however, the only options available to me is that there be no God at all or the god of the Bible is real, exactly as the Bible tells about him, then I would rather there be no God. Of course, what I want is irrelevant. What truly matters is what is real, and we should seek to understand what is true, not what we wish to be true.

One of the most-often-levied accusations against those who don't believe in God is that we don't believe in anything (which really is a nonsense observation). In light of this, I suppose that before proceeding to why I stopped believing in a god or gods, I should provide at least some idea of what I do believe and why. What I believe vis-à-vis religion is quite simple really. There probably is no God, arguments for God are almost always intellectually dishonest, and our only source document for belief in the Christian god, the Bible, is inconsistent, full of errors, of dubious origin, and is morally ambiguous at best. While I do not care that much if others believe in God—aside from the intrinsic value of truth and the harm done by religion—I do care deeply if a friend of religion tells me and others that we must also believe as they do, especially if he gives really bad reasons that we must believe. I consider your religion to be much like your genitalia—you can do whatever you want with it in private, but when you start waving it around in public, I don't mind telling you that it just looks funny to me, it's not nearly as impressive as you seem to think it is, and you should put it away.

While I will address these points extensively in the following chapters, a brief elaboration of what I believe looks something like this:

I. Everything that happens has a naturalistic explanation. We may not yet know and may not ever know the explanation for everything that happens, but all explanations are naturalistic, whether we know what they are or not. While we can't explain everything, we can explain a great many things that we once attributed to supernatural causes, and *in every single case* where we found the real explanation, it turned out to be a natural explanation. God, being supernatural, is one of the things in which I do not believe, and God has no explanatory power in the natural world.

II. I do not believe in a god or gods for the same reason I do not believe in ET,[3] fairies, Santa, the Easter Bunny, or unicorns.

    a. Absence of evidence. There simply is no evidence whatsoever for the existence of a god. Some may argue that there actually is evidence, but simply that it is not good evidence. I am not among them. Really bad evidence is no evidence at all. Granted, this is a point of semantics and not one upon which I am willing to elaborate further.

    b. Evidence of absence. While Carl Sagan was a great personal hero, I do disagree with something he once said. While talking about his own lack of belief in God, Sagan pointed out that the absence of evidence does not constitute the evidence of absence. However, absence of evidence in a situation where you should expect to see lots and lots of evidence does indeed count as evidence for absence. If a personal god, who suspends the laws of nature to grant

---

3 I do believe there is most likely life on other planets. I just do not believe in the alien visitation stories that are commonly told by people here on this planet.

intercessory prayers and perform miracles, is real, there should be lots of evidence. There is none.

c. The problem of evil. This is such a serious problem for the religious that there is a complete field within theology, called theodicy, which seeks to explain away the problem of evil in a world allegedly created by a perfect, all-loving, and all-powerful God. Theodicy fails to adequately explain away the problem of evil. In fact, theodicy not only fails to adequately address the problem of evil, it compounds it. This will be addressed more in chapter 1.

d. The evolution of morality. In spite of claims by the religious that we were created by God with objective morality, which God also created (and this is used as a "proof" of God), there are clear evolutionary origins of morality in humans (and other animals). Careful study of fossils and other anthropological evidence shows that our earliest ancestors cared for each other enough to protect their kin from predation and ensured they had enough to eat during times when they were ill or injured and could not fend for themselves. Much more recently, we see an evolution—in social terms, though not in biological terms—of morality in our species such that a great many of the teachings of the Bible are repugnant to us today and are ignored by even the most fundamentalist among us. This will be addressed at some length in chapters 3 and 4.

III. It is important to address the truth-value of religious claims for a number of reasons.

a. Important decisions, which affect people other than the decision-makers, are made all too often based on nothing other than religious convictions even when rational evidence mitigates toward an alternative course of action.

b. The terms of disquisition are unfairly stacked in favor of friends of religion in the United States and many other

nations, and this is harmful to rational discourse, education, and our collective moral compass.

c. The harm done by religious people, for specifically religious motivations, cannot be effectively addressed and corrected until religion is evaluated fairly and honestly.

I began thinking about this book while in Iraq in 2004 for reasons I will explain later. Long before that, I came to the realization
that while I don't mind if people believe in imaginary things, I do
mind if they use exceedingly poor logic, evidence, and reason to ask
me to also believe those things. I had been reading on this topic and
discussing it casually for some time before 2004, and I have been a
skeptic for much of my life. But it was not until December 2008 that
I thought I would actually do more than just talk and read casually
on this subject that I find so fascinating. I didn't know where to start,
but while sitting in my study, wondering where to begin, I remembered a story told to me by a friend. Her grandmother always told
her, "If you want to draw a tiger but don't know how or where to
start, just start drawing. Maybe your end result will be a cat with a
litter of kittens or a lion and not the tiger you wanted, but you will
at least have something. Until you begin to draw, you have nothing."
I started drawing.

I spent the next couple of years or so conducting research, inter-
views, and reading extensively for this book and actually began putting pen to paper in 2010. It has been a tremendously rewarding
journey—a journey that has taken far longer than I ever expected. In
fact, I am now sitting in a coffee shop in Seoul, South Korea, doing
a final edit of this book, and it is June 2015.[4] As so often happens
with such pursuits, life has just sort of gotten in the way from time
to time. I have been very fortunate to have jobs that allowed me to
see much more of the world than most people ever dream of. Parts
of this book were actually written on four continents; in forty-one

---

[4] As it turns out, it is now October 2016 as I am typing these words, and now
working on another edit in Manhattan's NoHo neighborhood.

countries,[5] including an active combat zone (so forget the lie about no atheists in foxholes), and a number of the United States.

My sincerest wish is that this book brings some small pleasure and even understanding to you as it has me. If you agree with my conclusions or not isn't nearly as important to me as it is that you critically consider what you believe and why. A common theme I try to weave throughout this book is the idea that the great majority of people who claim that a belief in god is the most important aspect of their lives have rarely, if ever, really given those beliefs any critical evaluation. If you truly consider, critically, your belief systems and conclude I am wrong, that is fine. If you conclude I am right, I will, of course, be pleased. However, if you believe without critically thinking about those beliefs, how deeply can you truly claim to believe? If you are among those who feel threatened by my ideas, then your faith must surely be built upon a foundation of sand.

A friend who read an early draft of this book asked a pertinent question—one that shouldn't have needed asking, I am ashamed to say. "Who are you writing this book for?" Upon reflection, I had to admit this is a largely self-serving endeavor. The book was written for me. Not only for me, here and now, however. It was written for me as I have evolved over nearly five decades of belief, questioning, serious doubt, searching, and eventually outright rejection of religion. Not only the religion into which I was born but all religions, the very nature of religious thinking, and any attendant supernatural claims, but also the me that respects deeply the rights of those who do believe in a god or gods.

---

5   The bulk of the research and writing took place in the United States with the majority of the editing taking place in South Korea. The remaining thirty-nine countries saw a mix of heavy lifting, such as writing much of a chapter in Singapore, and very minor tweaks (such as what I am updating as I type these words) in the Czech Republic. An example of other contributions from various countries is the myriad conversations I had with members of various faith traditions around the world—Christians in the United States and the Philippines, Buddhists in Cambodia and Thailand, Hindus in India and Bali, and Muslims in Iraq, Jordan, Turkey, and Kuwait, just to offer a few examples.

This book is then, by extension, written for almost any reader. If you are among the devout and cannot imagine why anyone would not believe as you do, I explain that part of my journey in chapter 1. Perhaps you wonder what the Bible may have to offer on important social issues or maybe why one may find it unconvincing. Chapter 3 addresses this. If you are already skeptical of religious claims yet find arguments in favor of religion troubling but aren't quite sure why (as I once felt), then chapter 4 may be for you. Many who eventually come to sincerely reject religious claims feel compelled to talk about it and express why this subject should matter to all of us—chapters 5 and 6 explains this, at least from one person's perspective.

If I were to put a label on myself, it would be a quite long label. I would say I am an agnostic, atheist, antitheist, strong defender of religious liberties. The chapters of this book show how each part of that label came to apply to me and do so chronologically except for the defender of religious liberties portion. That is a thread that runs throughout my entire journey from devout Christian to one with nascent doubts to nonbeliever to vocal critic of religion. At every step, I have staunchly defended the rights of others to follow any religion or no religion at all. The importance of this is difficult to overstate, and it is often lost on friends of religion. Nonbelievers are often the strongest defenders of the rights of others to follow their conscience no matter where it may lead. It is the adherents of religion, not unbelievers, who (often) say that to not believe as they do will condemn you to hell. It is the truly devout who try to force others to believe as they do, not the unbelievers.

Finally, this book is written in hopes of sharing the realization that most believers and nonbelievers share a great deal more common ground than many of us realize, at least if we simply look beneath the surface proclamations of belief or lack of belief. I have come to realize it is a false dichotomy that you either believe, and in which case you are all-in or you don't believe, in which case you feel religion has nothing at all to offer. In fact, the vast majority of us share a great many values, norms and mores whether we believe in God or not. Most of the people I meet who say they believe in God agree with the vast majority of what I say; they simply disagree with my conclusion about the existence of God. I hope this becomes clear as you read on.

While I am searching for common ground, I do so uncompromisingly. I am not willing to accept that there is no conflict between science and religion, for example. Science is, without question or fear of contradiction, the best way we have for describing how the universe (to include our daily lives, not just black holes, dark matter, and quantum mechanics) works. The common ground I seek is between my fellow human beings, religious or not. It is not between scientific truths and religious superstitions. Again, a topic to be made clear in the following pages.

CHAPTER 1

Devolution of Faith

When I was a child, I spake as a child, I understood as a child, I thought as a child: but when I became a man, I put away childish things.

—1 Corinthians 13:11

The invisible and the non-existent look very much alike.

—Delos B. McKown

What could motivate a former Southern Baptist Bible Banger (SB³) to write a book denouncing belief in, and worship of, an invisible god? After all, there is a huge difference between simply having doubts and actually going to the trouble, considerable work frankly, of writing a book explaining and defending those doubts. Also, it is quite intimidating to openly question what so many hold to be their most important and deeply held beliefs. This is especially true as someone who grew up in the buckle of the Bible Belt, where public professions of love of Jesus are so much a part of daily conversations. I'm reminded of Voltaire's cautionary observation, "It is dangerous to be right in matters on which the established authorities are wrong."

I receive e-mails, hear personal comments, or see posts on Facebook and other social media almost daily from friends and relatives on the importance of showing gratitude to, and praise of, God. We are, if these sentiments are to be believed, obliged to God for all the good things that happen to us daily. Conveniently, the reason for all the bad that we hear about is often attributed to those, like me, who don't properly praise God, and as a result, atheists are among the most discriminated against and despised of all groups in the United

States (Edgell, Gerteis, and Hartmann 2006), ranking somewhere below communists and somewhere above pedophiles according to some studies. The belief not only that God is real but that he is infinitely good and that unbelievers are inherently bad is to some a foregone conclusion. It would be easier to remain silent frankly, but to do so brings to mind another caution from Voltaire that "every man is guilty of all the good he did not do," and I truly do feel this is a good and worthy endeavor.

Offered here are a few personal stories that may help shed light on my personal journey from faith to reason. I feel these glimpses are relevant because the question I am perhaps asked more than any other is "Why did you stop believing in God?" Perhaps the second most-asked question is "Why bother even talking about it if you don't believe?" Both fair, if not well thought out, questions that I feel have very legitimate answers. I am often tempted to answer the first question with "Why did you ever start believing?" and the second with "Why does God need you and other believers to tell his story and defend his positions if he is real?" After all, shouldn't the burden of proof be on the person making the claim of things unseen (this goes to the first question)? And Christians are rarely shy about telling anyone who will listen about their love for Jesus, so why should I feel shy about simply stating why I don't share that belief? (This goes to the second question.) While I address the question of why I bother talking about this in great detail in chapters 5 and 6, I will try to address the first question, why I stopped believing in God, here in this chapter.

This book is at least partially a response to the countless attempts by others to convince me that I am wrong not to believe. My consternation lies not only in the attempts at persuasion, for those attempts are normally motivated from the best of intentions, but rather in the weakness of the arguments repeatedly presented and my surprise at learning of the weakness of all available arguments. I am troubled not only by the weakness and repetition of the arguments but also the occasional contempt displayed toward me when I have the audacity to challenge the arguments and not just blindly accept them.

I have often been, and continue to be, treated as if I am some-how unable to think rationally because I don't see the "truth" before me when I am told that the evidence is undeniable. While I continue to respect each individual's right to believe as they choose, I find it increasingly difficult to respect the cognitive jiu-jitsu necessary to rationalize the things in which some theists say they believe. As I have often heard Christians say, "Hate the sin but love the sinner," my mantra has become, "Respect the believer, but challenge the belief."

One of the things I like to do when talking to the devout is ask why they believe as they do and how they perceive God's nature. It is amazing, to me at least, how difficult it is for the average believer to articulate what God means to them in real terms and to convey an argument for God that does not rely on circular logic, begging the question and bare assertion fallacies. Circular logic, or *circulus in probando*, which is Latin for "circle in proving," was probably first discussed in Aristotle's *Prior Analytics*. An example of circular logic is "Jesus is the Messiah. I know this because it says so in the Bible. I know the Bible is true because Jesus says so. I know Jesus spoke the truth because he is the Messiah." Begging the question, or *petitio principii*, "assuming the initial point," is often confused with circu-lar logic but is different according to Aristotle, who identified it as a fallacy closely related but distinct from circular logic. An example of begging the question is seen in the cosmological argument when the claim is made that the universe could not have always been here and could not have started itself, therefore there must have been an all-powerful cause of the universe, and this we call God. The ques-tion being begged is, Where did God come from, or who created the creator? The fact is that once you get past the bumper-sticker comments and one-liners, most people who say they believe are chal-lenged greatly when asked to say what it is that they actually believe and why.

Just as I ask the believer to consider her reasons for believing, I do not argue for an unthinking *lack* of belief but rather for a crit-ical interrogation of the facts, wherever that might take you. I am simply convinced that if you honestly consider the evidence, or lack thereof, without the pressure of "wishful thinking," or *argumentum ad consequentiam*—the idea that a belief should be true (or untrue) because of how much I like (or dislike) the consequences of it being true—unbelief is the natural consequence.

This idea of wishful thinking, so far as I am able to discern, is the only compelling reason to *want* to believe in God. Note that I did not say it is a compelling reason to actually believe in God; merely, it is a compelling reason to *want* to believe in God. Wishful thinking is often manifested in proclamations such as, "I don't want to live in a world without God." I understand the desire to want to live in a world where there is a god who looks out for you. It is a fact, however, that what we want to be true has no bearing on what actually is true. I might not want to live in a world in which Jessica Alba does not want to bear my children (and my wife might not want to live in a world in which I say such silly nonsense), but what I want in this case is irrelevant. I could also take this argument to the next level of religious excuse making and say that believing that Jessica Alba wants to run away with me gives my life meaning and purpose and is the reason I can make it through tough times. Does this sound familiar? Remember, if you believe in God because you want to see loved ones after you die, while a powerful motive for wanting God to be real, is not rational or based on evidence and is simply a bad reason for believing he actually is real.

I once believed in God. I never really had a good reason for believing it. It was not a conscious decision really. I was just told it was true when I was a child and that to believe otherwise was not only incorrect but would make me a bad person deserving of punishment. There was no evaluation of the evidence that led me to consider myself a Christian. I was simply always told this was true, and when everyone around me believed the same thing, it was easy to continue believing.

Over the years, however, a series of epiphanies brought to light certain flaws in the belief system of my childhood. I would like to offer a retelling of some of these events to lend context to the rest of this book. Some of the observations I offer are personal reflections on people of faith and their various actions; others are ideas and concepts presented by others with the intention of buttressing my faith, often with the opposite effect. Some of these are admittedly quite silly, and I offer them for entertainment value if nothing else. Keep in mind that no matter how silly these examples may seem, they were often offered by persons of authority to me and were believed by those who offered them and were offered for the purpose of reinforcing a belief in God.

This last point perhaps bears a bit of clarification. While not all Christians believe the same things, the examples I offer are not isolated beliefs no matter how nonsensical they may seem to some readers. I realize, of course, that not all Christians agree on all beliefs. In fact, religious beliefs vary from time and place even within the same religious tradition. There are a great many things that went to the very heart of Christian dogma for the vast majority of Christianity's history that are not taken seriously today by most Christians. This does not change the fact that many people believe the things I recount here even today, and they tried to convince me to believe these things as well.

This is one of the challenges for the nonbeliever when discussing such issues with believers, isn't it? What kind of believer are they? Fundamentalist? Evangelical? Liberal? Moderate? There are really only a few things that all have in common, most important among these, to me at least, is that they claim to have a special book given to them by God and in which he tells them how he wants us all to live. We are told that in this book is all the really important information that we need to know about the creator of the universe and all that he wants for us and from us. It is believed that this book is a very good book, a perfect book, and we know this to be true because God says so, and he says so in this book.

Like the vast majority of Christians, I never read this book when I actually was a Christian, at least not in its entirety. I was able to quote chapter and verse of some of the really heartwarming stories to be sure. These were the things that I learned in Sunday school. But have you read this book entirely? Scary stuff! In it are dragons[6]

---

[6] While there really are dragons in the Bible (Revelation 12:3), I am using the term here rather as an analog for other scary things like evil visited upon man

and worse! It is because of this book that for much of the past two thousand years some men have felt empowered to tell other men how to live and often to torture and kill those who fail to follow the rules of this special book. Quite honestly and to my great surprise, when I actually bothered to read the book for myself, I found that not only was it not a good book, it was replete with errors, contradictions, and inconsistencies. I began to wonder, How could so many intelligent people use a book of this nature as a basis for their worldview? Certainly, this book was not the thing that made me first begin asking questions. Quite to the contrary, it was only after having questions that I turned to this book for the answers. I eventually came to believe that the Holy Bible, if read honestly, may be the single greatest force for nonbelief available to us, and I will explain why in chapter 3.

Preambles and caveats complete, what follows are just some of the things that led me to question, and ultimately reject, the idea that God is likely real. Chapters 3 and 4 will drive home why I became more confident in my lack of belief. Here I only share those simple everyday things that caused me to start to at least wonder about possibility of God's nonexistence.

The Argument from Incomplete Annihilation (God Is so Merciful for Saving That Baby in the Plane Crash!)

What clear-thinking person doesn't do a facepalm every time a Grammy winner thanks God for picking them over all the others. What of athletes who do the same thing? What did God have against all the opponents of Tim Tebow and the New York Jets in 2012? Tebow thanked God for his divine assistance after every successful play, so the Jets must have been God's favorites. Right? So why wasn't it God's fault when Tim Tebow got sacked (pun intended) by the New York Jets in 2013? If God was responsible for Tebow's success,

---

by other men at God's direction.

wasn't God also responsible for his failures? God gets a free pass on all the bad but credit for all the good. A pretty sweet deal!

While they may seem unconnected, these examples are related to what is sometimes referred to as the argument from incomplete annihilation (or destruction). An example of this is seen when an airplane crashes killing all aboard except for one single passenger and an outpouring of thanks for God's great mercy results. After all, so goes the argument, only God's intervention could have saved this lone individual. What is rarely asked is why did God cause the plane to crash in the first place? Surely, if it is only through his infinite and just love that one can be saved, it is only through his malevolent involvement or uncaring refusal to act that the tragedy occurred in the first place. Why was God not inclined to save all the other passengers on that flight? Was he angry at them? Maybe the Westborough Baptist Church folks have it almost right and God really hates frequent fliers and not fags.

Ideas such as this were among my earliest influences to begin questioning the involvement of God in our daily lives. The free pass given to God when bad things happen coupled with the gushing praise given to God when good things happen (or when bad things happen to an incomplete extent) just seems to be taking the easy way out cognitively speaking. Before you fall into the trap set by some theists that God should be praised for all the good but God is not really responsible for the bad, I offer this from the "Good Book": "Are not two sparrows sold for a farthing? And one of them shall not fall on the ground without your Father" (Matthew 10:29). The point being that nothing happens without God's will. If God is truly in control, then he is responsible for all the good that does not occur. To simply praise God for the good and blame ourselves for the bad does not pass muster in my mind.

God's Problem[7] (the Problem of Evil—Theodicy Anyone?)

> Religion is a byproduct of fear. For much of human history, it may have been a necessary evil, but why was it more evil than necessary? Isn't killing people in the name of God a pretty good definition of insanity?
>
> —Arthur C. Clarke

In the beginning, at least the beginning as best we can understand it so far, there was a sudden expansion of all the stuff that makes up our current observable universe. This has come to be known colloquially as the big bang. Scientists are, after all, rather practical folk and "a homogeneous universe of constant mass and growing radius" doesn't quite roll off the tongue like "the big bang." Big bang cosmology is supported by every fact of every field of science that has anything to say on the matter, and while some fundamentalists deny it, even sophisticated theists see this as how the universe, as we currently know it, was created (Knapp, 2012), they simply disagree with atheists in that they believe God caused it. Since I began writing this book, there have been amazing discoveries that further confirm the big bang model of cosmology. For example, researchers using the BICEP2 (Background Imaging of Cosmic Extragalactic Polarization 2) telescope at Amundsen-Scott South Pole Station has discovered direct evidence of gravitational waves, believed to be a result of the big bang and something that Albert Einstein predicted in his general theory of relativity. I won't defend big bang cosmology any further aside from saying that not only does all the evidence support it, there isn't a shred of evidence against it nor are there any alternative explanations for cosmic origins that are taken seriously.

While our understanding is very limited of what may have happened at the very moment of the big bang or even before (if such a concept has any real meaning) our understanding of what has

---

[7] For an entire book-length discussion on the problem of evil, see *God's Problem* by Professor Bart Ehrman.

happened in the intervening nearly 14 billion years is beautiful and inspiring—incomplete, yes, but constantly growing and refining. We understand, for example, that planets like our home form through a process called accretion in the disks of gas, dust, and organic matter that coalesce around forming stars. We also know that our home could not have formed in the very early universe because other stars had not yet formed the heavy elements necessary for planet formation. When the conditions were set, however, the stuff of which our planet is made did indeed conjoin around a rather ordinary star, just one of 200 billion others, in a rather ordinary galaxy, again among hundreds of billions of other galaxies.

Our planet formed about 4.5 billion years ago, and as it cooled, tectonic plates were created upon which the continents slowly drift. Oceans, rivers, and lakes formed; and a hydrologic cycle began. The movement of continents and the movement of water are both powered by energy, the former mostly from inside the earth and the latter from the Sun. Remember this last point if ever an apologist tries to tell you that evolution violates the second law of thermodynamics (or any other law for that matter).

On this planet, life emerged not that long after the planet itself was formed (at least not long in geologic timescales). Just as with the exact moment of the big bang (or before) and what exactly caused it, we don't know exactly how the first life began. We know how this life-starting event, known as abiogenisis, *could* have happened, but we do not know yet for sure how it actually did happen, and we may never know for sure. What we do understand (and again for extremely good reasons) is how life evolved after it did get its start and that evolutionary process has led to us. Actually, we were not the purpose of evolution as evolution has no higher purpose; it simply is. It has led to a great many other forms of life as well, but we are one result of that evolutionary process, and I for one am happy that it worked out that way.

One of the interesting and underappreciated facts of how life here developed and how that process directly yet almost imperceptibly affects us is that there are ten times more microorganisms in the average human than there are human cells (National Institutes of

Health 2012). This means that as much as six pounds of a two-hundred-pound adult is made up of bacteria! Most of these microorganisms are not only harmless, they live symbiotically with us and serve important functions, but this is not always the case. A seemingly irrelevant point of gee-whiz-neat-trivia perhaps, but I have a reason for bringing it up that I hope will be clear in a moment.

By now, you may be wondering what my admittedly brief and extremely over-simplistic discussion of both cosmic and human evolution (two very different things to be sure) has to do with the problem of evil. The point is simply this—all of what religions have come to view as "evil" has purely naturalistic explanations and no recourse to a god is necessary. There are natural consequences of life on a cooling planet with shifting tectonic plates (earthquakes, tsunamis); a hydrologic cycle and climate influenced by the heating of the sun, pressure systems and the Coriolis force of a rotating Earth (hurricanes, tornadoes, flooding); and the times when biology and microorganisms do not work for us but rather against us (birth defects and disease). We once attributed all these things to the will of the gods; we now know better.

All of this *heartache and the thousand natural shocks that flesh is heir to* was once believed to be the result of our not living in accordance with God's will. Some people still believe this. Earthquake? God is upset about something we did or failed to do. Flood? Again, it's our fault for not pleasing God. Likewise for disease, pestilence, birth defects, and any other undesired outcome of our inability (or unwillingness) to live up to God's expectations. This would actually be extremely troubling if it were true. Part and parcel to belief in God is that he created us with full knowledge that he would eventually cast us out of Eden, later flood the earth to kill almost all life on it, later still destroy entire cities, and throughout time afflict us with disease and famine, all because we failed to resist the temptations he willingly placed right in front of us. The good news is that through our efforts alone, we have managed a situation in which we have mitigated much of this suffering, and we now live longer, healthier, and happier lives than at any time in human history. We owe our longer, healthier, happier lives to our understanding of natural processes, not the will of God.

Again you may wonder, what does all this have to do with the problem of evil, and why is it God's problem? Simply this: all the bad things described (the undesired consequences, the human suffering) occur because either God willed it, God failed to prevent it, or God isn't real and this is just a consequence of nature. No amount of equivocation, special pleading, or mental gymnastics can change this. It is also important to remember that all the bad things that sometimes happen to us do so at the same rate for Christians as for Muslims, as for Hindus, as for atheists. This is not what one would expect if God were real. As it turns out, the universe behaves exactly as we would expect if God is not real. It could be understood if bad things happened to bad people and good things happened to good people. It could maybe (just barely but maybe) be understood if there were some greater good served by this suffering and bad things consistently happened to good people (as a test of their faith for example), but this is not the case. Good and bad things happen to both good and bad people, and with the exception of human-imposed justice, there is no rhyme or reason to how much good or bad happens to good or bad people.

Remember the convergence of climatic circumstances that leads to tornados described above? As I was working on this part of this very book, a tragic natural disaster struck the good people of Moore, Oklahoma. An EF5 tornado devastated that city and left a path of destruction two kilometers wide and thirty kilometers long. An estimated 2 billion dollars in damage paled in comparison with the loss of twenty-four priceless human beings, among them ten children. This was not, however, the result of an angry god teaching a lesson to atheists. (One survivor, Rebecca Vitsmun, replied, "I'm actually an atheist," when CNN's Wolf Blitzer asked her if she thanked the Lord for her survival.) Most of the victims were Christians. No doubt many of those who were killed prayed just as hard and with as much sincerity as those who survived.

The tornado that caused such destruction in Moore Oklahoma was on the ground an estimated forty minutes. In that same forty minutes, an estimated two hundred children died worldwide of starvation. Extend that forty minutes to a year. Annually 2.6 million children starve to death, a situation characterized by the World Health Organization as the single gravest threat to human health globally. How can one conceive of an all-powerful, all-knowing, and completely good God being real and still allowing that to happen? And like the tornado victims in Oklahoma, the parents of these children often pray just as sincerely as those whose children have enough to eat. Their belief in God is just as devout. Again, life carries on just as we would expect in a world where there is no God. This is not a problem for the nonbeliever, but it is a very big problem for anyone who believes that God is real. This is a problem for so many reasons. Why did a perfectly good God create such an imperfect world? Why so much suffering? Why does this suffering affect those who love him most just as much and with the same frequency as those who reject his very existence? This is the problem of evil. It was the problem of evil as much as anything else that started me on the journey from devout Christian to nonbeliever.

Recall the opening paragraphs of this book and the fate of most of us should the world come to an end. After considering the implications of Christian dogma taken to its logical conclusion and the realization that most of the people who have ever lived are going to hell in the Christian world view, I began having serious doubts not only about what I believed about the nature of God but about the possibility he may not be real. It was not only my inability to understand how an omniscient, omnipotent, and perfectly good god would allow most of us to end up in hell; it was also the suffering we see here in this life. I began to realize that at least some aspects of this belief system must be wrong.

There are attempts to explain away this and other problems, but none of them are at all convincing. Some say that suffering is required for spiritual growth—this rings hollow when there is supposed to be no suffering in heaven. Would only fully grown (spiritually speaking) beings be in heaven? Then what's up with Satan? He started out in heaven! Some argue that suffering results from our free will. God doesn't want us to hurt each other, but he doesn't want automatons either, so he gave us free will—that is why some people do bad things. Free will is not only a bad explanation for the problem of evil; it is a problem in its own right. It is also the explanation most often given for the problem of evil.

The Paradox of Free Will (You are free to choose, and go to hell for it)

The rationale for citing free will as the source of our evil is actually rather simplistic. While God is perfect, all-powerful, and all-knowing, and could have created us such that sinning was impossible for us, he also wanted us to be free to choose. Free to choose to follow him, free to choose right from wrong, free to choose salvation or damnation. Were it not for this free will, then there would be little value in us behaving "morally" because we wouldn't be consciously deciding to do that; we would simply be doing it robotically. This, so goes the argument, is not what God wants. He wants us to choose between good and evil.

Free will is cited not only as the source of evil, it is also often cited as the reason God chooses not to reveal himself to us absolutely. To complicate matters, he wants us to choose to believe in him on faith, but if he actually appeared to each of us, then we would lose the free will to choose. This is yet another really bad argument—one that I will elaborate on in a moment. While the free-will argument attempts to explain some suffering, such as rape and murder (bad things happen because people choose to do them), it does nothing to explain why these things still happen to good people as well as bad, why these bad acts are statistically committed more often by believers than by nonbelievers (Niose 2011). It doesn't address natural disasters, such as tornadoes and earthquakes. It also falls short of its intended mark because an infinitely powerful and wise being could create a universe in which we still have free will (we could still *want* to rape and murder) while restricting our freedom of action (we couldn't actually *do* it). This would allow God's judgment of those who chose evil in their hearts while not allowing harm to the innocent, at least in terms of man's inhumanity to man. The natural disasters don't result from anyone's free will other than God's, so the ball is in his court to stop those things if he is real.

I mentioned Satan a moment ago, and further reference to Satan is helpful to illustrate this point as well. If the reason God refuses to reveal himself to us, or maintains "epistemic distance" from us, is because that would interfere with our freedom to choose, then how was it possible that Satan made the choices he made. Assuming that Satan is real, there can be no doubt at all that Satan must be absolutely convinced of God's reality, yet he (and apparently a host of other lesser imps and demons) decided to turn his back on God. Not only that. He has continued to defy God throughout all the ages of man, from Adam and Eve right up until today, all with the unmistakable knowledge that God is real. Unless of course none of this is true.

The idea of free will is problematic (theologically speaking) for other reasons as well. According to this concept, we are free to choose, yet if we choose incorrectly and don't believe in God, the punishment is not just terrible, it is eternal. There is a very strong case to be made that we don't *choose* what we believe anyway; we simply believe. We may choose which actions to take based on our beliefs, but we don't actually choose *what* we believe. But assume we do have the freedom to believe whatever we wish. When we do choose, do we really have freedom to choose if we know that an unspeakable punishment is waiting if we choose other than what we are told is the correct choice? A silly example perhaps, but what if I place a Pepsi and a Coke in front of you and tell you that you are free to choose either one, but just as you reach for the Pepsi I put a gun to your head and say if you don't choose the Coke I will pull the trigger. Do you really have free will in this case? Of course, you are not free to choose, at least not if you wish to avoid sudden terminal lead poisoning. In the Christian view, we are told we have free will, and following God is a choice, but if we choose incorrectly and don't follow God, we will go to hell for that choice. Some choice! Some free will!

Mistakes of an Omniscient God (Practice makes perfect... eventually... maybe)

Religion has gotten a great deal wrong that we can verify and prove. On most issues, in fact, where we can actually prove a matter true or false, religion has normally gotten it wrong. Why then should we place undue confidence in the religious claims that remain unresolved when the track record so far is so poor? It is a fact that never in history has religion ever offered reliable evidence for any supernatural claim whatsoever. It is also a fact that the claims of religion exist now only in the shadows cast by the light of reason, and that light is getting ever brighter and more pervasive—the shadows, more evasive.

Science is a human development, and as such, it is imperfect, but it is our best way for determining truth. God, if he were real, would have to be, by definition, a lot less prone to making mistakes than would his creations with their petty scientific knowledge. I pull up just short of saying that a god must be perfect by definition, because some of the gods people have believed in were not claimed to be perfect, only very powerful. The god Christians believe in, however, is claimed to be perfect and possessing of such traits as omniscience (knowing everything), omnipotence (the ability to do anything and everything), omnibenevolent (limitless in his care for us), and others.

Here again, we are presented with a Christian dilemma (number 6). If the Bible is to be believed, God makes a lot of mistakes for an omniscient and omnipotent being. Read the Bible and take note of all the times that God either had no choice in some matter (troubling for claims of omnipotence) or was uncaring enough not to destroy almost all of his creation (troubling for claims of omnibenevolence) because it had not gone the way he expected (troubling for claims of omniscience). The Noahic flood and the destruction of Sodom and Gomorra (just to name two examples) illustrate this. And let us not forget that the start of all the suffering just discussed in the last section stemmed from the flawed design in God's greatest creation, mankind, and our inability to keep our hands off the one thing God told us not to eat in the Garden of Eden. While this last example would not count as destruction, it certainly would make God an assassin of human happiness for all eternity.

God created us so flawed that we immediately betrayed him by eating the forbidden fruit and the first person ever born to God's first two human creations (Cain) killed his younger brother (Abel). This was preceded by one of God's earlier and most beautiful creations (Lucifer) turning on God and becoming the very incarnation of evil. Not a good track record for a perfect god.

At least God was willing to admit he made mistakes and demonstrated remorse (very human of him) for creating man, a mistake he corrected (though not completely) by committing global genocide in the already mentioned great flood (Genesis 6:6–7). If, in all of humanity, Jesus was the only person who ever lived who was without sin, then this certainly does not argue for a perfect creator. Remember that the Population Reference Bureau estimated there have been about 108 billion people who have ever lived. Out of all these people, there has only been one who was perfect. This means that a perfect creator actually had a 0.0000000000092593 percent success rate in creating perfection. And to achieve this, he cheated by sending down part of himself, which has always existed anyway and was already perfect, to die a horrific death so that he could allow himself to forgive us for not being perfect—even though he had chosen to create us imperfectly. Of course, an honest reading of the Bible, even if it is true (and I am not arguing that it is), indicates that Jesus was probably not perfect either and probably had the same human failings as the rest of us, as will be discussed in chapter 3.

In light of his allegedly perfect nature why must God go about correcting his mistakes so often? There is actually a logical and philosophical impossibility inherent in the belief that God is perfect, omnipotent, and omniscient yet must continually set things right by granting prayers. How, for example, can an all-knowing and all-powerful god create a world in which he will have to intervene (using his omnipotence) in the future (in which case his omniscience seems to have failed)? If he is all-knowing, then he must have known what was to happen but was perhaps powerless to do a better job from the start; hence, we have reason to suspect he is either not omnipotent, not omniscient, or lacking in both areas—or far more likely, he's just not real.

The fact that even if God were real, he is demonstrably not perfect was yet another chink in the armor of my faith. This was not the straw that broke the proverbial camel's back, but it was yet another step toward disbelief.

Natural Selection Map of Religion (Worship Our Local God or Go to Hell)

Geographic distribution is one of the great many convincing evidences of evolution through the mechanism of natural selection, genetic drift, random mutation, and other factors explained by evolutionary theory. Geographic distribution is seen when animals that evolved in a given area are seen primarily in that area, and where those animals exist in other areas, you can normally tell from the fossil record approximately when that particular animal spread out from its native habitat and often why. The further from where an animal evolved, the less likely you are to see that particular animal in nature, unless of course there are environmental influences to cause things to be otherwise.

Just like the way we rarely see marsupials outside of Australia, it is interesting to see how a sort of religious evolution and geographic distribution has taken place. If you look at a religious map of the world, you will see Catholicism is very common in Europe and North America, South America, and the Philippines (along with the "fossil record" of Spanish conquest in the latter two examples). Islam dominant in much of the Middle East and Indonesia, Hinduism in India, and so forth. If an all-powerful, infinitely wise god actually wanted us all to be in fellowship with him, why such a mess of things in terms of religious geographic distribution? Clearly, this is a natural evolution of human religious influence and not the design of an all-powerful god with a purpose in mind.

Obviously, not all religious claims can be true, and in all likelihood, even if one religion is true, it is the only one that is. All the others then are almost certainly wrong. Few adherents of Christianity would hesitate to admit they are skeptical of claims made by followers of Islam, Hinduism, Daoism, Buddhism[8] or any of the other religions; and the same goes for the believers in each of those faith systems with respect to Christianity. This "my god-centric view of the world" presents a problem for the followers of any one particular religion, because their god chose not to, or was unable to, share his good word with all those followers of other religions due to geographic isolation. This presents the seventh dilemma—that an all-powerful deity whose truth is self-evident and who wants his truth to be known is only worshipped in certain parts of the world, only at certain times, and by certain people.

Related to the geographic distribution of religion, at least from the perspective of a challenge to religious belief, is the distribution of dogmatic claims about the nature of each religion. This is why we have so many denominations within Christianity. I could not help but ask myself when I was young why there are so many religions and, even focusing closer to home, why there are so many different Christian denominations. A bit more on this later, but suffice it to say there are over thirty-three thousand different denominations in Christianity alone. How could God allow that if he is real?

The way geographic dispersion of religious beliefs has developed versus the way that scientific knowledge has grown is also interesting. Penn Jillette made the point in his book *Every Day is an Atheist Holiday* (and elsewhere) that if all the world's religions were to disappear, they would not develop again the same way. They would be replaced by other religions surely, but the same beliefs would not come back the same way almost certainly. If we lost all scientific knowledge, on the other hand, someday someone somewhere would rediscover the exact same scientific truths. This will be revisited and elaborated on in chapter 6. I have often thought about the differences in religion and science. There is a very good reason for this geographic and cultural segregation (generally speaking) of religious

---

[8]   It may not be entirely accurate to refer to Buddhism as a religion as there is no god in orthodox Buddhism and Buddhists don't actually worship the Buddha.

beliefs and an equally good reason that science does not follow this trend—science is borne out by the evidence, and religion is the cultural handiwork of people who do not know better.

The Nature of Religious Arguments (Because I Said So, That's Why)

Religious arguments do not submit to the same rigor as one can reasonably expect from other forms of discourse. If they did, they would not last long. This has become something of a heuristic maxim for me and so consistently true that I have frankly stopped spending much time on religious arguments. Believe it or not, this is one of the reasons I wrote this book. Counterintuitive as it may seem, writing this book-length argument is meant to take the place of my frequent informal religious debates. If a religious person tries to tell me the Bible is good and true, I ask them to read chapter 3. If they attempt an apologetic argument, I commend chapter 4, etc. Of course, most proselytizers will not take the time to read my entire book. But I took the time to write it, and if they don't take the time to at least read the portions that are relevant to the particular disagreement, then at least I've done my part. I have spent years now listening intently to anyone willing to offer evidence for God, and in every single case, no exceptions at all, the arguments have proved unconvincing; and in most cases, they have also been intellectually dishonest. Not only have they been unconvincing and intellectually dishonest, they have almost always been inconsistent with even the religious defender's own view of evidence and reason if only they were talking about anything other than religion or even of another religion.

Religious arguments are almost always circular in nature, proceed from an already established premise in mind (God is real), ignore all contrary evidence; and those who offer such arguments gladly use techniques they would not allow for others with dissenting views. Basically, every rule that one should be expected to follow in honest rational discourse is conveniently ignored if it does not bolster one's own religious belief. Specifics of this include quote mining, ad hominem attacks, usurping of scientific facts for clearly unscientific reasons, nebulous explanations that don't really explain anything, and others, all discussed further in the following pages. For now, I will only briefly address the *nature* of religious arguments as one of the early influences on my lack of religious belief and not the actual formal religious arguments. The specifics of many religious arguments will be addressed in chapter 4.

Contrast the nature of religious arguments with that of scientific arguments, which propose testable predictions, theories with great explanatory power, ideas which are falsifiable, and ultimately which have provided everything which defines and identifies ours as a modern society. This is a point that is difficult to overemphasize. Freethinkers are sometimes accused of having blind faith in science, which is a desperate misuse of language. I have no faith at all in science. Because of the proven track record of science and all the tangible benefit that we have gleaned from it, I have reasonable confidence that scientific explanations are tremendously more likely to be true than are religious arguments. Faith does not enter into the calculus at any point. I will delve deeper into this fact in the discussion of the Bible versus science in chapter 3.

This understanding of the weakness of religions arguments versus scientific arguments is certainly not something I was first to discover. Honest thinkers have long known this. I have known it since my youth, even when I still believed in God. I recall as a child, somewhere around middle school, learning how scientific knowledge is collected (empirical observation, testing, falsifiability, repeatability of test results, peer review, etc.), and I couldn't help but notice that religion does not submit to this way of evaluating knowledge. If it did, I suspect we wouldn't long have religion. One thing I would ask the religious believer to do is consider "bad ideas" outside your own religious tradition—things like astrology or religions other than your own, for example—and then look closely at how the supporters of those ideas defend their positions. Compare this with how rational pursuits, such as science, history, etc., differ. If you then see the disparity of reasons, you will then see how I view the nature of religious arguments.

What if you are wrong?

I once had a very dear friend, a devout Christian, who often said that if she is wrong about her belief, then there is nothing to lose. But she said, if the unbeliever is wrong, then he has everything to lose. I didn't know it at the time, but this is known as Pascal's wager, so named because Blaise Pascal argued that even if there may not be overwhelming evidence for the existence of God, it is still a safer bet to profess belief in him since to bet against him and be wrong could result in eternal damnation, whereas to bet in favor of belief and to be wrong simply means you worshiped a god who wasn't there and then you died just like everyone else but nothing more.

This actually seemed a valid argument to me at the time, but it is not, and I will explain why in chapter 4. Suffice it to say here that once I actually thought about it I realized that not only is this clearly unconvincing, it has harmful implications, again to be elaborated on later. It is also one of the most often used arguments by theists against nontheists. The only other point to be made on Pascal's wager for now is that it reveals another important feature of religious arguments and the way they are presented. Friends of religion consistently show an inability or at least unwillingness to distinguish between arguing for what actually is true and what they wish were true. Remember the earlier statement, "I don't want to live in a world without God!" which theists often make. This is actually presented by some as evidence for God. No, this is evidence that you wish for something to be true, not that it is in fact true.

Figures Lie and Liars Figure

> Just going to church doesn't make you a Christian any more than standing in your garage makes you a car.
>
> —G. K. Chesterton

> Nothing has a greater tendency to lessen the reverence which mankind ought to have for the

Supreme Being than a careless repetition of his name upon every trifling occasion.

—Noah Webster

On a Fox News interview I once heard, Rick Warren said something to the effect of 2.5 billion people in the world believe in God, and they can't all be idiots. For anyone who does not know, Rick Warren is the author of the wildly successful *The Purpose Driven Life*. I've been told by a couple of Christian friends that this is a great read that helps to give one a sense of purpose, hence the title. I've not yet read it, though I plan to, so I will withhold any other comment on the book other than to say it is very successful.

What of the reference to the 2.5 billion people who can't be idiots though. A couple of points I'd like to make here. First, if numbers are the measure of the validity of a given premise, then we should consider the roughly 5 billion people who don't believe in the same God (Jesus Christ specifically) that Mr. Warren was talking about. Are they all idiots? Warren went on in this interview to point out that 85 percent of Americans say they are Christians. This is an example of using figures liberally to prove your preconceived point. Sure, most Americans are "cultural Christians," but I know for certain that nothing approaching 85 percent of Americans are in church each Sunday. One would think church attendance is pretty important if you truly believe that Jesus is the only begotten son of God, one with him in the Holy Trinity along with the Holy Spirit, sent to die for our sins so that we may have everlasting life, etc., but such is not the case.

I suspect that the numbers of just how many Christians assume that title are a bit inflated. The way that polls are conducted is sometimes misleading. To be sure, most Americans if asked, "Do you believe in a higher power?" would say yes without hesitation, or if asked, "Are you an atheist?" would say no, but there is clearly more to the story. If a poll were to be conducted in which we begin with the question, "Do you believe in God?" and the answer is no, then the poll is over. If the answer is yes, then the questions should become more interesting. The nature of that belief is important. For example, imagine that we then ask, "Are you a Christian?" and if the answer is in the affirmative, we then ask, "Can you tell me about the concept of the triune nature of God?" If the self-identified Christian can't, then there might be a problem. This is after all one of the central concepts of Christianity. I have met a number of Christians who don't even pretend get the concept of the Trinity, and I've yet to meet one who can explain it to me clearly.[9] Many Christians just assume it is clearly spelled out somewhere in the Bible and has always been at the core of their faith tradition. It is interesting how many Christians are surprised to learn that it wasn't until the Council of Nicaea (in 325 CE—more on this in chapter 3) that this idea was formally codified and officially accepted as a central tenet of faith in the Church. Not all Christians, in all times, have believed in the Trinity.

I have admittedly gotten slightly off topic here, but the point to remember is that numbers quoted by people like Rick Warren as some sort of evidence for the truth of their religion should be considered skeptically. When one of the most influential religious leaders in America uses as evidence that a large number of people believe as he does, when in fact most of the people alive don't believe as he does, then his argument is actually self-defeating if looked at honestly. In spite of this, perhaps the challenge most offered to my skepticism of religious claims is that most people believe in God.

Rain Dances and Prayers to Joe Pesci

Comedian George Carlin used to have a very funny bit about why he prayed to Joe Pesci. According to Carlin, "I noticed that all the prayers I used to offer to God, and all the prayers that I now offer to Joe Pesci, are now being answered at about the same 50 percent rate. Half the time I get what I want. Half the time I don't. Same as

---

[9]   I think the best attempt at explaining the Trinity (not a good attempt, only the best of the bad explanations) was to compare it to water. Water, I was told, can exist as a solid, liquid, or gas; but it is always water. I hope that it is not necessary to explain why this, admittedly creative, explanation does not "hold water."

God, 50–50. Same as the four-leaf clover, the horse shoe, the wishing well and the rabbit's foot. Same as the mojo man. Same as the voodoo lady who tells your fortune by squeezing a goat's testicles. It's all the same; 50–50. So just pick your superstitions, sit back, make a wish and enjoy yourself."

This position, while funny when presented by George Carlin, is a valid one borne out by any research ever conducted into the efficacy of prayer. Consider results of the "Study of the Therapeutic Effects of Intercessory Prayer (STEP)," also known as the Templeton Prayer Study (Benson 2006), perhaps the most scientifically rigorous study ever conducted on the results of prayer. The method used in this study was that at six US hospitals, patients were randomly assigned to one of three groups. Of these, 604 patients were prayed for after being told they may or may not be prayed for; 597 patients in another group were not prayed for after also being told they may or may not be prayed for. In the final group, 601 patients were prayed for after being told that they would be prayed for. Intercessory prayers were offered for the chosen patients for fourteen days, beginning the night before receiving coronary artery bypass graft (CABG) surgery. When evaluating a primary outcome of "presence of any complication within thirty days of CABG" and secondary outcomes of "any major event and mortality," the results were not what the religious would have hoped for or expected.

This study not only found no effect at all on the recovery of patients who were prayed for, it actually found a higher rate of postoperative complications among patients who knew they were being prayed for. The simple fact is that there is no evidence at all to indicate that prayer ever works, and in every single case where prayer was critically evaluated, it came up short. Worse yet, there was at least anecdotal evidence in this study that belief in prayer can be harmful!

In spite of the clear lack of evidence that prayer works, the governor of Texas, Rick Perry, a former serious contender for the Republican nomination for US president, used his office to issue an official proclamation (Perry 2011) that there shall be three official days of prayer in Texas. While this might seem harmless to many, I offer a different perspective. Just imagine the good that could have been done if all those hands folded in prayer had actually been put into action to do tangible good for their fellow Texans. Also consider the bureaucratic time, effort, and cost that went into drafting that official declaration—resources that could have been used far more constructively for the good of Texas.

For the record, the rains did not come when Perry called for prayer in late April. What did happen was that a series of wildfires erupted that destroyed lives and homes (*International Business Times* 2011), and this went on for months after the prayer proclamation. Then on October 7, the Texas Freethought Convention began in Houston with such atheist, agnostic, and freethinking speakers as Richard Dawkins and Christopher Hitches. On the second day of the convention, it rained. Some areas of Texas even received record rainfalls on the same weekend as the Freethought Convention. Now I am in no way saying that it rained because of the Freethought Convention! But I am saying that praying for rain clearly failed.

The clear rate of unanswered prayers was a major factor in my deconversion story. Does the fact that prayers to God are answered at the same rate as if you prayed to your pet rock, your dog, to the memory of Nat King Cole, or Charlie Chaplin mean that there is no God? No, it does not. It does mean, however, that there is no reason at all to expect prayers to be answered, so I decided to stop trying and to focus on what I know does actually work—my own actions and those of other human beings.

As I write this paragraph, it is early morning in South Korea. I just took a short break to look out the window of my twenty-ninth-floor apartment. While looking out across the city and thinking about the day ahead, I realize that I have the ability to make a positive impact in the lives of others. The only thing that will prevent that from occurring is for me to not try or simply refuse to do so. What if, on the other hand, I spent the day in prayer? All evidence indicates that my time is better spent working in the real world to make it a better place. That is where I focus my efforts. If I simply resolve to do at least one good thing today, one simple act of kindness, then my day will have been infinitely better than had it been spent in prayer. Some friends of religion tell me that praying is actually for the person who prays. It makes them feel better. Well, doing good for others makes me feel better, too, but also does tangible good for the object of my efforts, so actually doing good seems to me at least twice as good as prayer.

A final thought on prayer, and this goes back to the nature of religious arguments. Wouldn't it be great if each of us could get the same breaks that God is given? If you want something badly, then just pray for it we are told. God always answers prayers, don't you know! But then when you don't get what you prayed for, did God let you down? No! God, in his infinite wisdom, realized that is not what was best for you, and so he actually *did* answer your prayer by not doing what you asked for. This is how you shift the goalposts such that God can't lose, or as I once heard Sam Harris observe, "This is how you play tennis without the net."

Christian Karate (the Paragon of Hypocrisy)

So what could karate possibly have to do with Christianity or a book of this nature? Good question, and the correct answer is "Not much," at least the two shouldn't be related. Before spending a year in Iraq, I would have said they have nothing at all. Actually, I still can't give a reasonable answer why the two should have any correlation at all, but what I can do is tell you what some seriously confused people think the connection is.

I offer for your consideration an experience that I had while spending a year in that sunny part of the world with the US military conducting tactical human intelligence operations. The fact that I was in Iraq is only relevant to the story in that I was something of a captive audience for the other players in this little story. We were all often confined to the base to which we were assigned, and there wasn't a lot to do there that didn't require our mutual interaction. I didn't realize it at the time, but this chance encounter would turn out to be life-changing for me because it served as something of a "final straw" and the event that convinced me that I had remained quiet for too long when being told in what and how I must believe.

This encounter was with an Army chaplain who happened to be teaching a karate class at the gym on the base. My interaction with him ran from amicable to guarded, to annoying, and finally to outright contempt. I have tried to capture the better part of a year's worth of interaction into a few salient points. Some of what follows were face-to-face conversations; some were via e-mail. All are true and accurate to the best of my recollection, and much was written down at the time so this is a pretty reliable account.

When I first heard there was a karate class being taught on the base, I went to meet the instructor. I wanted to be very tactful as I was also a black belt and had been teaching karate myself for some time and didn't want to appear to be moving in on his turf. When we met in person, I quickly realized that his qualifications for teaching karate were less than adequate (not as irrelevant as it may at first seem), but this was his class, and it was not my place really to upset his apple cart. I thought I would give it a try and at least get in some good workout sessions. This was a combat zone in Iraq, and my options were limited after all and only a temporary situation.

He had a few questions for me about my prior karate training—who I had trained with, where and for how long, things of that nature, the standard sort of information one would expect to be asked when going to a new karate class. But what he was most concerned with was my beliefs about God. He was less concerned that I had trained with some of the most senior and highly respected instructors in Europe, the US, and Japan than he was if I believed that Jesus died for my sins.

While belief in Jesus is an important issue in church, I didn't see its relevance for a karate class. He told me this was relevant because he teaches for the Christian Karate Association (I later learned not the only Christian Karate Association) and a "statement of faith" is an important aspect of their karate training. He went on to say that I didn't have to be a Christian to start training with them but that eventually I would have to accept Christ if I wanted to progress in the organization. Since progressing in their organization was not a desire that I had, this seemed to be a non-issue at the time.

As it turns out, part of the training was Christian indoctrination. I was expected to entertain his lessons in apologetics, and I agreed to at least listen but did not agree to blindly accept anything on face value. While little of what he said really passed any "reasonable person" test, there was a single event during this time that convinced me it was time to stop allowing religious propaganda to go unchallenged. This single event was an assertion he made one day in his office about the divinity of Christ and the nature of evidence. My position was that while his religious beliefs are fine and his right to have these beliefs should be respected, religious faith is not something that can be proven with evidence. If anyone offers a sound argument against this position, I assured him, I welcome it.

What he did was to prove my point better than I ever had by demonstrating the common willingness to create new "facts" to support religious beliefs. "Who do you think was the first president of the United States?"[10] he asked me. Thinking I knew where he was going with this, I cautiously answered, "George Washington." I was cautious not because I doubted my answer but because of where I thought he was going next. And for a brief moment, he didn't let me down. He followed up with, "And how do you know that since you've never met George Washington?" He was making the same mistakes of critical reasoning I have heard for so long when discussing belief with Christians. Since I never met Washington and the chaplain never actually met Christ, then the two perspectives must have equal merit, or at least that is the tack often used by friends of

---

[10] A point on the use of quotation marks here. As I am doing a final edit of this book, I am reminded of something Sebastian Junger notes in his book *Tribe* (Junger 2016). "Ordinarily speech enclosed by quotation marks should be documented with a tape recorder or notebook, and any event should be written down as it happened or shortly thereafter. In the case of these few stories, however, I had to rely entirely upon memory. After giving the matter much thought, I decided that doing so was within my journalistic standards as long as I was clear with my readers about my lack of documentation." I am in much the same position in this case. Much of my interaction with this chaplain was via e-mails which I still have. Others I wrote down at the time; others still I am pulling from memory but have endeavored to be as accurate as possible in all cases.

religion, and that is where I thought his argument would rest. That would have been bad enough, but what came next was much worse.

In an attempt to head off his faulty reasoning, I offered as carefully worded a response as I could muster on the spot. I stated that I believe George Washington was our first president. I believe this because of the undeniable historical evidence from a variety of different sources, each mutually supportive, coupled with the lack of any reliable evidence to the contrary. Also, as it is only logical to assume that since we've had more than forty presidents in our history, some still alive and a couple I've actually seen in person, there had to be a first. This is a claim of a routine event, nothing extraordinary so no extraordinary evidence is needed. Finally, while this event seems very long ago when we casually discuss it today, two hundred years ago is really not that long, historically speaking. It is possible that there are people alive today whose great-great-great-grandfather might have known Washington.[11]

The chaplain's reply was shocking. He informed me that there is more evidence that Jesus rose from the dead after his crucifixion than there is that George Washington ever even existed in the first place. I thought at first I must have misheard him. I asked him to repeat what he had said. He did, and my ears had not deceived me. This man, who so proudly talked about the morality that God had instilled in him the strength of character that comes with being a follower of Christ, not to mention the doctorate degree he claimed to have, was actually telling me, with a straight face, that the weight of the evidence is stronger for the bodily resurrection of Christ than that the father of our nation had ever even existed.

---

[11] And no, I didn't actually do the math at the time of this original conversation to sketch out the average length of a generation to see if it was indeed only five generations or so removed, and I admit that I do not recall exactly how many *greats* I placed before *grandfather* at the time, but I hope the point is well made. Just as a point of reference in how some events in history may not be as far removed from us as we often think, as of the time of this writing, there is still one single living dependent of a soldier who is receiving veteran's benefits from the Civil War (Bidwell 2013).

I must confess to a personal failing on this point. My reaction was so emotional (perhaps that was his intent?) that I didn't have the presence of mind to ask what evidence he was talking about, and I never did ask that question. To this day I don't know how any sane person can argue this point. On the one hand, I should have walked away from any further discussions with this man at this point. On the other, I am glad I did not because our future conversations proved very informative for the path I have chosen since that time.

Allow a digression on this topic of evidence for George Washington versus Jesus's resurrection just to illustrate the seriousness of this problem. Owing to sheer coincidence, the chaplain from my higher headquarters back at my home station was visiting Iraq. Because I was bothered by what the other chaplain had told me (and frankly, I felt it might be some sort of ethical violation that perhaps needed to be reported), I shared the story. I was shocked by the other chaplain's reply when I told him what the first chaplain had said about there being more evidence for the resurrection that the existence of George Washington. He actually agreed that there actually *is* more evidence for the resurrection of Christ than for the existence of Washington!

Now it has taken me a while to arrive at the heart of why "Christian karate" should matter to the reader, even for those who have no interest in the martial arts. This man, who as a chaplain and Army officer, holds a position of considerable influence in the lives of others. As such, he advises people on issues as important as their immortal soul (their belief, not mine) and is often deferred to on issues of ethics and morality. Yet he looked me in the eye and, with a serious tone, told me that farcical story about the evidence of Christ's resurrection relative to that for our first president's very existence. It is difficult to not see such intellectual dishonesty as anything other than a lie. As this book is an appeal for honesty in the terms of religious (in fact all) disquisition, it is important to point out and to reiterate frequently that dishonesty is not only the overt telling of something you know to be untrue, it is also the repeating of things you have every reason to accept are untrue but are simply unwilling to admit it. I would certainly lose all respect for atheists who resort to lying to achieve their ends and from a man who professes a faith in which lying is defined as a sin. I find it reprehensible.

As a retired Army officer now looking back on this situation, what really concerns me most is that this man had a position of honor, trust, and respect as an Army officer. He had this position not because of proficiency in military art and science nor because of, as do doctors and lawyers, a critical skill in a profession such as law or medicine. He had this position because he is in a field characterized by its participant's claims of having an invisible friend and of claims to know things about the cosmos that are simply not knowable. Further, because he had this position, he was empowered to wield influence on the lives of others far out of proportion to that of many other military officers whose authority comes only from the president of the United States and our Constitution, and not the creator of the cosmos (again, their claim, not mine).

I feel it necessary to point out that I have known, and still know, a number of chaplains who are wonderful people and who do a great service in helping our service members make it through tough times. I am not arguing for an abolition of the Chaplains Corps, something advocated by some atheists and free thinkers. I am simply relaying my personal opinion about select experiences I have had that influenced my current thinking.

My experience with the chaplain karate teacher was also instructional for me as it demonstrated one of the most troubling traits often witnessed among theists, and that is the tendency to give credibility to people in areas completely unrelated to religion simply because they are religious. This was brought fully to bear after the chaplain was not present for one class, and I, as the only other black belt, taught the class in his absence. All seemed well until I received an e-mail from the chaplain a couple of days later informing me that in his absence I am not to teach the class because I have not yet accepted their statement of faith and that another student, a yellow belt (a beginner), was to teach the class.

While this might seem to some a completely pointless story, it is actually relevant to all our lives. This mind-set is not limited to a karate class in Iraq. Frankly, if it was limited to that one experience, I would not expect anyone else to care. However, just consider how many times in your life you have heard listed among someone's qualifications to do something, "He's a good Christian." If you have not heard this, then you are the minority (and in all likelihood, you actually did hear it and you've just forgotten). The simple fact is that being a Christian qualifies you for nothing at all other than being a Christian. Aside from your Christianity, you may indeed be a very qualified doctor, lawyer, manager at Denny's, or sniper for a SEAL Team for all I know, but you are qualified at those other things because you have a great deal of experience at those things. It is not innate in the fact that you also believe in a particular god.

Religious Illiteracy[12] (I Don't Know What I Believe, but I Believe It with All My Heart)

Remember dilemmas 2 and 3, that most true believers can't really articulate why they believe and that most Christians know very little about what is actually in the Bible? This ignorance of religion often seems to be more acute for those who are religious than for those who are not. The evidence indicates that most religious folks know less about religion than atheists do. This is problematic when they often insist on telling the rest of us that we must believe as they do. In fact, one of the most consistent (and most troubling) themes I've come across in the God debates is the inverse relationship between what people actually know about religion and the degree to which they are willing to tell others what they must believe based on what God wants.

It is rare indeed for a friend of religion, always eager to tell me I must believe the Bible and follow Jesus, to actually be well versed in what it is they so freely push on others. Countless times, my views have been challenged with "Where does it say that in the Bible?" or more likely, "That's not in *my* Bible." This is why such care has been

---

[12] For an interesting read on the topic of religious literacy (or lack thereof), see Stephen Prothero's book *Religious Literacy*.

taken to actually provide chapter and verse in this book where appropriate. It is no secret that most Christians know surprisingly little about their most revered book. What may be surprising, however, is that atheists usually fair better than devoutly religious people on tests of religious knowledge (Dennett D. 2010).

Most graduates of theological and biblical studies programs at legitimate institutions of higher learning are aware of everything that I will say about the Bible. This information is still a surprise to most churchgoers, however. It is interesting to consider the possible ramifications of a wider understanding of what really is, and is not, in the Bible. Could it be that church attendance would drop precipitously? One of the reasons I so often question the intellectual honesty of religious leaders is that most preachers who hold theological degrees know of the problems raised in chapter 3, yet their congregations remain ignorant. Are they simply not sharing this information, and if not, why not? This lack of understanding of what each religion actually stands for, what is actually in their holy books and of the history of the various religions served as yet another catalyst for my unbelief.

Drive-By Proselytization

I once walked into a Virginia Beach coffee shop to catch up on some reading. I was about halfway through *A History of God* by Karen Armstrong and looking forward to making a little more progress on it. As is often the case, most of the good seats were taken, but there was one in the corner that was free, so I dropped my book there to save the seat while I went to get a cup of coffee. When I turned for my seat, there was a pleasant-looking lady standing in front of me who I at first thought wanted to get past me. When I tried to move out of her way, we at first did that little dance people often do when trying to decide which way to go around another person but you each keep going the same way. However, it became apparent she was actually waiting for me and blocking my way intentionally. I was about to be the victim of a drive-by proselytization!

Standing there, smiling, she asked if that was my book at the corner table. Without thinking about it, I answered that it was. She asked what it's about. I told her that it is a history of the three major monotheistic religions, how they developed, their similarities and differences, and how their adherents all worship the same God, albeit in different ways (apologies to Karen Armstrong if I've done a disservice in my off-the-cuff explanation). "Oh, it's not the same God! You know that, right?" she ejaculated. I was getting a bad feeling about this and felt that I had been ambushed. I informed her that Judaism, Christianity, and Islam all do indeed worship the same God, though in different ways, some minor and some quite profound. She was not having this.

She asked me what I believe. While I knew exactly what she meant, I was half-tempted to attempt a regurgitation of the line Kevin Costner's character in the movie *Bull Durham* used when asked the same question, deleting the initial reference to the soul of course.[13] I informed her that I was "spiritually unaffiliated" but willing to learn from anyone of any faith as long as they were offering something I'd not already heard and dismissed. As it turns out, she had apparently already decided that if I was bothering with something like Armstrong's book about God, I was badly confused and in need of spiritual guidance.

This lady offered to teach me about how I was wrong and to tell me the truth that God wanted me to hear. "Can't God tell me?" I asked. "I am listening." This seemed reasonable to me after all. God knows I am easy to get along with and easy to talk to. He even knows when I am bored and lonely and most apt to be receptive to the company. Why would he need her to tell me about his truths? I am also a lot more likely to believe it coming from him rather than

---

[13] "I believe in the soul... the small of a woman's back, the hanging curveball, high fiber, good scotch, that the novels of Susan Sontag are self-indulgent, overrated crap. I believe Lee Harvey Oswald acted alone. I believe there ought to be a constitutional amendment outlawing Astroturf and the designated hitter. I believe in the sweet spot, soft-core pornography, opening your presents Christmas morning rather than Christmas Eve, and I believe in long, slow, deep, soft, wet kisses that last three days."

some church lady in Starbucks. And why on earth would God send someone so unconvincing and uninteresting to persuade me of his ultimate truth? God needs a marketing campaign!

Understand that at this point in my life I'd already been subjected to this sort of thing quite a bit. Not only with the previously mentioned chaplain in Iraq but frequently throughout the Bible Belt and even on occasion in various countries in Europe and East Asia. I was just about to the point that I had stopped feeling I somehow owe it to people to lie to them and pretend I believe as they do just to save their feelings, especially if they invade my personal space and impose on my personal time to talk about God. After all, if their beliefs are built on a solid foundation, then surely it wouldn't hurt to ask honest questions so long as I did it in a respectful way. Right?

The church lady offered to pray with me, to which I replied that I thought this would be a wasted effort as any omnipotent God already knows what we were going to say in prayer, so to actually say it would be redundant. I also felt that if God is real, then things are going to unfold according to his plan, and for us to pray for him to change his plan is frankly a bit presumptuous. And besides, since I didn't share her beliefs, I didn't think prayer would be appropriate anyway. It would be a bit hypocritical in my estimation. Though I didn't realize it at the time, I was at something of a turning point in my life. While I had taken part in the previously mentioned discussions with the chaplain and a couple of friends over the years about my nascent skepticism, I was slowly beginning to feel empowered to actually tell people that I don't believe in their religion and why, though I was not yet very good at it.

What eventually broke up our conversation was my offer for her to join me and have an open and honest discussion about the merits of our views. Initially, she seemed open to it until I said we would start with her defending my simple question, "Why was Jesus necessary?" She looked as if I had punched her in the throat. You know, that wrinkled face look, the expression of someone who's just had a mosquito fly in her mouth. She finally managed to demand that I explain what kind of question that was. "A simple one, actually, and a fair one at that," I continued. After all, my reasoning went, if

God is omnipotent, why did he need to send a part of himself to die a horrific (albeit temporary) death so that he would be able to allow himself to forgive us for doing what he already know we were going to do before he created us (yes, I am repeating a point here, but it is worth repeating, and at that time, it was the first time I'd ever made it to anyone). Not only was his reported death horrific, it all transpired in such a manner that most of humanity would doubt the whole resurrection story anyway. Couldn't God have just decided we are forgiven for all our transgressions if that's what he wanted to happen anyway?

If God did feel some action, other than simple forgiveness was necessary, couldn't he have done something a little more convincing and lasting and known to a wider audience? A bit of a digression here and not part of my conversation with the church lady, but perhaps God could have been on the moon waiting for Neil Armstrong with a message for all humanity in all languages, perhaps even etched on a material not found anywhere on Earth? Can you imagine it? "One small step for man, one giant leap for… GOD, DAMMIT! WHERE DID THAT COME FROM?" A message delivered in this way would almost certainly remove doubt from most skeptics like me.

OK, back to the church lady. This seemed a bit much for her and her irritation was beginning to show. She clearly was not going to entertain such blasphemy. She left me to my book but not before issuing a challenge. She told me that if I would simply go get any book by Lee Strobel and read it, then my life would be changed and I would become convinced of the error of my thinking and would have no choice but to accept Christ.

She concluded by saying she'd pray for me and forced a smile and walked away, her demeanor and way of carrying herself slightly different now. This is why I have come to refer to this as a drive-by proselytization because it almost always follows the same pattern. First, there is the slow approach—friendly, with the appearance that there might be something else entirely going on, sort of like an Amway salesman. Second, establishing rapport: "Oh, you're a skeptic? Me too!" Third, the hard sell: "Jesus loves you so much he died for you. You don't want to go to hell for not loving him back, do you?" Fourth, the special pleading: "Scientific evidence supports the existence of God. What? It doesn't? Well, scientists are often wrong, and they are always changing their minds anyway." Fifth, the speedy getaway: "Oh, you won't accept my unsupported religious claims, so you must be close-minded. I love you anyway, so I'm gonna pray for you!"

I call this pattern "feel, felt, found, and fuck you." The "feel, felt, found" is a technique I was taught while attending the US Army Recruiting Command Company Commander's Course. Yes, a mouthful, but it was a course designed to prepare captains for command of recruiting companies in the Army. "Feel, felt, found" is a technique used when overcoming objections to a sale (in this case, selling a career in the Army). When someone states an objection, you say, "Oh, I know exactly how you *feel*. I *felt* that way once myself. But what I *found* was…" and then explain away their concern. Drive-by proselytizers do this all the time. "Oh, you are a skeptic? I know exactly how you feel. I am a skeptic too! I once doubted God. But guess what I found. I was wrong!" Then of course, when their consistently unconvincing arguments don't sway you, then comes the "fuck you." Of course, it almost never actually comes in those exact words. It is normally an extremely condescending, "Well, I love you, and I will pray for you." I'd rather have an honest "fuck you."

An interesting (to me at least, and this is my book) side note is that I did get an honest "fuck you" once from a drive-by proselytizer after she said, "Well, I'll pray for you," and I replied, "Thanks, and I'll think for you." I remember quite clearly that not only did I get a heartfelt "Fuck you" but was immediately preceded by an equally heartfelt, "I don't need you to think for me, motherfucker." Yep, I was feeling the love on that particular day. Fortunately, the vast majority of religious people do not feel compelled to force their beliefs on others, but this in itself presents its own problem.

Here is a good place to address the eighth Christian dilemma. You must both be insufficiently caring and uncommitted to your faith and leave people to their beliefs, or you must be so obnoxiously "in their face" about your convictions that you alienate yourself from nearly everyone you know. It seems a nearly insolvable problem for the Christian who wants to take a "live and let live" approach popular among modern, moderate Christians because this violates the very core of their religious dogmas. If you truly believe in your heart that my inability or unwillingness to accept Jesus into my heart means that I go to hell forever, how can you possibly ever let me just live as I wish? This is after all the Great Commission given by Jesus in Matthew 28:18–20 to spread his teaching to all the nations of the world:

> Then Jesus came to them and said, "All authority in heaven and on earth has been given to me. Therefore go and make disciples of all nations, baptizing them in the name of the Father and of the Son and of the Holy Spirit, and teaching them to obey everything I have commanded you. And surely I am with you always, to the very end of the age."

You would never allow a friend to stand on the tracks in front of an oncoming train simply because he said to do so gave his life meaning and purpose and he truly did believe it's the right thing to do. You would physically stop him from doing this! Yet on much weightier matters, eternal salvation or damnation, most Christians today see this as "personal business" and don't say anything. This reminds me of what H. L. Mencken had to say about Protestants: "The only really respectable Protestants are the fundamentalists. Unfortunately, they are also palpable idiots." His point being that while you must admit to believing some pretty wild things to be a fundamentalist, at least you have the courage of your convictions.

For the reasons recounted here and many others, I long ago stopped believing in the things I was taught in church. Anytime I think about how I once believed and how that all changed, I can't help but think of the passage from 1 Corinthians 13:11 that I used to introduce this chapter: "When I was a child, I spake as a child, I understood as a child, I thought as a child: but when I became a man, I put away childish things." Like most atheists, I don't deny there are parts of the Bible that are actually useful and that contain wisdom worthy of emulation. Taken in isolation, this example from Corinthians is one of those useful passages. It is just amazing to me that I have seen Christian apologists use this passage as somehow supporting their position and that it is only clear-thinking adults who see the truth of their religious beliefs. Herein lies another dilemma (number 9 for those who are counting). Quotes and passages of this nature from ancient texts, of apparent depth and profundity, are rarely unambiguous and can often be used by literally anyone to bolster virtually any position on nearly any argument.

My lack of faith has evolved over time to something much more than simple skepticism toward the truth-value of religious claims. What was initially just a personal doubt, a feeling that perhaps my preachers had just misunderstood what the Bible really has to say about the nature of God, became much more. I became concerned about the influence that I saw exercised over daily life in America by the religious right. The incredible political power exercised by a certain group of Americans who see to it that decisions affecting us all are all too often based on religious considerations is very disconcerting. I will come back to this point in chapter 6.

CHAPTER 2

Epistemology: How We Know What We Know (and How We Know You Can't Really Know What You Claim to Know)

If you would be a real seeker after truth, it is necessary that at least once in your life you doubt, as far as possible, all things.

—René Descartes

Epistemology is the study of knowledge. By what conduit do we know what we know?

—Theodore Bikel

We owe much to the scientific method. It is in fact one of the most underappreciated developments in the history of our species. If you doubt it is underappreciated, just spend a short time online or at your local bookstore or library researching how the average American, especially those predisposed to fundamentalist religious thinking, feels about science when compared to religion as a "way of knowing." Look at the way that great thinkers such as Charles Darwin have been vilified for putting forth their extraordinary ideas. Then consider that were it not for the scientific method you would not, in all likelihood, be able to read the opinions that you found against the scientific method in the first place. In our modern age, the odds are very great, indeed, that if you actually did research opinions opposed to the scientific method, you did so by googling it on the internet. This is science in action, not religion. None of the great advances in our civilization would be possible without the desire to peer into the abyss of the unknown and rationally seek answers. Not answers that make us feel good or only those that reinforce our preconceived notions but answers derived from the observation and critical analysis of empirical data. In short, answers that actually work, answers that are true.

If you doubt the importance of the scientific method, stop reading, go out into the woods with a shovel, dig a very deep hole, and bury yourself in it. Some things are just so mind-bogglingly irrefutable that if you still refute them then I don't want you to finish reading this book. Give it to a friend, preferably a clear-thinking friend, perhaps as payment for filling in the hole after you jump in!

It is important to keep in mind the imperfection of human language. To be sure, words have meanings, but not always with sufficient clarity to stand on their own. I often mention science, and in every case, I am talking about the rational interrogation of evidence using facts, evidence, reason, and logic. I may not in every case be referring to the things that are strictly done by formally trained scientists working in scientific labs or in what we may define as "hard science" disciplines. I, for example, am a fan of science—a science groupie—and I try to think scientifically, but I am in no formal way a scientist. I was told that Richard Feynman observed, "Science is what we have learned about how to keep from fooling ourselves."

I have often thought of how this approach is applicable to disparate fields and recently came across the statement in Sam Harris's book *Waking Up*: "There are no real boundaries between science and any other discipline that attempts to make valid claims about the world on the basis of evidence and logic. When such claims and their methods of verification can admit of experiment and / or mathematical description, we tend to say that our concerns are scientific. When they relate to matters more abstract or to the consistency of our thinking itself we often say that we are being philosophical. When we merely want to know how people behaved in the past we dub our interest historical or journalistic. And when a person's commitment to evidence and logic grows dangerously thin or simply snaps under the burden of fear, wishful thinking, tribalism, or ecstasy, we recognize he is being religious" (Harris, *Waking Up: A Guide to Spirituality Without Religion*, 2014).

While the scientific method is a superior way of knowing it is important to be aware of some of the other ways, we might know things as this aids in understanding how we so readily accept bad ideas. Charles Sanders Pierce in the latter part of the nineteenth century outlined some of these ways of knowing. Specifically, there were three methods of knowing that he pointed to and addressed some key characteristics of each. These three ways of knowing were *authority*, *tenacity*, and *a priori* (Kantowitz, Roediger, and Elmes 2001).

The simplest of these is *authority*. With this method, we accept information as true simply because we are told it is so, normally by someone we trust, some *authority* figure such as our parents. As we grow older, there may be other authority figures who replace our parents—teachers, a boss, anyone really who we trust to tell us the truth. Very often this method of knowing, however, becomes untenable for much of what we think we know, at least if there is any significant degree of contrary evidence. When we are very young, we believe our parents completely when they tell us about Santa Claus or the Tooth Fairy or God. But remember that feeling you got when you were first told, normally by a precocious older relative, that Santa isn't real? How about when he tried to destroy that cherished myth by asking questions like, "Have you ever seen Santa?" or "Think about it, how can he visit every child in the world in one night?" or "How did he get in your house last night when you don't have a chimney?" That stressful feeling when confronted with information that (reliably) contradicted what you *knew* to be true is called cognitive dissonance.

About the method of authority, Kantowitz, Roediger, and Elmes (in their textbook on Experimental Psychology) point out, "Provided nothing happens to raise doubts about the competence of the authority setting the beliefs, this method offers the great advantages of minimum effort and substantial security. It is most pleasant in a troubled world to have complete faith in beliefs handed down to you." Could one ask for a more potent explanation for the religious beliefs most of us hold dear than the indoctrination of our early life? Our parents told most of us when we were young that Jesus is God's son and he loves us perfectly, so we believed it. I have been told by more than one Christian that this is not true for them and their parents never even mentioned God. I would submit (and this is open to debate) that if you grew up in America, you were almost certainly indoctrinated to some degree by society to believe in the god of Christianity even if your parents were not highly religious.

Religion, however, has a built-in advantage that makes it difficult, even when we grow up, to question its authority. Eventually, the realization comes to us that our parents are not perfect, and eventually they die, but many of us can't make the conceptual leap to assume the other great authority, God, might also be imperfect (or nonexistent). God is something we can't disprove, but unlike Santa or the Tooth Fairy, we are rarely told God isn't real. God also comes with something that Santa did not, the threat of eternal torture should you not believe. The worst that will happen if you stop believing in Santa is that you get crappy presents or none at all. No, the safe position, if we want to avoid the dreaded cognitive dissonance, is to simply ignore evidence to the contrary.

There is some goodness in knowing things by authority, especially for young children. When your parents tell you not to touch a hot stove or not to play in the street, it is good that we don't normally test their demands and just believe they are right. There are good reasons to believe that Darwinian evolution explains how this method of believing developed in our ancestors, and there is a wealth of scientific and popular literature that supports this view. Two recent popular books by prominent experts in this field that I commend are *Why Evolution Is True* by Jerry Coyne and *The Greatest Show on Earth* by Richard Dawkins.

It is not difficult to imagine how long ago, when predation was a major concern to early man, those children who did as their parents directed and did not wander too far from the relative safety of the group or too near cliffs or other dangerous areas tended to live long enough to reproduce in larger numbers than those who did not do as their parents directed. This argues for the evolutionary advantage of authority, but there also comes a time when it can be a hindrance to progress. There is much to be said for the survival advantage of blindly following what you are taught by your elders if you are an early hominid. It is also clear that this approach can greatly retard deeper understanding of those things upon which the authorities may be wrong in the modern world. Eventually, we must grow up and test the assertions of those in authority and cast off ideas that don't hold up to experience. Without doing so, progress is limited.

When we doggedly cling to ideas we wish to be true (ideas normally instilled by authority), regardless of countervailing information, this may fall under the way of knowing sometimes called *tenacity*. Religious dedication can be an example of this, but it is by no means the only one. Racial bigotry and chauvinism are examples of tenacity. When a bigot believes his race to be superior to another, even in the presence of counterexamples, this is due to tenacity. This approach is highly illogical and can be corrosive to rational thinking. Tenacity accounts in no small measure for the existence of very intelligent people, with legitimate degrees from accredited institutions in scientific disciplines, who still are not considered proper scientists by their peers. This is because they demonstrate a propensity to cling to what they wish to be true in spite of reliable evidence to the contrary. There is a huge difference between being an innovator, a maverick even, within your field and not being a proper scientist because your judgment is badly skewed by ideological dogma. If, for example, you are a geologist who claims that Earth is no more than six thousand years old, you are not a proper scientist, no matter how many degrees you may receive from accredited institutions. This is because you are ignoring all available scientific evidence and instead taking your cues from a religious text that has repeatedly been proven unreliable in matters of science. More on this in the chapter 3 discussion on The Bible Versus Science.

The desire to avoid the psychological discomfort that goes along with learning that you have been wrong about deeply cherished ideas is strong, indeed. Counterintuitively, any honest religious person should be highly supportive of rational inquiry and avoid tenacity and authority as ways of knowing. That is, at least, if they truly believe their religion has any truth-value to speak of. Free, critical, and rational inquiry should be important to the religious as well as the secular person for obvious reasons. If religious claims are actually true and have merit, they will survive being subjected to intellectually rigorous investigation, and the same should be demanded of the claims of other religions. In a world of mutually exclusive religious claims, most, if not all, of these claims must of necessity be false, and if yours are true, then you've nothing to fear from an honest evaluation of the facts and evidence. If, on the other hand, one particular set of beliefs is granted immunity from skeptical challenge, then what is to keep others from claiming similar immunity?

We are presented here with a tenth dilemma of religion. There is nothing inherent in any religion that should make it immune to honest questions and appeals to reason, and to recognize this with other religions and not one's own is simply hypocrisy. The dilemma lies in the fact that it is difficult for the religious person to strongly challenge the claims of other religions for fear of admitting to the same weaknesses in one's own belief system. As a result, we often see adherents of one religion giving a free pass to, or even defending, demonstrably false claims by members of other religions for fear of opening up their own religious claims to scrutiny.

The third way of knowing addressed by Peirce and equally applicable to the dogmatic attachment to religious beliefs is known as the *a priori* method. This occurs in much the same way as *authority*, but with *a priori*, there is not a single authority figure, such as a parent, that tells you what to believe, but rather, it is simply how things "appear to be." In essence, the way things appear to be is the authority, and it can be a powerful one. This is perhaps the biggest hurdle to solid empiricism because the propositions being discussed often don't behave as they appear on the surface. True scientific explanations are often frankly counterintuitive.

We have all heard examples of this; even if we were unaware we were being exposed to the *a priori* method at the time. The sun comes up in the morning and sets at night, right? Well, it is obvious really that Earth is firmly fixed in one place while the Sun revolves around the Earth. That is *apparently* what happens anyway, and in the absence of evidence to the contrary, it seemed perfectly reasonable for our ancestors to think just that for a very long time. The very obvious problem this poses is that no matter how creative our ancestors were in trying to understand why and how the Sun orbited the Earth they were simply seeking to answer the wrong question and no matter how ingenious their attempts were, the answers could not help but to be wrong.

Fortunately, we are (sometimes) able to overcome this tendency to believe that things must be as they appear. With respect to the example of the Sun circling the Earth, Copernicus managed to overcome conclusions based on *authority, tenacity,* and *a priori* thinking. Consider the opposition to Copernicus's idea that Earth was not really at the center of the universe with everything revolving around it. Copernicus was not alone in being correct that Earth was not at the center of the cosmos, nor was he the first to believe this. Aristarchus of Samos, for example, proposed a heliocentric model of our solar system nearly 2,300 years ago. For purposes of this book, however, Copernicus is a good example. It was with Copernicus that the groundwork was laid to finally overthrow the geocentric view of the solar system to which we had so long subscribed.

The idea that Earth was in fact revolving around the sun, right along with the rest of the solar system, was threatening to the church's idea that God had placed us firmly at the center of all his creation. Biblical verses that were used by the church to support and enforce the geocentric view of the cosmos, like with so many other topics, can be a bit vague and are clearly open to interpretation. I was asked recently by a Christian friend, "Where does it say in the Bible that the Earth is at the center?" while discussing this topic. When I offered Joshua 10:13, Judges 5:31, and others, he offered, "I don't read it that way." Well, neither do I, but it was verses like these that the church used to justify the suppression of scientific advancement for centuries and maintain that the Earth is indeed at the center of the cosmos (remember dilemma number 9). The fact that very few Christians today believe in a geocentric universe does not change the fact that the Church, and Protestant religious leaders, such as Martin Luther, enforced this view for a very long time and relied on the Bible as evidence for that position.

Copernicus's book *De Revolutionibus Orbium Coelestium* (*On the Revolutions of the Heavenly Spheres*) was suppressed by the Catholic Church, which placed it on the *Index Librorum Prohibitorum*, or *Index of Forbidden Books*, in March 1616 (*Encyclopædia Britannica* 2015). Not only the Catholic Church was displeased with Copernicus, Martin Luther stated, "People gave ear to an upstart astrologer who strove to show that the earth revolves, not the heavens or the firmament, the sun and the moon... This fool wishes to reverse the entire science of astronomy; but sacred Scripture tells us [Joshua 10:13] that Joshua commanded the sun to stand still, and not the earth" (Kuhn 1957).

While it took the church centuries to refine their censorship techniques, this practice goes back to the beginning (and before) of Christianity. Censorship of a sort was apparently instrumental in the early spread of the word. According to Acts 19:19–20, "A number who had practiced sorcery brought their scrolls together and burned them publicly. When they calculated the value of the scrolls, the total came to fifty thousand drachmas. In this way the word of the Lord spread widely and grew in power." Lest you be tempted to think such draconian measures as publishing an index of forbidden books is ancient history, this index was only abolished seven years after the first manmade object landed on the moon!

A priori thinking can be a powerful impediment to progress. A model of the universe used until Copernicus's ideas prevailed was given to us by Claudius Ptolemy (90–168 CE), who proceeded from the presupposition that the earth was at the center of the universe. Consequently, he went to great lengths to reconcile the erratic movements of the planets, devising a very clever theory of planetary motion. His explanation was brilliant and lasted until Copernicus came up with a better model, later elaborated upon by Kepler and finally proven observationally by Galileo. Unfortunately, Ptolemy, while extraordinarily clever, was also extraordinarily wrong. Such is the danger of relying on *authority*, *tenacity*, and *a priori*. Such is the danger of trying to answer the wrong question.

The Scientific Method—More Than Just Science

The historic struggle between faith in a god or gods and rational inquiry has been a slow, sometimes halting, but inexorable and irrefutable eroding away of justifications for God as an explanation for the mysteries of nature. "God did it" doesn't quite satisfy when we have more far eloquent and convincing explanations for just about everything, explanations that work just fine without the arbitrary imposition of the god hypothesis. Unfortunately, these scientific advances may not be necessarily irreversible. Society and human learning have endured devastating setbacks in the past, and this can happen in the future. Civilization is not inevitable and linear. It is for this reason that rational inquiry is so worthy of a vigorous defense.

We once accepted that only through a special act of creation could humans—clearly the only creatures we know of that are capable of conceiving of a god—have come into being. Darwin, Wallace[14] and a great many others in the intervening years have shown, with exquisite clarity, detail, and often even beauty, how we came to be—all without the need of divine assistance. We cannot yet fully account for the initial inception of life, but once life got its start, we no longer had any reason to turn to God as an explanation. LaPlace is said to have remarked to Napoleon when asked where God fits into his model of the cosmos, "Sir, I have no need of that hypothesis." It is entirely possible this report is apocryphal and is sometimes refuted by religious authorities with LaPlace's religious conviction being pointed out. What is significant about LaPlace's observation, if he did in fact utter the reported words, is not that he denied the existence of God but only that he didn't see the need to invoke God to explain planetary motion. Like LaPlace, we have time and time again found no need for the god hypothesis.

---

[14] Alfred Russell Wallace, a contemporary of Charles Darwin, was a co-discoverer of evolution through natural selection. Wallace developed this theory independent of Charles Darwin, and it was this that spurred Darwin to publish his work on the origin of species.

While neither perfect nor complete (nor is it likely to ever be) science, it is the best tool we have for discerning bad ideas from good and good ideas from better ones. If we never went beyond knowledge from authority, tenacity, and a priori, we would still see ourselves as apart from nature and not part of the animal kingdom as we now know to be true. We would still see ourselves firmly set at the center of the universe, unmoving, watching the sun, stars, and other planets revolving around us as seems to be indicated in the Bible (addressed in chapter 3). Science offers explanations that are demonstrably concordant with reality and therefore more reliable and consistent than religious explanations. The scientific explanations are practical and often make our lives better for the knowledge they provide.

Religion has traditionally laid claim to many of the explanations that are now clearly within the magisteria of science. Before science, religion attempted to explain such issues as where we came from, how go the heavens, when, and why; how we should treat each other; what moral behavior is; and what happens to us when we die. Our religious impulse developed at a time of great naiveté for our species, by a people for whom even the most rudimentary glimpses of twenty-first-century technology would surely have seemed the work of gods.

No less inherently intelligent than we are today, though not yet blessed with the gift of science and the accumulated knowledge of countless generations, our ancestors of a few thousand years ago tried to explain mysteries with the tools at their disposal. Our tools are better today. Well-intentioned as our forebears may have been, they were ill-equipped to understand the complexities of our cosmos, and as a result, superstition reigned supreme. It has often been said that nature abhors a vacuum. Surely, it is true that human understanding, too, abhors a vacuum. We evolved a natural curiosity—we desire explanations. Unfortunately, this often leads many of us to be more satisfied with very bad answers than with no answers at all.

Even as science carries with it an explanatory power far superior to that of superstition, religion clings tenaciously to the idea that the really important issues are still theirs alone to address. While science is able to explain with piercing clarity the movements of the heavens, the inner workings of the atom and the various "flavors" of quarks from which the subatomic particles are made, religion offers an anemic protest. "Ah, but the really big stuff is ours still," say the religious apologists. "Sure, science can tell us how the diversity of biology came about, but can it tell us how that life started in the first place?" the religious devotee may implore. To this, they might add that science can't tell us *why* life was created in the first place or *how* or *why* the big bang happened. "This is our domain," they argue. To which I have a simple question. What are the answers that religion offers to these questions, and what evidence supports those answers?

The apologist may offer, "God did it," in any instance where science may not have ready answers or more likely in instances where the apologist doesn't understand or rejects the scientific explanations that are offered. However, "God did it" is a bare assertion with no evidence upon which to base the claim. I can just as easily assert that the flying spaghetti monster or the invisible pink unicorn did it. My evidence is every bit as certain as any offered by the believers of any deity either now or in the past.

This is, I think, as good a place as any to introduce Christian dilemma number 11. This dilemma, which is a centerpiece of religious apologetics, is largely informed by what is sometimes called the "God of the gaps argument." This particular argument is an attempt to benefit from the inability of science to explain "life, the universe and everything" (to borrow a term from Douglas Adams). The gaps that science cannot yet fill are where friends of religion often attempt to insert God. The "God of the gaps" argument is a form of an argument from ignorance, what John Locke described in *An Essay Concerning Human Understanding* as *argumentum ad ignoratiam*. How this becomes a dilemma specifically for the theist is this; science has always been and continues to be so incredibly efficient at filling in the gaps in our understanding, leaving no room for God. Any attempt to insert God into the gaps of scientific explanations only draws sharp focus to the exact location from which God will likely be next evicted. By attempting to appeal to the gaps of scientific knowledge, attention is only drawn to the realization that while science can't explain everything, religion explains nothing at all.

I am at a loss to come up with a single example of an answer once given by science for which religion now provides a suitable alternative. Conversely, there is a long and ever-growing list of questions with attempted answers, however weak, once provided by religion for which science now delivers the only workable explanations. There has been an inverse relationship to science's ability and religion's inability to explain the cosmos. Where scientific knowledge has become more elegant, powerful, sublime, and beneficial and has answered the previously unanswerable, religion has time and again retreated into the shadowy gaps cast by the light of science. The scriptures are replete with false claims, broken promises, and explanations for the natural world that have been proven untrue to the degree that it cannot be ignored by any person thinking reasonably on this subject.[15] While I cannot say with certainty that science may not someday yield ground to a better explanation forthcoming from religion, the opposite trend has been so consistently true for so long that it seems unreasonable to suspect that it may someday reverse itself.

Science's inability to explain something now does not mean science will not answer it someday, so to resort to "God did it" and just leave it at that is intellectually lazy and has at times retarded scientific advancement. As Dr. Peter Atkins put it, "The adipose argument is that God did it. That of course is the lazy man's elixir. A cocktail made up of a swig of credulity and a teaspoon full of unwillingness to think. In short, it is an explanation that avoids explanation" (Atkins and Craig 2011).

Neil deGrasse Tyson has spoken and written about the perimeter of ignorance (Tyson) and the choice faced by scientists to either "invoke a deity or continue the quest for knowledge." He offers several examples, but the most pertinent in my mind is that of Isaac Newton, who Tyson considers to be the greatest genius in the his-

---

[15] My original wording for this sentence was "It cannot be ignored by a reasonable person," but I changed it because a central theme I hope to convey is how perfectly reasonable and highly intelligent people are often highly religious but are only so because of the ability to suspend or ignore reason on certain issues and by subjugating their intelligence and reason to faith, at least on matters of religion.

tory of our species. In order to explain why planets move in ellipses, Newton simply invented by himself integral and differential calculus when he was twenty-five years old! Newton was able to explain, with uncanny precision, the motions of heavenly bodies as other heavenly bodies act upon them—the Earth orbiting the Sun, the Moon around the Earth, and the like. However, when the effects of other bodies (such as the effect of Mars's gravity on the Earth) were thrown into the mix, Isaac Newton failed to get the right answers.

Newton's great mistake? He invoked God as an answer to the problem. He essentially gave up his quest for knowledge and decided God was the answer, and this was exactly the wrong answer. How do we know this? Just over a century later, another genius, though one who was not in the league of Newton, the previously mentioned LaPlace, developed perturbation theory to explain how planetary motion continues unimpeded by all these little gravitational tugs of the many celestial bodies in our solar system. Isaac Newton could have done this with half his brain tied behind his back if he had not decided that this was the purview of God and stopped trying. Given enough time and sufficient intellectual rigor naturalistic explanations have always succeeded where supernatural explanations failed. The best religion can hope for is a tie at "We both don't know," but even this is temporary.

According to the *New Oxford American Dictionary*, the scientific method is "a method or procedure that has characterized natural science since the 17th century, consisting in systematic observation, measurement, experiment, the formulation, testing, and modification of hypothesis." What follows is personal commentary but reasonable and defensible nonetheless.

If there is a single word that can sum up the scientific method and crystallize what really sets it apart from other ways of knowing, I would submit that that word is *honesty*. The scientific method demands complete and sometimes brutal honesty in following where the compass of empirical data points. It does not matter how good a desired experimental outcome would make you feel, how emotionally attached you are to a particular hypothesis, or how esteemed a particular scientist is who supports a given position. It doesn't matter that believing in something gives your life meaning and purpose, that having your entire family believe it along with you might bring your family closer together. None of this is at all relevant to the scientific method. All that matters is ferocious honesty in light of the evidence. On this, Richard Feynman asked us to:

> Compare the consequences [of your theory] to experience... if it disagrees with experience, the guess is wrong. In that simple statement is the key to science. It doesn't matter how beautiful your guess is or how smart you are or what your name is. If it disagrees with experience, it's wrong. That's all there is to it... Don't invent elaborate calculus to make your guess seem right, or claim intervention by a higher power. Just admit you're wrong.

During the question-and-answer period following a lecture in Lynchburg, Virginia, Richard Dawkins was issued a challenge. He was asked to explain why he rejects the incomprehensible concept of the Holy Trinity but freely accepts the (perhaps) equally-hard-to-grasp implications of quantum theory. The reply was not what the questioner expected, I am sure. While conceding the difficulty the human mind has in actually visualizing the inner workings of quantum strangeness, Dawkins pointed out that the two concepts are in no way comparable. The Trinity offers no explanations about the world around us, makes no testable predictions or in any other way offers a way of empirically testing its merit. On the other hand, "Quantum theory yields experimental predictions which have been verified to an accuracy of a number of decimal places, so accurate that the great theoretical physicist Richard Feynman compared it to the accuracy of predicting the width of North America to the accuracy of the width of one human hair. That is why quantum theory has to be taken seriously."

This leads us to dilemma number 12 faced by the religious person. Science not only contradicts religion in a great many ways; science also actually works! Science not only works, it does so *miraculously* well. In light of this, the theist is often found trying to undermine science in an attempt to defend the faith. This is a dilemma because friends of religion, like all of us, enjoy the gifts of science—they even embrace science when they feel it can be used to support their claims. When science poses a threat, however, apologists attempt to throw science under the proverbial bus.

This was, perhaps, the final straw for me with respect to belief in God. A great many things—some that I have written about in this book, many that I have not—caused me to question the existence of God, but the constant one-way, regression of God into the gaps of human ignorance (and those gaps are getting smaller all the time) has left me no choice but to abandon the god hypothesis. Consider again all those things for which we once turned to religion as a source of explanation and what happens when we instead look to science. Science provides better explanations every single time. Either God is not real or he has taken great pains to create a universe that behaves exactly as if he is not real. In either case, we are well advised to behave as if he is not real until better evidence arises.

Why Religion?

> The very nature of our brains evolved to guess the most plausible interpretation of the limited evidence available makes it almost inevitable that without the discipline of scientific research we will often jump to wrong conclusions, especially about rather abstract matters.
> —Francis Crick

> I am satisfied, and sufficiently occupied with the things which are, without tormenting or troubling myself about those which may indeed be, but of which I have no evidence.
> —Thomas Jefferson

> If God did not exist, it would be necessary to invent Him.
>
> —Voltaire

Think back to the opening pages of this book when I mentioned that there are approximately two billion people on the earth today who are identified as Christian, another 1.2 billion or so Muslims, and so forth. Most of us believe in some sort of god or other supernatural claims. Clearly, atheists really are in the minority. But why is this so if, as I contend, there really is no rational or convincing argument available to support the god hypothesis? Why are so many intelligent people so enamored of the idea of a god or gods? In actuality, it really isn't so hard to imagine how the idea of something beyond us came to be in our collective psyche. It seems the creation of gods is simply a natural byproduct of our evolved intelligence and imagination.

There is a clear survival advantage of higher intelligence and the ability to think abstractly. Imagine three sets of footprints on the beach, one large set, one slightly smaller, and a third smaller still. There is no reason to believe that any animal, beyond man, can gather much from these prints other than something came through here and maybe "they went that-a-way." We, on the other hand, can imagine the man, woman, and child that came through here. Not only can we picture this family in our minds, we can wonder about them abstractly and creatively. We might wonder if the woman is beautiful, the man strong, and the child precocious. We might even project these thoughts into the future. Will the child, we might wonder, grow up to be like his father or her mother?

There are much more pragmatic advantages that come with this ability to daydream about things unseen. Our ancestors were quite aware of the dangers all around them. Early man, just as we are, was weaker and slower than many of the predators in his environment. Then, as now, we were not equipped with sharp claws or large canine teeth to use as formidable weapons. We lacked the elephant's strength, the cheetah's speed, and the bird's flight. What we did have was our superior intelligence. And not just the "know how" for crafting weapons. Early man surely used the ability described earlier (to wonder about the future of the child who left the tracks in the sand) to a different end.

This ability served us well for avoiding predation as well as for being better predators ourselves, alone and in groups. We evolved to see dangers early enough to avoid them or to anticipate the location and behavior of prey early enough to secure our next meal. Sometimes we do this just a bit too well, and we perceive things that are not there. This evolved imagination, with its inherent flaws, goes even further, to something known as a hyperactive agency detection device, or HADD, which is the tendency to attribute intervention in human affairs to an intelligent force that may not be real. This is easy to understand if you take evolution into account and there is a distinct survival advantage to this believe it or not, even though it sometimes leads us to wrong conclusions.

Imagine if you will two human ancestors. One tends to see predators in the bushes even when predators are not there and keeps a safe distance. As a result of avoiding perceived danger, he also sometimes avoids real danger. The other human ancestor, the one that does not perceive danger where none exists, does not react to actual danger until it is an unmistakable, legitimate threat, often too late, and is less likely to propagate his genetic makeup (and his risk-taking tendencies). While it might seem counterintuitive on a certain level that we would evolve the tendency to be wrong about something like this, it is really not so hard to comprehend when you take a cost-benefit analysis into account. There is little cost for guessing there is a tiger in the bushes and avoiding the bushes even if there is no tiger (known as a type I error). The cost for not imagining there is a threat in the bushes when there is one (a type II error) and getting too close as a result is that one helps to propagate the tiger's genes by becoming a nourishing meal.

There is also a phenomenon known as pareidolia, or the tendency to see or hear things that aren't really there or to assign significance where none is warranted. Psychologists are quite familiar with this and understand it fairly well. This trait is often associated with seeing human faces in common objects, though it is not limited to faces. I recall one such event that happened to me while jogging once near my home in Virginia. As I rounded a curve in the trail, I looked ahead and saw a bicycle leaning against a tree. I very clearly saw a road-racing-style bicycle there ahead of me. It was red in color. I assumed the cyclist must be answering the call of nature off in the woods nearby. I then wondered why someone would be riding a street bike on a rough trail like this. Also, at this particular trail, there are signs posted saying no bicycles are allowed. But aside from this, I could imagine a mountain bike, but not this particular type of bike, being used on this trail. It was only after I got closer that I realized it wasn't a bicycle at all but a bunch of twisted vines and tree branches. As strange as it may seem for anyone reading these words, this really did appear, at least briefly, like a bicycle. From this simple bunch of naturally occurring vines and branches, I not only imagined a non-existent bicycle; but I had also started to develop a concept of the cyclist in my mind, even going so far as to question why he may be in such an unlikely location, why be on a rough trail with a road bike, and why ignore the signs.

Back to the evolutionary survival advantage and just keeping with the example of sometimes seeing faces where there are none. There are clear advantages to being extremely good at recognizing faces. The ability to discern not only a face but to distinguish between friend and foe very quickly is quite a handy ability. Again, this ability comes with the additional baggage of sometimes seeing faces that are not there or perhaps "recognizing" someone you've never actually met. As social creatures, we are better in groups than alone, and this imagination also helped us work together in groups. Our ability to empathize with other humans, to realize they are aware just as we are and imagine how they feel, is critical to this cooperation. A healthy imagination was just that—healthy. It was, in fact, essential to our survival. This imagination comes at a cost, however. We sometimes imagine things that aren't really there. Is it any wonder then that our imagination sometimes gets the better of us?

Another aspect of evolved human psychology that served us well from a survival advantage perspective but that also carries with it certain less advantageous side effects is self-awareness. This is actually one of the more interesting subjects (and sometimes very confusing) to study in human psychology. For example, first-order consciousness is simply that I am self-aware. Second-order is when I am aware that you are aware. Third-order is that I am aware that you are aware that I am aware, etc. Self-awareness and our ability to imagine future events, combined with even the most casual observation of how nature works, leads us to a very disconcerting realization—awareness of our own mortality. The realization that we are ephemeral in nature, combined with our strong survival instinct, leads to some very serious emotional repercussions. Faced with the simple fact that there is absolutely nothing at all we can do about this, we seek ways to deal with this emotional distress. But how?

Consider all that we've discussed about how we know what we know and how we perceive the world around us, as well as what we understand of human nature. We are pattern-seeking primates born with an incredible innate curiosity. We have a natural aversion to not knowing. We crave answers, even bad ones. We would prefer a bad explanation to no explanation at all. Again, this is something that gave us a huge survival advantage, but the survival advantage is simply to survive to reproductive age, not to be happy about the consequences of our own mortality or of not knowing. It is not at all difficult to see how our religious impulse developed when you consider the implications of pareidolia, hyperactive agency detection, awareness of our own mortality, as well as the mortality of those we love (and the desire to see them again after death), and our strong desire for explanations.

It is little wonder that so many of us believe in things unseen, even in the absence of any evidence all to support those beliefs. However, that we believe in God in large numbers does not in any way lend to the probability that God is real. David Hume famously said, "A wise man proportions his belief to the evidence" (Hume, *An Enquiry Concerning Human Understanding*, 2006) Beliefs in incredible things require incredibly convincing evidence.

PART II

Failure of Reason and Lack of Evidence

CHAPTER 3

Cognitive Dissonance: The True Nature of the Good Book

The God of the Old Testament is arguably the most unpleasant character in all fiction: jealous and proud of it; a petty, unjust, unforgiving control-freak; a vindictive, bloodthirsty ethnic cleanser; a misogynistic, homophobic, racist, infanticidal, genocidal, filicidal, pestilential, megalomaniacal, sadomasochistic, capriciously malevolent bully.

—Richard Dawkins

I say I bet you didn't know this came in the Bible... god isn't God a shit!

—Randolph Churchill

Assume you grow weary of all the uncertainties of life. You find yourself needing a source of true knowledge that is reliable, consistent, enlightening, and comforting. Not to worry, dear friend, the all-knowing creator of the universe gave us a special book. This book not only tells us how to deal with the difficulties we face; it is ineffable, perfect in every way—no better book has ever been written. However, when you read this book yourself and try to discern the meaning and importance of the contents, something seems amiss. Perhaps, like me, you found reason to question the veracity of this book. Perhaps some of the stories just don't add up. Perhaps this book, the Bible, isn't really the Good Book after all.

As someone who grew up in the deeply religious American South, I could not help but wince at the quote from Richard Dawkins that opens this chapter. I did not like it when I first heard it even though I was already an unbeliever. I thought it was unfair. I don't know a single Christian (personally) who could be described in this way or even be mistaken for someone who would follow a god like that. But there is a problem. If you want to take issue with Professor Dawkins on this, you'd better have more than the Bible on your side, because there is ample justification for all of his statements. In fact, the Bible clearly supports his assertion almost word-for-word.

Do you doubt me? Let's look at the quote again, this time inserting biblical citations for each claim: "The God of the Old Testament is arguably the most unpleasant character in all fiction [This is the one subjective statement, but Dawkins did qualify it with "arguably."]: jealous and proud of it [Exodus 34:14]; a petty [Deuteronomy 13:15], unjust [too many examples to list, but consider just two: original sin (Romans 5:12–21) and substitutionary atonement (1 Peter 2:24)], unforgiving control freak [Matthew 12:32, Mark 3:29], a vindictive [Genesis 6:7], bloodthirsty ethnic cleanser [Deuteronomy 20:17; Judges 11:32–33]; a misogynistic [1 Corinthians 11:3–5, 1 Corinthians 14:34–35], homophobic [Leviticus 20:13], racist [Leviticus 20:1–3], infanticidal [Exodus 13:2], genocidal [Deuteronomy 7:1–3], filicidal [Genesis 22:2, Judges 11:39], pestilential [Ezekiel 14:19], megalomaniacal [Deuteronomy 7:4], sadomasochistic [Exodus 21:20–21], capriciously malevolent bully [Leviticus 27:28–29]."[16]

Here we find a thirteenth Christian dilemma. Christians (most theists for that matter) have painted themselves into a corner morally/philosophically speaking. If you ask most theists about the values, norms, and mores they hold dear—or ask them what kind of people they wish their children to become—and then critically read the Bible in search of those values, you might be amazed at what you

---

[16] As I've already mentioned, this book was written over several years and in many places. Most of this chapter was written when I was still an active duty Army officer (I retired in 2011). Since then, Dan Barker has written an entire book on this same topic, *God: The Most Unpleasant Character in All Fiction*. While I have not (as I type these words) read this particular book from Barker, I have every reason to believe it is worth reading.

find. The characteristics most Christians want in their children are often more in keeping with the writings of Epicurus, Democritus, Siddhartha Gautama, and Confucius (and a host of more modern moral philosophers) than with the Bible. This is a dual dilemma for the Christians who claim that our morality comes from God when the Bible is not only morally ambiguous (to be generous), it is the sole source of what Christians claim to know about God's moral nature.

I wrote earlier about the psychological discomfort we experience when confronted with evidence that effectively challenges a cherished myth—cognitive dissonance. This psychological discomfort exists for a number of reasons, not least of which is that we *desire* these beliefs to be true. When we not only believe something is true but also desperately hope that it is true, we are bothered by evidence that indicates we may be wrong. Another reason for the unease with which countervailing evidence is greeted is that we have often fashioned our lives and actions around these beliefs—we've "invested" in these beliefs. We often have much to lose if we admit we are wrong. We also, however, have much to gain if we honestly accept our errors. So while it is often difficult, intellectual honesty should always be our goal. Let us now honestly discuss the Bible.

How many among us have ever honestly contemplated the assertion that the Bible is the Good Book even though it directs us to kill insubordinate children (Deuteronomy 21:18–21), sanctions human sacrifice to God for his assistance in killing other human beings (Judges 11:30–39), and directs the victim of rape to marry her rapist (Deuteronomy 22:28–29) or that she be killed for not resisting hard enough (Deuteronomy 22:23–24).

This task is approached in the spirit of Benedict de Spinoza when considering his own similar task: "I determined to examine the Bible afresh in a careful, impartial, and unfettered spirit, making no assumptions concerning it, and attributing to it no doctrines, which I do not find clearly therein set down." His last thought is especially critical: "attributing to it no doctrines, which I do not find clearly therein set down." Yes, it was worth repeating. When the Bible clearly says to kill an entire race of people, man woman, and child, that is genocide; and any theologian or apologist who argues "that's really not what God meant" is simply misusing words and what he's saying is meaningless palaver. If there are exegetical issues of mitigation or extenuation which make genocide, rape, slavery, and other evils, actually conducive to a "greater good," that is one thing—a thing for which I have seen no evidence by the way—but it is a position which at least does not deny the fact that these things are presented in the Bible as God's will.

With the exception of framing the biblical discussion with a few introductory thoughts, I have taken care to write nothing here that is not actually found in the pages of the Bible. Of necessity, I will begin with a discussion of biblical origins and touch on the broader nature of biblical claims, reliability, and consistency before addressing specific biblical positions on important issues. I have also not taken things out of context, no doubt an accusation I will receive. I have normally not even provided a context but only reported what's in the book.

Some may consider this lack of context a failing, but the intent is not to argue theology in this chapter but rather to educate the reader about what is actually in the Bible. Interestingly, the "context" excuse is only used when addressing the "bad parts" of the Bible. Conveniently, for the parts of the Bible that actually are good, context is never needed; the words are okay on their own.

Finally, some may find what follows as a sort of ad hominem attack on God. But there is no other way to address the actual nature of the Christian god, if there is a god, than to refer to the pages of the Bible. We can argue about the possible existence of God, discussing the pros and cons of the cosmological and teleological arguments (addressed in the following chapter) for example, but these conversations only address the possibility that *some* god may or may not exist. They do not really talk about his nature. If we are to talk about what we believe God might be like, we must turn to the scriptures. It is the Christian operator's manual! The only possible exception to this is found in the use of the argument from morality, which I will address in chapter 4 and explain why this does not stand up to scrutiny.

When we actually read the entire Bible and do not just cherry-pick "the good parts," we are left with the question asked about God by Kenneth C. Davis:

> Is it the angry, jealous, temperamental, punishing Yahweh? The war God celebrated by Moses? The God who swept life off the face of the earth in the Flood, killed the first born in Egypt, helped conquer the people of Jericho and had them put to the sword, and silently accepted the sacrifice of Jephthah's daughter? The God who took pleasure from the smell of burnt animal flesh?
>
> Or is it the merciful, just, patient, forgiving God? The tender Shepherd of the Twenty-third Psalm? The hunky 'lover' of Song of Solomon? The "perfect" Father of Jesus? And could they all possibly be the same God? (Davis 1998)

The Bible, from Whence Did It Come? (Here's a Hint: Probably Not Where You Think)

> When I think of all the harm [the Bible] has done, I despair of ever writing anything to equal it.
> —Oscar Wilde

> Properly read, the Bible is the most potent force for atheism ever conceived.
> —Isaac Asimov

The Bible is understood to be different things by different people. To some, particularly fundamentalist Christians, it is the divinely inspired literal truth of the almighty creator of the universe—the perfect word of a perfect, just, and loving God. To some less conservative Christians, it is a set of (largely) allegorical or metaphorical stories given to us by men, albeit inspired by God, as a source of guidance on how we deal with him and with each other. To others, it is poetically beautiful, historically significant, and morally relevant but not divine in nature. To others still (and I count myself among this group), it is a poorly written amalgamation of prescriptions and proscriptions for the control of a group of people at a time when plate tectonics, the germ theory of disease, cosmology, astronomy, and physics were not yet understood—a book written when it was the best we could do but, in spite of this, still worthy of study as literature and for its cultural and historical significance.

Because of these vastly differing perceptions of the Bible, it is difficult to embark upon a discussion about it that makes sense to all people. No matter where you come down on the spectrum of biblical impression described above or somewhere else completely with respect to the Bible (as it is difficult to capture all the possibilities), one must concede that, as the sole foundational source document on the authority and historicity of Christianity, it must be addressed.

Some may argue that the Bible is not the "sole foundational source document" for the dominant world religion. While it is true that theologians and philosophers such as Maimonides and Augustine had a huge impact on the interpretation of scripture, they were still interpreting the same scripture. At least it was essentially the same scripture by the time of Augustine (354–430 CE) and Maimonides (1135–1204 CE). In fact, it is probably fair to include Judaism (especially since I just mentioned Maimonides) and Islam into this as well. The Old Testament is, to a large extent, the Jewish Bible, and while Muslims might claim the Quran as the divine word of God, theirs is still a religion based upon the foundation of the much older Judaic and Christian traditions. It is also worth pointing out that all the failings (save for its questionable authorship) of the Bible are found also in the Quran.

It is not my contention in the sometimes-harsh critique that follows that there is nothing of value to be found in the Bible. I've already conceded that there is *some* poetic beauty, wisdom, moral virtue, historical accuracy, and literary goodness to be found in the pages of the Bible. We find all the aforementioned qualities of merit in writings by a great many men throughout history, however, and with no claim to holy nature. Cervantes penned *Don Quixote*—selected by the Nobel Institute as "the best work of fiction ever written" (BBC News 2002)—in the seventeenth century. The depth and quality of many of the works of Shakespeare are believed by almost anyone, not judging from the perspective of a true believer and on religious grounds, to be far superior to anything found in the Bible. The logical consistency in the Bible, the narrative flow, the ability to command the rapt attention of the reader are no better than that of a below-average author today. Frankly, it is hard to imagine anyone being able to get the Bible published if it were written today. Could you imagine me trying to get this book past a publisher if I had entire sections that addressed nothing other than my paternal genealogy going back dozens of generations? I would have been summarily dismissed from consideration. Yet the Bible (to some Christians at least) is considered divine and inerrant, the greatest book ever written.

It is not surprising in the least that there is some redeeming value in the Bible. It was man's best attempt (at least this particular group of men) to describe the world in which they lived. A great many very intelligent (though theologically wrong in my opinion) men then had many centuries to improve upon it. What *is* surprising is that there is so much else there that is not redeeming in any way. Consider that, arguably the most powerful institution ever created by man, historically speaking, the Church has had twenty centuries in which to improve upon the Bible (longer for the Old Testament), and still we are told that the Earth was created before the Sun and other stars, plants also came before the Sun, whales appeared before reptiles, and a great many things we now know to be quite wrong.

Just to unpack one of these claims, let's address the notion that whales came before reptiles. This comes from Genesis 1:21–24. Whales are aquatic mammals, which evolved from land mammals. Reptiles are, well, reptiles. We now know the first reptiles (just to use one "creeping thing" mentioned in Genesis) appeared approximately 315 million years ago. The first mammals did not appear until approximately 225 million years ago, and the first whales not until approximately 35 million years ago. Granted these are *very* approximate ages of reptiles, mammals, and whales due to the nature of evolution and the fact that there was not just a magical appearance one day of any single animal. If the Bible were from the perfect creator of the universe, there would be no need for correction. God would be the ultimate copy editor.

Contrary to what many may assume at this point, it is not my position that time spent reading and even diligently studying the Bible is time wasted. To be sure, if you dedicate your life to the Bible as the sole book worthy of study, you have wasted a significant portion of your life, but for all its flaws, the Bible is actually a fascinating book, especially if you put it in the proper historical context. The Bible should be read and understood for a very simple reason first and foremost—it is probably the most influential (yet possibly the least read and most poorly understood) book in the history of man.

This concession does not attest to the reliability of supernatural claims in the Bible in any way. A very strong case can be made that the tremendous success and influence of the Bible and of Christianity has had far more to do with astute political decisions of ruling elites who happened to be Christian (or at least titular Christians and who co-opted the religion for their own political ends) than any deep conviction that the religious truth claims are reliable. Just consider the single example of the Roman Emperor Constantine (Flavius Valerius Aurelius Constantine, or Constantine the Great, 272–337 CE), whose conversion to and legitimization of Christianity likely did more to promote the faith than all the alleged miracles combined. Or consider perhaps the role played by Theodosius I (Flavius Theodosius Augustus, 347–395 CE), who made Christianity the official state religion of the Roman Empire. Both Constantine and Theodosius, with all their tremendous influence on the future of Christianity, were human leaders, not divine miracle workers.

Another reason that I commend a thorough reading of the Bible is that the very things that cause me to question the reliability of the Bible say some very interesting things about those who wrote it. The Gospel narratives each tell a different story if read closely, for example, and these different narratives both help us understand and are informed by the shifting tides of Christian-Jewish relations as well as the understanding of how Christians viewed the nature of

Jesus Christ. For a deeper understanding of this, I commend Bart D. Ehrman's books *Jesus, Interrupted: Revealing the Hidden Contradictions in the Bible (and Why We Don't Know about Them)* and *How Jesus Became God: The Exaltation of a Jewish Preacher from Galilee.*

Is the Bible Consistent and Reliable? (Consistently the Answer Is No)

> And God created the pongidids and hominids with 98 percent genetic similarity, naming two of them Adam and Eve. In the book in which God explained how He did all this, in one chapter He said he created Adam and Eve together out of the dust at the same time, but in another chapter He said He created Adam first, then later created Eve out of one of Adam's ribs. This caused confusion in the valley of the shadow of doubt, so God created theologians to sort it out.
>
> —Michael Shermer

One of the first and most important things to understand about the Bible is that it is not a single book; it is a collection of many. The Old Testament is made up of thirty-nine books, and the New Testament twenty-seven. I am here talking about the version of the Bible used by the churches of my youth and by most Protestant denominations. There are other versions, of course, and have been many other versions throughout history. Until the Protestant Reformation, the Catholic Bible was the official Bible. The Catholic Bible has seventy-three books total, with forty-six in the Old Testament and twenty-seven in the New Testament. For simplicity, I will refer primarily to the sixty-six-book Protestant version here. Most, if not all, claims apply equally to both the Protestant and Catholic versions.

Within the pages of these sixty-six books are no fewer than 439 internal contradictions. These are beautifully demonstrated in a graphic depiction developed by Steve Wells for the Reason Project with an arc going from each verse that contradicts another verse in the Bible with the result looking much like a photo of solar flares (Wells 2009). In light of this, any serious historian would have no choice but to call into question the veracity of the entire document, especially when it makes claims of an extraordinary nature. Remember at this point that these contradictions are just that, examples of biblical passages that contradict or are contradicted by other biblical passages. This does not even speak to the examples of things in the Bible which might be wrong but are not demonstrated to be so by other passages in the same book.

Clearly, if parts of the Bible blatantly contradict other parts of the Bible, then we have every reason to conclude that at least one part of the Bible is wrong in each of these cases. After all, this is not a case of a skeptic saying a biblical reference is wrong based on his opinion; it is actually one part of the Bible presenting information that indicates another part of the Bible is wrong—or possibly both parts. We also have good reason to question other things found in the Bible that are not direct contradictions. We simply have far more reliable ways of knowing things today than we did when the Bible was cobbled together.

It is also important to realize how little we actually do know about the Bible and its authors. This might seem a bit obvious to many, but I am constantly surprised by the number of people who don't seem to realize how little we actually know about who wrote which parts of the Bible (Moses didn't write the five "books of Moses," for example, certainly not all five of them) (Ehrman B. D. 2009), when the Bible was actually written (over a period of seven hundred years or more—perhaps a lot more, but certainly not thousands of years), and what themes and messages are actually written in the Bible (should we love our neighbor as we are told in Mark 12:31 or kill every man, woman, and child among them as was told in Deuteronomy 2:33–34). I stand by my conviction that more of us should read the Bible more often, but to get what the Bible really has to offer (cultural context, human understanding, and even *some* accurate history), we have to understand it for what it is. To look at it as a single book, perfect and inspired by the architect of the cosmos, cannot help but diminish its already limited potential to inform.

The Nature of Biblical Claims

Miraculous claims require much more reliable evidence that do claims of ordinary human experience. If your college roommate who is not from a wealthy family tells you he just bought a used Toyota with money he saved up at his part-time job, there is really no reason to be skeptical of this (unless he is a known pathological liar), and most reasonable people would just take his word for it. After all, people with limited incomes often buy used Toyotas. If, however, that same friend told you he just bought a new Lamborghini, you would most likely want to actually go out and see this car for yourself before believing him. Even this claim, however, is not outside the realm of human possibility. People sometimes win lotteries or engage in illicit activities that bring rapid and unexplained wealth (normally temporarily). The more extraordinary the claim, the more extraordinary the evidence most of us would require in order to believe it. If your friend said he had been dead for three days but he's much better now, you would likely call the authorities, hide all sharp objects, and fashion a tin foil hat for him to wear while waiting for the nice men with the heavy sedation and white jacket with extra-long sleeves.

Things like meetings and conversations between biblical characters, reports of battles, births, deaths, and other things that routinely occur as part of the human experience require ordinary evidence because these are rather mundane claims. One may be forgiven for not questioning such things even in cases where there is little or no corroborating evidence. These are things that happen all the time, always have, and always will; but even for these things, we don't take the information as infallible and are quick to doubt if it is contradicted by better evidence.

Many of the claims found in the Bible require a very different sort of evidence, however. The evidence should comport with the claims one seeks to prove. I never cease to be amazed at how readily many apologists talk about the evidence that Jesus was crucified (there isn't any really good evidence for this by the way) as if it were proof of the divinity of Christ. Even if there were verifiable, absolute, undeniable proof that Jesus really existed and died on the cross, this proves only one thing—that a human named Jesus was born, and he lived and died just like every other human. The supernatural claim that he rose from the dead or that he is divine is where the really compelling evidence is necessary, and this really compelling evidence should not be contradicted by better evidence.

Likewise, the fact that some things in the Bible are historically accurate is often used by friends of religion as some sort of evidence of the miraculous biblical claims. It is quite strange, however, for someone to argue that a biblical account of a miracle should be believed simply because in another part of the Bible there is mention of a mundane historical event or an ordinary geographic location that happens to be reliable. I have heard skeptics challenge this approach by pointing out that in the *Spider-Man* comic books, Peter Parker lives in New York City. The geekier among us (and yes, I suppose that includes me) may even know that Peter Parker specifically lived in the Forest Hills area of Queens. The fact that Forest Hills, Queens, or New York City all exist in no way adds to the credibility of believing that a teenager was bitten by a radioactive spider and now has superpowers. Why then should we believe supernatural claims in the Bible just because some (but certainly not all) of the historical events and places discussed have some degree of historical verisimilitude?

Religion often gets a free pass on its inability to provide even ordinary evidence for miraculous claims. What we often see in religious texts is a strange phenomenon in which those things that are hardest to accept (for nonbelievers or believers of other faiths), such as miracles, are the accounts for which there is the least evidence (and most often no evidence at all). Surprisingly, these are also most often those things that are believed (or at least claimed to be believed) most strongly by adherents. There is often a strange inverse relationship between the strength of belief and the measure of evidence (remember dilemma 2). For example, to many Christians, the fact that a person known as Gaius Julius Caesar existed is often not as deeply held as is the belief that Jesus rose from the dead. Many Christians actually argue that they believe more strongly in the bodily resurrection of Christ than in the existence of Caesar. Yet there is no evidence at all that Jesus did in fact rise from the dead (and surprisingly little that he even existed). The entire history of the Roman Republic, on the other hand, is incomplete without the existence of Caesar.

Even if I started out with enough faith to accept that the Bible is God's word (which I did long ago) and believed the stories in its pages, what is inside would still have to be consistent, non-contradictory, and supported by evidence to continue to believe it. Further, the nature ascribed to it, meaning the Bible is actually the Good Book, would actually have to be *consistently* good for me to subscribe to its teachings as the Good Book. Submitted for your consideration are those things that caused me to question if the Bible lives up to the expectations that it be true and that it be good. As the reliability of the Bible is clearly brought into question, consider something very important. If not for the Bible, why would you believe that God is real, that Jesus is not only his son but actually one and the same with him and the Holy Spirit, co-equal and eternal, and that there are people among us who know what this God wants with such precision that they can tell us how to live?

Is the Bible Consistent?

Even a cursory reading of the Bible reveals a number of inconsistencies, some rather minor and unimportant, others quite challenging. Just the Gospels, for example, reveal a number of direct contradictions if they are actually compared with one another side-by-side rather than simply reading uncritically in a linear fashion. Who, for example, was Jesus brought before in order to be tried, and how did he respond to his questioning? All four Gospel accounts tell us Jesus was taken before Pontius Pilate so that his fate may be determined. This is a good start as all four Gospels agree on this point, but the consistency quickly breaks down. In Luke alone, for example, it is mentioned that Pilate realizes that Jesus is Galilean and therefore under Herod's jurisdiction. Pontius Pilate then sends Jesus before Herod to be tried.

What Jesus said during his questioning was a bit more problematic. Mark and Luke agree that "Thou sayest it" was Jesus's reply when asked by Pilate if he was the king of the Jews. Matthew and John both say that Jesus spoke not a word when asked this question. John goes on to say that Jesus replied to a later question but not about being the king of the Jews. The nature of this contradiction is interesting. Mark and Luke did not simply offer a slightly different verbiage than did Matthew and John, the latter two explicitly reported that Jesus said nothing in answer to this question. Explicitly stating that he said nothing is far different from simply neglecting to mention something he said.

What about after the decision was made to crucify Jesus and the events leading up to and during the crucifixion? Are the Gospel accounts less contradictory here? According to John, Jesus bore his own cross and carried it to where he was crucified. But according to the other three Gospel accounts, it was Simon, a Cyrenian, who was set upon to bear the cross. Then when the crucifixion was well underway and Jesus was on the cross, did the other two men being crucified alongside him both rebuke Jesus? According to Mark and Matthew, both men rebuked Jesus. John is silent on this, and Luke tells a very different story. According to Luke, one of the men said to Jesus, "Lord, remember me when thou commest into thy kingdom."

How about the empty tomb? This is really important stuff here that goes directly to the very heart of the Jesus narrative. No matter what claims are made by apologists using such attempts as the minimal facts argument (addressed in detail in chapter 4), the "fact" that Jesus was crucified and died proves absolutely nothing at all, except that he did what a large number of poor unfortunates did in those days, namely he got crucified and that he also did exactly what every other human who has ever been born has either done or will do—he died. If this is evidence of anything, it is that he was human, not divine. The resurrection, however, is a different story. If this part of the narrative is credible and can reliably and consistently support this story, then we might have something interesting.

Three days after the crucifixion, who went and found an empty tomb? Strictly speaking, only one person actually found an empty tomb. According to John, Mary Magdalene went alone to the tomb and found a whole lot of nothing. Mark, on the other hand, tells us that Mary Magdalene, Mary mother of James, and Salome went there together and found an angel who instructed them to tell the disciples to go to Galilee, where Jesus would meet them. Matthew tells us that it was two women, Mary Magdalene and the other Mary who went there, at which time there was an earthquake and they saw an angel roll the stone back and sat on the stone. And in Luke, we find yet another version of who found what, with a number of women, at least five, they being Mary Magdalene, Mary mother of James, Joanna, and other women. This last group found two men in shining garments who had no message about going to Galilee.

Finally, the Gospels are not at all consistent as to what the women who went to the tomb did afterward. Mark tells us the women did nothing for they were afraid. Matthew and Luke both tell that the women went to tell the disciples what had happened, and according to John, Mary Magdalene, who went to the tomb alone, told the disciples, "They have taken away the Lord."

What of the first sighting of the risen Jesus? This is the most troubling portion of the entire narrative in my opinion. Of all the things to get wrong, this is a biggie. The Gospels not only disagree on who saw Jesus first, but most of those who reportedly saw him didn't initially recognize him. According to Mark and John, it was Mary Magdalene, and according to John, she at first thought he was the gardener. (No kidding! The *gardener!* And this is not some corny, and possibly even racist, joke about it being Jesus, pronounced *Hayseus,* versus Jesus, pronounced *Jeezus.*) It was the two Marys who first saw Jesus after his resurrection according to Matthew. And in Luke, we read that Jesus first appeared to two men on their way to the village of Emmaus. But even as "Jesus himself drew near and went with them," they didn't know it was Jesus. It is not at all clear if they asked for gardening advice.

This was an admittedly terse treatment of the Gospel accounts of Jesus's trial, death, and resurrection and was only intended to draw attention to the inconsistencies contained therein. A more thorough discussion will follow later on the nature of Jesus according to the Bible and how arguments for the existence of God that rely on the "historical Jesus" are left wanting.

Inconsistency Aside, Is the Bible Reliable?

Any honest evaluation of source material has to look at, among other things, the degree to which the material is (or is not) reliably accurate. If a physics textbook listed the speed of light as 768 miles per hour as opposed to 186,242 miles per second in one single entry, one might assume this is an honest mistake—clearly wrong, but it could be an honest mistake as one is the speed of sound and one is the actual speed of light. Both might be commonly referred to in a physics text. An inattentive editor might not catch the error. However, if the book consistently makes mistakes of this nature, the credibility of the entire text can't help but to be called into question. You may point to all the possibly correct answers in the same text all you want, but a reference book does not have the luxury of being right much of the time; it must be consistently correct. Mistakes of this nature must be clear outliers, not the norm. Further, if you attempt equivocation and argue that this is not in error in spite of better evidence, your credibility cannot help but suffer.

As already mentioned, religious believers often point out what the Bible got right. Much of which is debatable, but it is rare, indeed, for them to accept the errors in the Bible. Addressed here are just three of the things the Bible seems to have gotten wrong (the age of the universe, human biology, and the order of creation). This small sample of the most egregious errors was chosen for two reasons. First, the ease with which these biblical claims are disproven—empirically and undeniably. Second, the degree to which these claims are wrong, sometimes in orders of magnitude. Easily verifiable, grossly egregious errors make this short list. A much longer list is, of course, possible, but hopefully, this point will be sufficiently, if tersely, made.

On the age of the universe, a literal interpretation of the book of Genesis indicates an age for the universe at somewhere in the range of six thousand years. This was, more or less, the accepted Church position for a very long time and is believed by many fundamentalist Christians to this day. More liberal Christians today may scoff when a skeptic points this out and say that they don't believe that. It may be true that many Christians today don't believe the Earth is about six thousand years old, but a great many do, and it bears repeating that it was the official church position until very recently. In our current day, this mind-bogglingly wrong age of the universe is argued for by Answers in Genesis, for example (Lisle 2008). This will be revisited later in the discussion of the Bible versus science. For now, I will just say that we have very good reasons to have confidence in the scientific consensus that the universe is actually about 13.8 billion years old, not six thousand years old.

On human biology, the Bible offers many cases in which people lived for hundreds of years. Just a few examples from Genesis include Adam (lived 930 years), Methuselah (lived 969 years), Noah (lived 950 years); and there are many others. We know this is not true due to an exquisite understanding of natural laws and biology. It is, in fact, very rare for anyone to live beyond 100 years of age today even though average life spans have increased by 30 percent (Zaccaro 2010) just since the 1900s. There is no evidence that anyone has ever lived well beyond that age, now or during biblical times. The longest-lived human that we have reliable records of is Jeanne Calment, who lived to be 122 (Whitney 1997). What is more likely, that the Bible is in error about humans living over nine hundred years or that the universe had a creator who, for no apparent reason, caused this to occur in the past, chose to no longer let it occur, and left us no evidence at all outside of the Bible that it ever happened? Not only is there no credible evidence that this ever happened. Every shred of evidence we do have indicates that it is simply not true.

The order of creation in Genesis conflicts with the evidence as well. According to Genesis, on day 1, God created light. This was before he created the things that cause light (Sun and other stars) on day 4. He also created plant life, on day 3, before the Sun. This is, I suppose, something that a supernatural creator of the universe could cause to occur if he has the power to create the universe ex nihilo. Based on the paucity of reliable evidence, however, it seems premature to assume the validity of supernatural claims of any sort. All available evidence indicates that not only did the stars come long before any form of life, including plants; the simple necessity of photosynthesis would require that the Sun come before plants. This is also discussed in more detail later when comparing the biblical knowledge to scientific knowledge as well as in the chapter 5 discussion of how wonderful and mysterious the universe is without resorting to a god.

When considering biblical claims, a question we should continually ask ourselves is this: what is more likely, that the gratuitous claims of the Bible are more accurate than modern science, with its proven track record of success, or that these are apocryphal stories written by a superstitious people at a time and place when better information was simply not to be had? When we consider that the Bible was written over the course of many hundred years at a time and by a people "for whom a wheelbarrow would have been a breathtaking example of emerging technology" (to borrow a phrase from Sam Harris), the evidence seems clearly stacked against the concept of biblical inerrancy.

An honest look at the Bible's position on a number of important issues follows. If you are a religious person and are reading these words, it might be enlightening to consider something as you read ahead. In all the sermons and Bible studies you've attended in your life, how often has a preacher, priest, theologian, or apologist pointed out to you the things I am about to? I would not expect a religious teacher to focus only on the negative aspects, logical inconsistencies, and outright contradictions in the Bible, of course, but to completely ignore them (or worse, pretend they don't exist) seems less than honest. Is it remotely possible that all the things I am about to point out, things I had to discover on my own, were unknown to all the religious teachers I've had in the past? This seems extraordinarily unlikely, if not impossible. There is a very good chance that you've never heard most of what I am going to share here. In fact, it is maddening the number of times I've heard, "That's not in the Bible!" or "Where is *that* in the Bible?" when I am doing nothing more than quoting directly from the Bible.

The Bible and Prophecy (Betcha the Prophets Didn't See This Coming!)

> It's tough to make predictions, especially about the future.
>
> —Yogi Berra

According to megachurch pastor John Hagee in an interview on the Glenn Beck program, "The Bible is the most phenomenal book that's ever been written, because when it was written twenty-five percent of it was prophetic—telling the future."[17] Think about that for a bit. According to Hagee, one reason the Bible is so remarkable is that when it was written, 25 percent of it was predictions about the future. So if I write a book today, 50 percent of which makes predictions about the future, would it be twice as remarkable as the Bible? When Michel de Nostradame (Nostradamus) penned *Almanacs* in 1550 or *Les Propheties* in 1555, they were essentially all predictions. Does this make these books more phenomenal still?

Simply asserting that a percentage of a book is predictions does not make it remarkable in any way. Now, if those predictions actually came true, clearly and unambiguously, then that could be remarkable, depending on the nature of the predictions. Predictions of things that routinely come to pass are not convincing even when they do come true. What we would need here is a prediction of a very unlikely event that comes true (again) clearly and unambiguously. In the case of the Bible, this is simply not the case, however. Just a little fun fact, but this is the same Hagee by the way who said, "Christians don't steal or lie, they don't get divorced or have abortions" (*World*

---

17 Video of this assertion available at http://www.youtube.com/watch?v= mOsYSwNrlBo.

without End 2010), and then did divorce the mother of his two children, but that is another story for another book. It is noted here only for perspective and color commentary.

Hagee was wrong about Christians and divorce, and he is wrong about biblical prophecy. The fact that he claims biblical prophesies have come true with conviction, and venom does not add to the degree to which it is true. I use Hagee as the poster child for biblical prophecy for one reason only—he is the example most often presented to me personally as a champion of biblical prophecy claims. Remember that one of the main motivations for writing this book is as an answer to all the Christians who feel compelled to tell me all the reasons why I should believe in God.

Hagee, like all who make similar claims, ignores the vague, nebulous nature of biblical prophecy. Biblical prophecy, just like other famous sources of prophecy, like the previously mentioned Nostradamus, was written in such non-lucid language that it can be interpreted to mean just about anything. In fact, it often has been interpreted to predict things that clearly did not happen—things such as the exact date for the end of the world, for example. When these predictions of the end of the world failed to be fulfilled rather than conceding the prophecy was wrong, it is simply reinterpreted and given a new date. Remember that the Seventh-Day Adventists has its roots in the Millerite movement, which predicted the return of Christ on October 22, 1844. This belief was based on biblical prophecy and did not come to pass. The interpretation of prophecy was simply changed when it proved to be wrong.

More recently, we have the example of Harold Camping, the Christian broadcaster whose interpretation of the Bible led him to announce that Jesus would return on May 21, 2011. When this did not transpire, he altered his prediction, issuing a retrodiction of sorts, saying that May 21 had actually witnessed a spiritual judgment and that the actual physical destruction of the universe would come on October 21, 2011. Camping made similar predictions nearly two decades earlier. While this is easily dismissed as the meandering musings of a not-too-stable mind, Camping's organization Family Radio has been heard in about 150 markets nationally. A great many people who believed what Camping was preaching lost their life's savings in such frivolous pursuits as helping to advertise the coming end times. In fact, Family Radio spent millions on billboard advertising and RVs that traveled around the country spreading the word of the end of the universe—money that could surely have been put to better use for the good of mankind.

Back to Hagee, who offers as proof of the coming end times a few prophecies that he claims are coming true before our very eyes. There is not enough space here to address just how much is wrong with each of his examples, but a few highlights are offered for elucidation. When he talks of the signs signifying the end of days, Hagee brings up the "knowledge explosion" that will come. Hagee even specifically (and incorrectly) quotes scripture, "And men shall run to and fro and there shall be a knowledge explosion." He then offers examples of how civilization changed very slowly for thousands of years until very recently, and now we have many modern wonders that demonstrate this knowledge explosion.

There are a couple of problems with Hagee's view. First, the Bible verse he is referring to is Daniel 12:4 and it *specifically* reads, "Many shall run to and fro, and knowledge shall be increased." There is a considerable difference between "Knowledge shall be increased" and "knowledge explosion." Knowledge has increased many times in the past two thousand years. Hagee's position is problematic for many reasons. Not least of which is that this increase in knowledge Hagee loves talking about is a gift of modern science—something that disproves most of Hagee's fundamentalist worldview. For example, it is interesting that when talking about the "knowledge explosion," he mentions things like landing man on the moon then states that nothing like this has happened since the Garden of Eden, part of a creation myth conclusively proven false by this same knowledge increase of science.

Hagee goes on to talk about other signs that are all around us today, such as pestilence and earthquakes. This demonstrates a singular ability to cherry-pick through ideas that support his view while completely ignoring solid evidence that contradicts his preconceived notions. Hagee, and others who think as he does, talk as if pestilence and earthquakes just now started occurring or have suddenly seen a dramatic uptick. I suppose the Black Death in the fourteenth century (25 million dead in Europe) and the Spanish flu in our own century (20–40 million dead) don't qualify as pestilence enough to be a sign. For perspective, the Black Death killed one-third of the world's population. If that happened today, it would result in over 2.3 billion deaths. The good news is that, contrary to this being a punishment from an angry god, we now know it to be a zoonotic disease, normally spread by infected fleas, and we now have effective antibacterial treatments.

How about these earthquakes he is talking about? Hagee claims that the number of earthquakes is on the rise saying, "I do have those numbers, and they have virtually doubled in the twentieth century." But according to the US Geological Survey, "As more and more seismographs are installed in the world, more earthquakes can be and have been *located*. However, the number of large earthquakes (magnitude 6.0 and greater) has stayed relatively constant" (USGS 2011)

I contacted John Hagee Ministries to offer him the opportunity to comment on any or all of what I have written above. That offer was not accepted.

For Christians, the coming of Jesus is believed to have answered a number of prophecies. According to John W. Loftus, there is a perfectly rational explanation for this, and it is not answered prophecy: "Early Christian preachers simply went into the Old Testament looking for verses that would support their view of Jesus." This seems a much more likely explanation than that the normal operation of the universe was suspended in order that Old Testament prophets could predict future events.

One of the most often repeated prophesies deals with Jesus being the Messiah who was to be a descendant of David. But as pointed out in the discussion of biblical consistency and reliability, this does not hold up to even the lightest of scrutiny. The only evidence presented to support this claim is the genealogies given for Jesus in Matthew 1:1–16 and Luke 3:23–28, and there are several significant problems with this. First, would any reasonable person actually believe miraculous claims in any book (outside their particular holy book) based on no other reason than that same book said it is true? This is a grievous case of circular logic. Remember always that the Bible is the claim or series of claims, not the evidence of a claim. Second, consider that the genealogies found in the New Testament go through Joseph, with whom we are told Jesus has no blood relation, and not his virgin mother. This seems a fatal flaw if the evidence for Jesus being a descendant of David is that Joseph was a descendant of David.

A third problem with the "descendant of David" claim is that, in spite of the fact that the Gospels of Matthew and Luke were written long after the death of Jesus and had every chance to get it right, they disagree greatly on the number of generations and differ greatly in the names of the descendants from David leading up to Joseph. These two accounts agree only on two of the names between David and Joseph (not counting David and Joseph which are a given), even disagreeing on the name of Jesus's own paternal grandfather. Matthew lists Jacob as the father of Joseph; Luke lists Heli. Among the other notable discrepancies is the son of David in this lineage. Matthew lists Solomon, who is not named at all in Luke's list. According to Luke, the son of David in this genealogy is Nathan.

It actually gets worse. Not only do all but two of the names not match, they are almost entirely different lists. This is not just a case of someone accidentally transposing a letter in a fit of dyslexia or two similar lists of names only slightly out of order; they are almost mutually exclusive lists. Twenty-three of the names that appear in Matthew's genealogy after David and before Joseph were not present in Luke's genealogy. That's correct; they weren't just out of order or misspelled, they were not there at all. Likewise, when you look at Luke's genealogy, there are thirty-eight names between David and Joseph that do not appear at all anywhere in Matthew's list. This is all graphically depicted in appendix B.

These discrepancies have not gone unnoticed, of course, and there are explanations offered that seek to answer the questions that are raised. More than one apologist has told me there is a perfectly logical explanation for this, in fact. The explanation usually goes something like this: You see, in the Middle East, even today, people use different names depending on the circumstance, time, and place; so it is easy to understand why many of the names don't exactly match. I am not making this up; this is the excuse most often offered, to me at least, for this discrepancy when I bring it up. Not to defend this position, but as a retired military intelligence officer with experience in the Middle East, I can attest to the difficulty in tracking terror suspects with multiple names. This is why biometric identification systems that record and correlate with specific individuals such things as fingerprints, retinal eye scans, and the like are such valuable tools in this effort. However, this is revealed as an untenable defense of the descent of David idea in the light of additional facts.

Interestingly, if you follow the genealogies in the other direction, from David back to Abraham rather than forward to Jesus, an amazing thing happens. There is only one letter in the entire list that is not a perfect match. Matthew lists Judas as the great-grandson of Abraham, where Luke lists Juda. Beyond that, the genealogies are identical from Abraham to David, and it is only after David (you know, the part that supports the claim that Jesus is the Messiah) where the names are almost completely contradictory. If the alternate name excuse were true (and it is not), it really needs to be explained why people at that time and place only started using alternate names after David, did so immediately, and did so nearly universally.

Even if the use of alternate names could explain the fact that only two of the names match on the two genealogies, this still does not explain the even greater discrepancy that Matthew lists twenty-eight generations from David to Jesus (if you include both David and Jesus) and Luke gives forty-three generations. So even by doing mental cheetah flips, cognitive jiu-jitsu, and using fuzzy reasoning to get the names to magically match up, you've still got nearly twice as many "sons of" in Luke as you've got "begots" in Matthew. That math didn't add up in Bronze Age Palestine any better than it does in modern-day America.

I consulted one Christian friend for his opinion, whose initial response was the idea of different names for the same persons addressed in the preceding paragraph. When I pointed out that even if alternate names are granted the fifteen extra generations is still problematic, he conceded the point and consulted his pastor, who advised that his theological training taught him that the real reason for the differences in names is because one Gospel traces the lineage through Mary and the other is traced through Joseph. I didn't have the presence of mind to ask my friend where he heard about the "alternate name" excuse if his pastor's theological training taught him that the real excuse was that the genealogy was traced through Joseph in one Gospel and through Mary in the other. Why wasn't the paternity versus maternity excuse the first on offer?

The idea that one genealogy is through Mary and the other through Joseph is also an unsatisfactory argument if you simply read the Gospels in question. For purposes of this discussion, we begin with David in both genealogies because the prophecy in question is that the Messiah would be a descendant of David. As previously mentioned, both genealogies go further back. In the Matthew account, the genealogy begins with Abraham and proceeds to Jesus, and in Luke, it begins with Jesus and works back all the way to Adam—well, actually back to God, because Adam was the son of God. Matthew words it thusly, "Abraham begat, Isaac; and Isaac begat Jacob; and Jacob begat Judas and his bretheren." And this continues to "And Jacob begat Joseph the husband of Mary, of whom was born Jesus, who is called Christ." Luke's wording is "And Jesus himself began to be about thirty years of age, being [as was supposed] the son of Joseph, which was the son of Heli" and so forth. Both identify Joseph as the father of Jesus. The wording clearly does not support a lineage through Mary. Both genealogies have two names in the middle that do actually match; both list paternal grandfathers for Jesus (which don't match). Apologists who try to chalk up the differences in genealogies to one of them running through Mary can't agree on which Gospel account goes through Mary and which through Joseph, and finally, this still does not address the huge difference in the number of generations in each account.

While some Christians may find this hard to believe, I truly am more concerned with finding the truth than with being right, so I searched further for an explanation of this discrepancy. Quite honestly, I found it amazing that such a glaring problem as this did not have a ready and satisfying answer. I asked a Christian apologist whom I befriended (and who asked not to be identified) about the discrepancies in the Gospels in general. He asked for specifics and why I was asking, so I showed him the genealogies in appendix B. He asked me if I had been given an explanation for this, to which I replied that I had and discounted the alternate names and lineage through Mary explanations.

Another teachable moment had presented itself. He said that maybe one genealogy went through actual paternal blood relation while the other went through "head of household," a situation in which a father might actually be Nathan, but the oldest brother of Nathan was Solomon, so one genealogy would perhaps say that "David begot Solomon who begot Roboam," where the other might say, "Mattatha, son of Nathan, who was son of David," to achieve the same ends.

This is an egregious case of special pleading. There is no reason to assume one author chose to switch methods of reporting "begots" or "sons of" from David to Jesus after both had used the same method from Abraham through to David. We also still have the troubling issue of twenty-eight generations in one Gospel and forty-three in the other. On this account, I would concede a couple of extra generations if Luke were to use the "oldest brother" lineage as those older brothers might die sooner, but this would not add fifteen generations! Finally, and this is the teachable moment, the attempt of my apologist friend to explain this away by any method that I would be naive enough to accept was a textbook example of the difference between the rational and religious minds. He stated the "older brother" excuse *might* be right, not that it *is* correct or that it is even an accepted explanation supported by evidence. He also said that any of the explanations work for him because it is a non-issue because even if the Bible is not accurate or consistent, he will still believe in the birth, death, and bodily resurrection of Christ. Can there be any clearer example of the triumph of superstitious blind faith over rational, evidence-based reasoning within one person's mind? Without the Bible, the accuracy of which he clearly stated was not an issue; he would not even know of the Jesus story in the first place.

Aside from the claimed prophesy of Jesus's arrival in the first place, there are prophecies that are claimed to have been answered by the coming of Jesus. One of the more entertaining prophecies comes from Zechariah 9:9, and it is that the Messiah would come into town, "riding upon an ass, and upon a colt the foal of an ass." This is "confirmed" in Luke 19:35 and other Gospel accounts. But not only would Jesus and the writer of the Gospel of Luke both have known that the Messiah was *supposed* to ride into town on a donkey; it is not like donkeys were an unusual means of conveyance in those days. Would it be that difficult to predict that the next time a relative comes to visit you he or she is likely to come in an automobile? Not only was this a very common form of conveyance during the life of Jesus, it seems that in Matthew 21:2–7 there is a clear admission that Jesus is requesting both a donkey and a colt to ride into Jerusalem in order to fit the prophecy from Zechariah. Verbiage such as "All this was done, that it might be fulfilled which was spoken by the prophet" is pretty telling. Jesus and the writers of the Gospels were quite familiar with Jewish religious writings of the time. Even if these Gospel accounts are accurate, which I doubt, they seem little more than self-fulfilling prophecies.

When looked at rationally, the very idea of prophecy is not only easily refuted; it brings up serious problems for the theist. If one believes in the idea of free will, very important to Christians, prophecy is a showstopper. If God's creations are free to choose on every decision that comes their way, how can it be that those who wrote the Bible already knew future decisions? The only way is for those decisions to have been already made, perhaps by God and therefore not open to change,[18] which is problematic for free will. Also, if prophecy is one of the ways for an omniscient, omnipotent, benevolent Creator God who wants us to be in harmony with him to let us know he is real, he picked some very vague clues to let us in on it. What would be so hard about saying, "In the land, not yet conceived, that shall

---

[18] According to Malachi 3:6, God doesn't change. Of course, other parts of the Bible indicate this is not the case, which is a central point to be made in this chapter—the Bible means just about whatever you want it to mean.

come to be known as the United States, the team to be known as the Yankees shall win the 2051 World Series"? Or how about at least doing as well as an aspiring author (me) who consults NASA's catalog of solar eclipses and make the prophecy that on July 16, 2186, there will be a total solar eclipse that will last seven minutes and twenty-nine seconds. The example from NASA is not only very specific; I would be willing to bet a substantial sum of money that it will come to pass exactly as predicted. Anyone willing to take the bet, please make the check payable to my great-great-great-great-great-grandson.

The Bible on Morality (Cherry Pickers Unite!)

> During many ages there were witches. The Bible said so. The Bible commanded that they should not be allowed to live. Therefore the Church, after doing its duty in but a lazy and indolent way for 800 years, gathered up its halters, thumbscrews, and firebrands, and set about its holy work in earnest. She worked hard at it night and day during nine centuries and imprisoned, tortured, hanged, and burned whole hordes and armies of witches, and washed the Christian world clean with their foul blood. Then it was discovered that there was no such thing as witches, and never had been. One does not know whether to laugh or to cry.
> —Mark Twain

There are entire books that address nothing more than the problems associated with looking to the Bible for moral clarity. Addressed here are only a small number of the moral quandaries found in the pages of the "Good Book." Perhaps the most potent source of cognitive dissonance for true believers who honestly read the Bible is the dearth of goodness and the wealth of immoral behavior sanctioned in the same book. I concede, yet again, there are examples of goodness in the Bible, but these examples are troubling not only for their scarcity but also because when there is goodness in the Bible, this goodness is not unique to the Bible. There is not a single example of goodness and morality found within the Bible that cannot be found elsewhere, often with greater clarity and without contradictions. The examples and degree of immoral and evil behavior also far outweigh the good found in the Bible. This is one of the most important dilemmas faced by Christians: How can you argue that your religion is the source of morality when your religion is based on a book of such moral ambiguity? This is a revisit of the thirteenth Christian dilemma.

A favorite start point for many nonbelievers, morally speaking, is the story of Abraham and Isaac. Actually, if this discussion of biblical morality were to stand alone, it would be necessary to begin "in the beginning," with the creation myth, fall from grace, and original sin that damned all of us until the human sacrifice of Jesus. Oh, and don't forget the intervening flood that killed almost all life on earth. As this does not stand alone, it is necessary to skip some parts of the story to avoid excessive redundancy. Most of us are familiar with the biblical account of Abraham and his willingness to slaughter his own son as an offering to God. Strangely, this is seen by theists as somehow a good thing. Abraham's willingness to follow God's command is proof of just how pious and devoted he was to God. Why this is not universally seen as proof of just how cruel, jealous, and petty the god of the Old Testament truly is and how devotion to such a god can lead to evil behavior escapes reasonable comprehension. It is important to consider that the story of Abraham and Isaac is also evidence that the god of the Old Testament is by no means omniscient. If God were all-knowing, there was no reason for him to test if Abraham really loves him—God would already know. Some try to argue around this point by saying the test was not to prove anything to God but to prove it to Abraham. I find this just as unconvincing as the test of God. Again, God would already know the answer to the test and could simply reassure Abraham in the off chance Abraham had any self-doubts. They were, after all, in personal dialogue.

Often an energetic defense of this story is mounted, accompanied by indignant condescension directed at the skeptic's ignorance for not realizing that God demonstrated his infinite mercy by not letting Abraham go through with it. Let's not give biblical morality a free pass simply because in this one story an angel stopped Abraham before he actually slaughtered his son. Just imagine the psychological harm that would be done to a child who had been tied down by his father to make it easier to kill him to please God. Also, keep in mind that in the book of Judges, there is a similar story about a man named Jephthah, who actually did kill his daughter as an offering to God in exchange for God's help in winning a battle, and God did not stop him. God sometimes actually does require human sacrifice of children (and not just his own). There will be more on the story of Jephthah in the later discussion of biblical family values.

If you are a Christian and want to allow the Bible an alibi on the Abraham and Isaac infanticidal near miss, just subject it to the outsider's test here and ask yourself if you would be so fast to see this as a moral story if you heard it told from the viewpoint of a Hindu. What if the elephant-headed god Ganesh demanded a human sacrifice and a pious Hindu lashed his son to a rock and prepared to disembowel him only to have his hand stayed at the last minute by an all-loving and merciful Ganesh? You'd most likely call foul on this story—as you should!

Many years ago, I was introduced to another interesting outsider's test while an undergraduate student. The professor shared the story of a group called the Nacirema, written about by Horace Miner. The Nacirema were described as "a North American group living in the territory between the Canadian Creel the Yaqui and Tarahumare of Mexico and the Carib and Arawak of the Antilles. Little is known of their origin, although tradition states that they came from the east." Miner went on to describe their strange body rituals, such things as spending a great deal of time in shrines in the home where private rituals are carried out, the use of charms or magical potions that are kept in a chest built into the wall of the shrine, and even seeking "a holy-mouth-man once or twice a year. These practitioners have an impressive set of paraphernalia, consisting of a variety of augers, awls, probes, and prods." At the end of this lecture, the professor asked me what I thought of the Nacirema. I replied with something, embarrassing in hindsight, about how I thought they sound "kinda weird." As it turns out Nacirema is American spelled backward, and Miner was talking about us. His point was to get us to think about how we might appear to someone not from our culture. The "shrine" is a bathroom, "magic potions" are cosmetics, and the "holy-mouth-man" is, of course, a dentist. This story made quite an impact on me, and I've always tried to apply what I only later heard John W. Loftus call the outsider's test (Loftus 2009) on any claim or practice of a religious or superstitious nature.

Tangent complete, back to the Bible. A careful review of the Bible reveals a set of moral sanctions that are in many ways perfectly maladaptive to a healthy society. Our moral intuitions are such that even the most religious among us cannot bring ourselves to adhere strictly to the behaviors prescribed in the Bible. As Sam Harris offered in his book *The Moral Landscape*: "It is worth noting in this context that the god of Abraham never told us to treat children with kindness, but He did tell us to kill them for talking back to us [Exodus 21:15, Leviticus 20:9, Deuteronomy 21:18–21, Mark 7:9–13, and Matthew 15:4–7]. And yet everyone finds this 'moral' imperative perfectly insane. Which is to say that no one— not even fundamentalist Christians and orthodox Jews—can so fully ignore the link between morality and human well-being as to be truly bound by God's law" (Harris, *The Moral Landscape: How Science Can Determine Human Values*, 2010).

It is difficult to escape an acute cognitive dissonance when actually reading the words that come with each of the examples Harris cited in his well-made point and still clinging to the notion that the Bible truly is the Good Book. In each biblical citation provided by Harris, clear, unambiguous direction is given that children are to be slain for as simple an act of insubordination as talking back to his parents. If you've never actually read these passages, I urge you to do so now. Permission is not simply given for such barbarity; you are expressly commanded to carry out these acts. Fortunately, our evolved moral zeitgeist (see Richard Dawkins's disquisition on the shifting moral zeitgeist in *The God Delusion*.) is such that we know the idea of killing children, for any reason at all, is repugnant, and those who do so normally go to jail for it.

Some friends of religion attempt to get around this quandary by arguing that the most important moral lessons, such as accepting Jesus as your savior or believing in God with all your heart, are actually crystal clear in and unique to the Bible. It is difficult, however, to see these as examples of morality when they do not actually increase human well-being or decrease suffering in any way. Morality cannot be defined as worship of a god that is not believed in by the majority of humanity and for which there is simply no evidence. Morality, most of us can agree, is something else entirely.

Francis Collins, the scientist who led the first successful effort to map the human genome, wrote about a higher moral law in his book *The Language of God*. Collins wrote that this higher moral law humans seem to have, almost universally, is among the most compelling reasons for his belief in God. While I can't agree with Collins that this is evidence for God (in fact, it seems to me to be exactly the opposite), I do agree that a moral sense is almost universal. Clearly, our sense of right and wrong has evolved to the point that we can recognize it is simply wrong to kill one's children. If this higher moral law comes from God, it seems somehow missing from the Bible, or at best, we would have to admit the good is muddled with the bad.

Albert Einstein reasoned that "a man's ethical behavior should be based effectually on sympathy, education and social ties; no religious basis is necessary. Man would indeed be in a poor way if he had to be restrained by fear or punishment and hope of reward after death." This is a much more solid foundation upon which to build a cogent morality than Bronze Age scriptures of moral ambiguity and questionable origin. I am often asked questions like "What is keeping you from going out and committing rape, robbery, and murder since you don't fear what will happen to you after you die?" Well, the fact is I simply don't want to do those things, and it frankly worries me that so many religious people seem to think they might just behave in that way if they didn't fear God may be taking notes. Not only do we not need to look to the Bible for our morality, we clearly ignore so much of what the Bible offers specifically because our morality is superior to scripture. It is transcendently clear that morality is moderated by our intellect and experiences, especially when those moral intuitions are so often in stark contrast to sanctions found in scripture. We simply refuse to abide by biblical morality when it violates the collective moral sensitivities of today.

Morality will be revisited in the following chapter in the critique of "the argument from morality." This is another area where I will be challenged to avoid excessive redundancy, but it is necessary to address morality both from the position of biblical reliability and as an alleged "proof of God."

The Bible on Genocide

> Deaths in the Bible. God: 2,270,365, not including the victims of Noah's flood, Sodom and Gomorrah, or the many plagues, famines, fiery serpents, etc. because no specific numbers were given. Satan: 10.
>
> —Unknown

"Thou shalt not kill," except for every single man, woman, and child among the various tribes who get in the way of the chosen people.

On the issues of morality, right and wrong, and justice, it is sometimes difficult to differentiate what is more disturbing—the actual words of the Bible or explanations given by modern-day good Christians for why things like genocide really aren't that bad when you understand the context. In conducting research for the discussion on genocide in the Bible, I was expecting to find some leaders in the Christian community who would argue that I am misreading the scriptures and that perhaps these are allegorical stories, not meant to be taken as literal acts carried out by God's chosen people on his orders. I found all this, but what I also found was an interesting (and troubling) perspective from Dr. William Lane Craig; that I feel he articulates, far better than I ever could, what exactly can go wrong when a brain is on religion. Dr. Craig, by the way, is someone I will refer to several times as he is one of the leading voices in Christian apologetics today.

Dr. Craig responds to a questioner (Craig W. L., *Question 16 Slaughter of the Canaanites*, 2007) who is troubled by the problem of evil when God commands the slaughter of entire ethnicities so that his chosen people can go into the land of their forefathers. Craig admits readily that this was God's will. He cites chapter and verse (Deuteronomy 7:1–2[19] and 20:16–18[20]) and is very clear in his belief that these acts were not just "war stories" but actual events and that it was God's will for the Israelite soldiers to often kill every man, woman, and child of a given tribe. How does Dr. Craig explain this in such a way as to make it sound anything other than barbaric? He argues the only reason that we find these stories offensive is because of the high moral standards we have as a result of our cultural heritage, which he sees as a gift of the Judeo-Christian tradition. You read correctly! The only reason we find God-directed genocide troubling is because the same God that directed us to commit genocide also left us with the moral sensibilities to know genocide is wrong. Huh?

According to Craig, "These stories offend our moral sensibilities. Ironically, however, our moral sensibilities in the West have been largely, and for many people unconsciously, shaped by our Judeo-Christian heritage, which has taught us the intrinsic value of human beings, the importance of dealing justly rather than capriciously,

---

[19] Deuteronomy 7:1–2: "When the LORD thy God shall bring thee into the land whither thou goest to possess it, and hath cast out many nations before thee, the Hittites, and the Girgashites, and the Amorites, and the Canaanites, and the Perizzites, and the Hivites, and the Jebusites, seven nations greater and mightier than thou; And when the LORD thy God shall deliver them before thee; thou shalt smite them, and utterly destroy them; thou shalt make no covenant with them, nor shew mercy unto them."

[20] Deuteronomy 20:16–18: "But of the cities of these people, which the LORD thy God doth give thee for an inheritance, thou shalt save alive nothing that breatheth: But thou shalt utterly destroy them; namely, the Hittites, and the Amorites, the Canaanites, and the Perizzites, the Hivites, and the Jebusites; as the LORD thy God hath commanded thee: That they teach you not to do after all their abominations, which they have done unto their Gods; so should ye sin against the LORD your God."

and the necessity of the punishment's fitting the crime." Understand what Craig is arguing here. It is perfectly okay to kill every man, woman, and child, completely wiping out complete societies; and the only reason it bothers you is because of the fine moral tradition that leapt from this genocidal backdrop. And notice his last statement: "And the importance of the punishment's fitting the crime." Just what was it that the Hittites, Girgashites, Amorites, Canaanites, Perizzites, Hivites, and the Jebusites did, even the children, which was a fitting crime that justified genocide? Apparently, the accident of being born on land that God wanted his chosen people to inhabit someday is a capital offense.

Craig goes on to say that "you can't read the Old Testament prophets without a sense of God's profound care for the poor, the oppressed, the down-trodden, the orphaned, and so on." If there is a stronger statement that illustrates what happens to the human intellect when bent to the task of equivocating religious beliefs, I am not aware of it. Religious beliefs do not necessarily make you unintelligent, but devotion to religious dogma, at the risk of human intellect and rational thought, does allow otherwise intelligent people to believe and say things of almost breathtaking stupidity. We really can't read the Old Testament without a sense of God's profound care... for the orphaned? Perhaps if God's people had not been so busy wiping out whole cities, there wouldn't have been so many orphans. But not to worry, they didn't have to be orphans for long, because the Israelites killed the orphans too. To do otherwise would have offended God. Just a few of the many injunctions from God to kill even children are found in such passages as Deuteronomy 13:13–19 (kill everything, even livestock, for worshipping other gods), Isaiah 14:21 (kill the children of wicked men so they do not inherit their father's possessions), and Ezekiel 9:5–7 (kill every man, woman and child who does not bear the mark).

Now, in case this didn't already confuse the issue enough, Craig goes on to muddy the waters even further. After stating that the only reason divinely sanctioned genocide bothers us is because we have divinely sanctioned morality from the Bible while stressing these events actually happened, but Craig turns around and offers that these things probably didn't really even happen. His reasoning is that such an order might be against God's nature and "the problem, it seems to me, is that if God could not have issued such a command, then the biblical stories must be false. Either the incidents never really happened but are just Israeli folklore; or else, if they did, then Israel, carried away in a fit of nationalistic fervor, thinking that God was on their side, claimed that God had commanded them to commit these atrocities, when in fact He had not. In other words, this problem is really an objection to biblical inerrancy."

Apparently, when we get into the real ethical and moral dilemmas, one excuse isn't enough. It is both a matter of our only being troubled by this because God told us what he commanded was wrong *and* it never really happened anyway *or* it happened but not because God commanded it, even though the Bible tells us he did. Some parts of the Bible you see are just made-up stories while other parts are inerrant. Which parts? Depends who you ask.

Two further points from Craig's perspective on just one instance of genocide (from Deuteronomy 7) attempt to mitigate God's culpability. God didn't do it; the Israelites did, and it was actually the right thing to do anyway. "So the problem isn't that God ended the Canaanites' lives. The problem is that he commanded the Israeli soldiers to end them. Isn't that like commanding someone to commit murder? No, it's not. Rather, since our moral duties are determined by God's commands, it is commanding someone to do something which, in the absence of a divine command, *would have been* murder. The act was morally obligatory for the Israeli soldiers in virtue of God's command, even though, had they undertaken it on their own initiative, it would have been wrong." So you see, God didn't kill the Canaanites; the Israeli soldiers did. And it doesn't matter anyway really because what would be completely evil for you and me is not only okay if God tells us to, but it is also a moral imperative. Forget "The devil made me do it." GOD made me do it, so I am not only excused—what I did was morally right.

I have heard Christopher Hitchens, Dan Barker, and others issue a challenge to name a moral act or injunction that can only come from or be done by a believer in God (and you won't be able to). The challenge then has a corollary, to name an evil act that is carried out specifically in the belief that it is the will of God, and this is actually quite easy to do. While Craig has challenged Hitchens on this, saying "love your enemy" is a moral act that only a Christian would carry out, I argue this is flawed on three counts. First, this is hardly a moral act when it is taken to its logical conclusion. It is injurious to societal progress and maintenance. I believe this may be an argument for treating your enemy humanely (don't torture him, for example), but there is no *moral* reason to love your enemy. Second, there is no evidence that non-Christians can't share this misguided sentiment. Third, if the history of religious warfare in Christendom is any indication, nothing more than lip service has been paid to this "moral injunction" in all Christian history. We should remember Voltaire's words: "As long as people believe absurdities, they will continue to commit atrocities."

A final reference to William Lane Craig in this discussion of genocide in the Bible is warranted before moving on. I suppose thanks are in order to Dr. Craig for making this topic such an easy one to discuss. After all, reading of horrible things in the Bible that was written thousands of years ago is one thing, but hearing one of the leading defenders of the faith telling us what he and many other Christians think of it today is priceless.

So who were the real victims of all this genocide? Well, if you had any softness in your heart for the children of the entire cities of seven different societies wiped out on God's orders, get that out of your head right now—they were not the true victims here. The true victims were the Israeli soldiers. After all, do you have any idea how hard it is on you to go about killing innocent women and children all day? Craig put it thusly, "So whom does God wrong in commanding the destruction of the Canaanites? Not the Canaanite adults, for they were corrupt and deserving of judgment. Not the children, for they inherit eternal life. So who is wronged? Ironically, I think the most difficult part of this whole debate is the apparent wrong done to the Israeli soldiers themselves. Can you imagine what it would be like to have to break into some house and kill a terrified woman and her children? The brutalizing effect on these Israeli soldiers is disturbing."

Let's not give Craig a pass with what he has done here. He offers a perfect crystallization of the previously mentioned challenge to name an act or injunction of evil carried out specifically because you believe it is the will of God. Craig is very quick to point out in other areas and discussions that anything God does is right as he is the creator and he can do anything he wishes, without it being judged as wrong. So killing entire civilizations is not wrong if God does it or commands it, but God does wrong the poor Israelite soldiers for commanding them to commit these acts. How does God wrong them? Well, they have to do something that violates the fine moral traditions bequeathed to them by God, of course. Just try to imagine what it means if Craig is correct in what he is saying. Consider also what Craig says here about killing the children not being wrong because the children inherit eternal life. If there were some way to know that the adult citizens of any city (let's say San Jose) were corrupt, then what would be the right thing to do? All the adults are deserving of judgment, so killing them is a just act, and you are actually doing the children a great service if you kill them also, "for they inherit eternal life." The right thing to do would be to go in there and kill every man, woman, and child; and the poor victims would actually not be the ones who were killed but the ones who did the killing. This is bugnutty, full-blown whackaloon, batshit crazy!

The Bible on Slavery

> Servants, obey in all things your masters according to the flesh; not with eyeservice, as menpleasers; but in singleness of heart, fearing God.
> —Colossians 3:22

> There is not one verse in the Bible inhibiting slavery, but many regulating it. It is not then, we conclude, immoral.
> —Rev. Alexander Campbell, Restoration Movement minister (Lowance 2003)

> The right of holding slaves is clearly established in the Holy Scriptures, both by precept and example.
> —Rev. R. Furman, D. D., Baptist of South Carolina (Early 2008)

Among the myriad reasons to doubt the Bible is the Good Book sanctioning slavery is a hard one to beat. Many are surprised to learn that the institution of slavery—the buying, selling, and treating as personal property no different from livestock of other human beings[21]—is never spoken against even once in the Holy Bible. In fact, in most biblical mentions of the institution of slavery, it is actually sanctioned, either explicitly or implicitly. I have often been challenged by Christians who argue, sometimes quite angrily, that the Bible most certainly does not "sanction" slavery. But really now, if I tell you all the different ways you can do something and never once tell you that you shouldn't actually do that thing, isn't that indicating that it is quite okay to do it? The nearest thing to a humane reference with respect to slavery may come in the instructions for how to treat (and often beat) your slaves. As it turns out, the Bible tells us that if we beat a slave so severely that he or she dies right away, then we have gone too far. If, however, the slave recovers after a couple of days, then all is right in the eyes of God (Exodus 21:20–21).

---

[21] It may seem unnecessary to actually define slavery in this way, but it is unfortunately quite necessary. This is due to the common Christian apologetic attempt to whitewash biblical slavery by characterizing slavery in the Bible as actually "indentured servitude"—merely a way to settle debts—and nothing at all like the trans-Atlantic slave trade. As we shall see, this is a poor defense.

The "proper" way to beat a slave is addressed in both Old and New Testaments. Surprisingly (perhaps not), this is often pointed to as an example of how the Bible is supposed to teach humanity, but what would have been so hard about simply saying we shouldn't beat anyone for any reason, and oh, by the way, owning slaves is a bad idea. Could you possibly imagine a husband beating his wife severely but not so severely that she died, or at least she only died after a couple of days, and then telling the judge, "Well, Your Honor, I was trying to teach my sons about being humane and that it's wrong to beat their wives too severely when they grow up."

If one wants to really try hard and is allowed to get away with it, the letter of Paul to Philemon may be used as a sort of abolitionist entreaty. While Paul does argue on behalf of Philemon's slave, Onesimus, he is only arguing on behalf of one slave, not against the institution of slavery. It should also be remembered that Paul only argued for the humane treatment of Onesimus and not for his freedom.

Some Christians attempt to distance themselves from the Old Testament harshness and actually argue that the New Testament is kinder and gentler, but this approach is self-defeating. In such passages as Luke 12:47–48, we see that slaves who do their duty should not be beaten as bad as slaves who do not. This hardly speaks in favor of the New Testament when it would have been just as easy and infinitely more moral to simply say, "Do not own slaves."

The Bible is quite clear on such matters as how long a Hebrew slave could be kept, as well as a convenient loophole that allowed him to be kept forever (Exodus 21:2–6)—the importance of slaves being obedient (1 Timothy 6:1–2)—and how to mark a human being as your personal property (Exodus 21:6). Is there really a more telling exposition of the nature of the Bible than multiple prescriptions on how to take, treat, buy and sell, and even beat slaves, yet no mention at all that it is wrong? If there is anything in the Bible of such moral clarity and socially redeeming value that it makes up for this, then it surely must fall within the category of "God's mysterious ways," because I certainly don't understand it.

At the risk of being redundant or appearing pedantic, there is a point I feel is important to reinforce. When critics and skeptics point out that slavery is sanctioned in the Bible, we are not referring to some obscure reference in the Bible. This is not something that is easily misunderstood, mistranslated, or taken out of context. The Bible is replete with guidance on how to take slaves, such as in Leviticus, where we read that God's chosen people may take slaves from the nations around them, and this human chattel may even be willed to descendants (Leviticus 25:46). This is not one of those issues where Christians can attempt the "well, that was the Old Testament" excuse either. Slaves are directed in the New Testament to obey their masters just as they would Christ himself (Ephesians 6:5). Obedience to masters, it seems, is important enough a detail to warrant inclusion in the Bible, but the fact that slavery is morally repugnant and not to be done is never mentioned. Jesus himself even talked about the beating of slaves according to the Bible (Luke 12:47–48), indicating that the slave who did not even realize he was doing wrong gets off with a lighter beating, but a beating just the same.

On this topic, Mark Twain offered an insightful evaluation: "There was no place in the land where the seeker could not find some small budding sign of pity for the slave. No place in all the land but one—the pulpit. It yielded last; it always does. It fought a strong and stubborn fight, and then did what it always does, joined the procession—at the tail end. Slavery fell. The slavery texts in the Bible remained; the practice changed; that was all" (Twain, *What Is Man? and Other Mark Twain Essays*, 2011). Twain was an honest observer of the human condition who recognized the harm done when there exists divine sanction for such barbarity.

The very words of the Bible provided ample justification to such humanitarian luminaries as Jefferson Davis, president of the Confederate States of America, when he said, "[Slavery] was established by decree of Almighty God... it is sanctioned in the Bible, in both Testaments, from Genesis to Revelation... it has existed in all ages, has been found among the people of the highest civilization, and in nations of the highest proficiency in the arts" (Rowland

1923). Is it any wonder that the practice of slavery in the United States was such a persistent part of our national heritage?

Criticism of the biblical stance on slavery is not limited to the nonbelievers among us. Even some honest church leaders have had to admit that if the issue of slavery in the West were determined only using the Bible as a guide, then abolitionists would have lacked a solid foundation. The website ReligiousTolerance.org quotes Vaughn Roste of the United Church of Canada as saying, "If we apply sola scriptura to slavery, I'm afraid the abolitionists are on relatively weak ground. Nowhere is slavery in the Bible lambasted as an oppressive and evil institution." The question this raises in my mind is this: If you have to admit such failings in your sole religious source document, how can you continue to follow that religion? At the very least, how can you continue to claim your religion is good? This is, of course, if you are among those who claim such things.

If the Bible is truly the divinely inspired word of God, slavery is not just a right, it is a moral imperative. Not to own slaves, it seems, just might be (or at least at one point might have been) a sin if the Bible is to be believed. Even in what is perhaps the most often cited example of biblical morality, the Ten Commandments, we see that slavery is not something that God sees fit to prohibit. When you read these commandments in their entirety and not just the first couple of lines of each one as most Christians do, you see that among the things you are not to covet are your neighbor's male and female slaves (Exodus 20:17). Again, how hard would it have been to instead command, "Thou shall not own slaves"?

There are Christians, some very dear friends among them, who take issue with the use of the word *sanction* with respect to slavery and the Bible. The rationale for using *sanction*, however, is not because the Bible explicitly reads, "Hey, this slavery thing is good-to-go and highly commended." While I've not found anywhere in the Bible the words "slavery is good," it is widely claimed that God is good, and it is true that God does allow and even direct the taking of slaves in the Bible. If the Bible is truly a moral guide for Christians—and it is difficult to find a Christian today who actually thinks (or at least will openly admit) slavery is a good thing—it is perplexing why the Bible does not very clearly, expressly, and eternally forbid slavery.

I offer as a final consideration one of the great defenders of slavery, Thornton Stringfellow (1788–1869), a Virginia pastor who published a lengthy defense of slavery, *Scriptural and Statistical Views in Favor of Slavery* (Stringfellow 1856). This defense was divided into two major sections, the first based solely on scriptural grounds and the second on statistical analysis of "the census of 1850 to make material claims for the expediency of slavery." Stringfellow's main points are captured in the summary of his treatise on the website "Documenting the American South" (University of South Caroline at Chapel Hill 2015) as follows:

> His four major points in this essay are as follows: 1) Slavery received the sanction of God in the time of the Patriarchs; 2) Slavery is incorporated as a part of the only commonwealth expressly established by God; 3) Slavery is recognized by Jesus Christ as legitimate; and 4) Slavery is full of mercy. In support of these contentions, Stringfellow calls attention especially to Abraham, Jewish Law, and the Pauline epistles in the New Testament.

We not only *can* do better than the Bible on most matters of morality, but we *actually do* better. It is difficult to imagine any work of philosophy, law, morality, or ethics written today that would leave this topic open-ended enough to even debate slavery. Consider, just for comparison, Article 4 of the United Nations Universal Declaration of Human Rights (Malik), which very clearly and unambiguously states, "No one shall be held in slavery or servitude, slavery and the slave trade shall be prohibited in all their forms." On this issue, I must conclude the final score to be "UN: 1. God: 0."

The Bible on Rape

> It ain't the parts of the Bible that I can't understand that bother me, it is the parts that I do understand.
>
> —Mark Twain

One of my challenges in writing this book was in deciding if it was best to address issues such as rape separately or as one comprehensive discussion on the issue of morality. I have tried (and I hope achieved some small measure of success) to strike a balance between both approaches. Rape is clearly an abhorrent violation of any reasonable person's view of moral virtue, so it was mentioned (along with genocide and slavery) in the discussion of biblical morality. It is also, however, addressed separately (again along with genocide and rape) for two very important reasons. First, these are clearly such abhorrently immoral acts that even friends of religion shy away from defending them in spite of what the Bible has to say in defense of such acts. Second, the Bible so clearly does defend these issues—I am simply drawing a big circle around the parts of the Bible were this defense is outlined.

To be clear, just as with slavery, I have found no place in the Bible where it explicitly says, "It is morally correct to forcibly have sex with a woman against her will." The Bible does offer, however, in Zechariah 14:1–2 that "a day of the LORD is coming, Jerusalem, when your possessions will be plundered and divided up within your very walls. I will gather all the nations to Jerusalem to fight against it; the city will be captured, the houses ransacked, and the women raped." An all-powerful, just, and loving god could easily prevent this day from coming, especially when he not only sees it coming but commands it through his omnipotent nature.

A disturbing biblical notion found in abundance is sanction for virgin females to be taken with the clear intention that they were to be done with as their captors wished. Just see Numbers 31:15–18, for example. After doing battle with the Midianites, it seems the Israelites had not done quite enough killing. They were challenged by Moses. "Have you allowed all the women to live?" he asked them. "They were the ones who followed Balaam's advice and enticed the Israelites to be unfaithful to the LORD in the Peor incident, so that a plague struck the LORD's people. Now kill all the boys. And kill every woman who has slept with a man, but save for yourselves every girl who has never slept with a man." I can't help but wonder what purpose Moses had in mind for these young girls who had not slept with a man. Can you imagine any young girl whose family has been slaughtered willfully doing anything with the man who killed her family members? It does not require a prodigious imagination to discern the intended fate of those virgin females.

At least the Bible does occasionally offer some justice for victims of rape. According to Deuteronomy 22:28–29 a man who gets caught raping a virgin has to pay a fine and marry the girl. "If a man happens to meet a virgin who is not pledged to be married and rapes her and they are discovered, he shall pay her father fifty shekels of silver. He must marry the young woman, for he has violated her." Isn't it a relief to know the poor rape victim at least gets a husband out of the deal? In light of the 2012 "legitimate rape" comments of Republican Senator Todd Akin (Abdullah 2012), I am left to wonder if the girl only has to marry her rapist if it was "legitimate rape." Perhaps if we were able to determine what constitutes "illegitimate rape," this could be grounds for an annulment.

In other cases, however, the rape victim doesn't get a husband; she gets stoned to death. "If a man happens to meet in a town a virgin pledged to be married and he sleeps with her, you shall take both of them to the gate of that town and stone them to death—the young woman because she was in a town and did not scream for help, and the man because he violated another man's wife. You must purge the evil from among you" (Deuteronomy 22:23–24). Note that the woman is to be killed because she was raped and didn't scream for help, and the man is stoned not because he raped the poor girl; he is stoned because he is mishandling another man's property.

Perhaps it is okay to do as you wish with a woman just so long as you call her your wife. According to Deuteronomy 21:10–11, "When you go to war against your enemies and the LORD your God delivers them into your hands and you take captives, if you notice among the captives a beautiful woman and are attracted to her, you may take her as your wife." Just as with the example of the young girl whose family was killed a few paragraphs previous, can you imagine a woman willingly marrying the killer and enslaver of her people?

The Bible on Equality for Women

> The Bible and the Church have been the greatest stumbling blocks in the way of women's emancipation.
> —Elizabeth Cady Stanton

In the beginning, there was misogyny. And God saw it, and it was good. And why shouldn't the hatred of women be good? It was, after all, Eve's actions that led to all the ills that we suffer to this day. Had she not tempted Adam (Genesis 3:6) to disobey God, then man would not have to survive by the sweat of his brow (Genesis 3:17–19) and woman would not have to suffer through childbirth (Genesis 3:16).

To be fair, this is by no means unique to Christianity. Remember that it was Pandora who opened the jar (often identified as a box), releasing all the ills and evils upon man from which we suffer to this day (see a pattern here?). Pandora, who was also the first woman and mother of all mankind, closed the jar, leaving inside only hope. Typical of the depiction of women in mythology—she not only released all that is bad, she then sealed off the jar before releasing that which is good. Many in America believe that in Islam the role of women is one of subservience and inequality. While a great many Muslims reject this view, it is taken to heart by far too many and with ample justification in the pages of the Quran. It would seem after all that a woman is worth only half that of a man (Quran 2.282). They are subject to a life sentence if men determine they are indecent (Quran 4.15), and a husband may beat his wife (Quran 4.34) if she is insubordinate.

Does the Good Book of Christianity fare any better than Islamic or Greek mythology in its views and prescribed treatment of women? After the rocky start in the Garden of Eden, it seems that one should be skeptical of any claims of equality for women based upon biblical guidance. As will be elaborated upon in the later discussion of family values, Lot, who was the only pious man in Sodom, offered his virgin daughters to be gang-raped (Genesis 19:8) so that two angels could be spared this fate at the hands of his neighbors. It seems difficult to find a positive moral to this story in terms of gender equality or family values. Of course, you should not allow two strangers to be gang-raped if you can stop it, but if the only solution you can imagine involves giving up your virgin daughters to the same fate, I suspect you care insufficiently for the women in your family.

It is not as if women serve no purpose, however. To revisit briefly the issue of slavery, women can, it seems, be useful in keeping male slaves in bondage longer than might otherwise be the case. According to Exodus, a male slave might be freed, and if he brought a wife with him, she might also be freed; but if the master gives the male slave a woman to be his wife, then she (and any children they bare) shall remain the personal property of the master (Exodus 21:2–6). This is the loophole mentioned in the previous section on slavery that allows a master to keep his Hebrew slaves longer than the prescribed six years.

If the Bible really is the word of God, then women are, in fact, not only the source of evil's introduction into the world, but they are inherently unclean. So unclean, in fact, that after the dirty act of childbirth, the woman must be ritually purified twice as long if giving birth to a female child than for a male child (Leviticus 12:1–5). So it seems that a woman, dirty by nature, is made doubly so by giving birth to another dirty female in a sort of compound interest on being unclean.

Some argue that this sort of misogyny is only found in the Old Testament and not to be followed today because this was all changed with the arrival of Jesus Christ. This view goes against the words of Saint Thomas Aquinas, one of Christianity's brightest lights, on the status of women. According to Aquinas, "As regards the individual nature, woman is defective and misbegotten, for the active power of the male seed tends to the production of a perfect likeness in the masculine sex; while the production of a woman comes from defect in the active power." These are the words of one of the most influential leaders in the history of Christianity.

The Bible on Justice

> Man will never be free until the last king is strangled with the entrails of the last priest.
> —Denis Diderot

> At his best, man is the noblest of all animals; separated from law and justice he is the worst.
> —Aristotle

Is the god of the Bible a *just* god? With the understanding already discussed that the Bible is the only guide we have on the nature of the Christian god, let us consider the nature of biblical justice. If the Bible truly is God's instruction to us on matters of justice, any follower of God who does not defer to the Bible on these matters (or anything else for that matter), then they surely has some explaining to do.

Before evaluating the justice in the Bible, first consider what it means to be just. One definition offered by *Webster* is "The maintenance or administration of what is just especially by the impartial adjustment of conflicting claims or the assignment of merited rewards or punishments." Of course, when speaking of justice, we are limited by the shorthand of language, challenged as we are to explain the complex in simple terms. As such, we are faced with competing definitions; none of which are likely to be fully satisfactory.

Justice involves more than simply providing merit, reward, or punishment. Most reasonable people would agree that a reward or punishment should be commensurate with the action committed. Proportionality of reward or punishment should surely be a component of justice. Before we get into specifics of biblical justice, I pose one overarching question: What crime could possibly be committed in one short lifetime that would warrant eternal, excruciating torture in a furnace of fire (Matthew 13:42 and 25:41)? Even if I were to commit the most horrible crimes anyone can think of, murder perhaps, does that warrant *eternal* punishment in hell? Even if I commit one murder each day for the rest of my life and I live another forty years (that is terrible to be sure), would it warrant eternity in the kind of hell described in the New Testament?

Now, imagine that I get the same eternal punishment, but this time, my only crime is that I used my abilities of reason to determine there is insufficient evidence for a belief in God or the divinity of Jesus Christ. While you are pondering this point, also consider that eternal punishment for finite crimes was brought to us by the kinder and gentler testament of Jesus Christ. Christians often tell me that the New Testament did away with all the "bad parts" of the Bible in the Old Testament. At least in the Old Testament, with all the rape, genocide, slavery, and human sacrifice, once you were dead, you were not tortured for eternity. It is not entirely clear if you would be tortured forever if the Muslim view of God's justice is correct. This is introduced in the New Testament and is not clearly carried over into the Quran.[22]

What are we to make of the common refrain that the god of Abraham is a just god? This is such an ingrained facet of religious disquisition in the United States that we are even told the very nature of justice and of our legal system in the United States flows from God's holy word as naturally as day follows night. This is a claim that stands

---

[22] Admittedly, some pretty serious qualifications are offered here—but of necessity. For example, surah 6 ayah 128 of the Quran reads, "And [mention, O Muhammad], the Day when He will gather them together [and say], 'O company of jinn, you have [misled] many of mankind.' And their allies among mankind will say, 'Our Lord, some of us made use of others, and we have [now] reached our term, which you appointed for us.' He will say, 'The Fire is your residence, wherein you will abide eternally, except for what Allah wills. Indeed, your Lord is Wise and Knowing.'" So hell is eternal, "except for what Allah wills." So there may be an end to the torture.

apart from the truth-value of supernatural religious claims. Perhaps God is real. Perhaps God is imaginary. Neither premise is falsifiable or provable. The claim that we have Holy Scripture to thank for our system of justice, on the other hand, is quite easy to hold up to the light of reason and arrive at some rather conclusive findings.

A quick Internet search reveals some interesting attempts to project justice onto the pages of the Bible, sometimes with creativity, sometimes with outright dishonesty and delusion. The Poverty and Justice Bible website (Word Vision Resources 2010) states, "Almost every page of the Bible speaks of God's heart for the poor. His concern for the marginalised. His compassion for the oppressed. His call for justice." But how can such a claim be honestly made for a book with myriad examples of genocide, rape, the killing of one's own children as a sacrifice to God, slavery, and misogyny? Do these things, all clearly sanctioned by God in the Bible, demonstrate concern and compassion for the oppressed and marginalized? It is one thing to attempt a theological exegesis showing a possible *underlying message* of justice and compassion for the oppressed in what seems otherwise indicated by the language, but claims like the one listed above seem somehow less than responsible and even overtly dishonest.

Platitudes and wishful thinking aside, what does the Bible actually teach us about justice? There are positive examples that, when taken in isolation, are worthy of emulation. For example, Leviticus admonishes us, "Do not pervert justice; do not show partiality to the poor or favoritism to the great, but judge your neighbor fairly." This is hard to argue against. At least until you consider that this is found within the same Bible which tells us that God killed a man simply for touching a box (the Ark of the Covenant) containing stone tablets (1 Chronicles 13:10). Who among us today would judge the simple act of laying hands on something to be an act worthy of capital punishment? It is also instructive to consider the Levitical prescription above is to judge your *neighbor* fairly. One may be justified in wondering if it is easier to be fair to one's neighbors after successive genocides have left only one's immediate relatives as neighbors to judge.

From the very beginning, it seems we get mixed signals when looking for biblical justice. For eating fruit (Genesis 3:6–19), Adam and Eve (and every human being who ever came after them) were made to suffer through all the excruciating maladies that accompany the human condition. Childbirth became a curse. Man had to toil to earn a living. There was enmity put between man and woman, death itself, and the associated loss. All these things are the punishment, in perpetuity, for all mankind, simply for two people having eaten fruit long ago. Yet for the act of committing humanity's very first premeditated murder, Cain was simply sent away (Genesis 4:11–12) to live someplace else and to have bad luck with his crops (Genesis 4:8).

Not only does God's punishment seem far less severe for murder than for eating fruit and touching arks. When Cain complained that the punishment was too severe because he feared "everyone that findeth me shall slay me" (Genesis 4:14), God put a mark on him so everyone would know to not harm Cain or else he (God) would punish them seven times over (Genesis 4:15). This, of course, brings up troubling issues both logical and moral. First, who were all these other people out there whom Cain feared? He was the son of the first man and woman ever created. Surely, there could not have been that many people out there to fear. Second, it seems a strange lesson in justice that if you touch an ark you get killed, if you eat fruit you and all your descendants are punished, but if you murder your own brother you are placed in a divine witness protection program. Surely, I can be forgiven for not buying into this.

A final point on the excessive and eternal punishment for Adam and Eve's gastronomic indiscretion should be considered. In spite of the cliché that ignorance of the law is no excuse, in many cases, an inability to know you are doing wrong actually is a matter of legal mitigation. Have you ever considered the nature of what Adam and Eve were supposed to have done? According to Genesis, there were two trees in the middle of the garden that God had created. Adam and Eve were free to eat of all the trees that were pleasing to the eye and good for food. There were two trees, however (you know, the ones that God placed conspicuously in the middle of the garden), that were forbidden. They were the tree of life and the tree of the knowledge of good and evil. It was not until Adam and Eve had eaten of the tree of the knowledge of good and evil that they knew right from wrong. This is clearly spelled out in chapter 3 verse 5, "For God knows that when you eat from it your eyes will be opened, and you will be like a god, knowing good and evil." Then in verse 7, after eating the fruit, "Then the eyes of both of them were opened, and they realized they were naked; so they sewed fig leaves together and made coverings for themselves." All of humanity since then, according to Christian theology, endure God's punishment when Adam and Eve could not have possibly even known they were doing anything wrong. How is this justice?

In other places, the Bible tells us that God just arbitrarily kills those he deems to be wicked, such as Er, Judah's firstborn (Genesis 38:7). No explanation is given for why Er was judged to be wicked, simply that he was, and he was slain by the Lord. Would the story not be of greater didactic utility if we had been advised what it was that constituted wickedness so that we might avoid similar behavior? It must surely have been something worse than the premeditated murder of one's brother that caused Cain to pull up stakes and move his tent under God's protection no less. Never mind the moral decision most of us today would make if we had godlike powers and simply not create Er wicked in the first place since in our omniscience we would know if we did that eventually we'd kill him for being wicked.

What of the Ten Commandments? Theists often claim they are the basis of the American justice system. Only through breathtaking ignorance (most likely willful ignorance) of both the Ten Commandments and US history can you arrive at this conclusion. The first four commandments have nothing at all to do with the law and are only meaningful if you believe in the god of Abraham. Why would an atheist, Hindu, Buddhist, or anyone not of the Abrahamic tradition care about a prohibition against worshipping gods other than Yahweh or keeping a certain day of the week holy because Yahweh allegedly said to do it? No, these first four commandments only serve to stroke God's divinely sensitive ego.

Numbers 5 (honor your parents) and 7 (don't cheat on your spouse) are often hard to argue against on moral grounds, but neither are illegal. Okay, adultery may have legal ramifications in some situations, but under most circumstances, you need not fear jail time for this offense. Numbers 6 (killing) and 8 (stealing) are illegal in most circumstances, and number 9 (bearing false witness) is illegal in some circumstances, but these seem to be universal human ideas of what should be illegal and have never been limited to Christian societies. Number 10, dealing with not coveting what your neighbor has, is simply bad advice. It is the very act of coveting what others have that motivates us to succeed in life.

This last commandment (at least in this version it is number 10—there are different versions of the Decalogue found in the Bible and 613 commandments in all, and these are simply the ten most talked about) is actually grossly immoral if considered in its entirety. As already pointed out, among the items of property a neighbor may own that we are not to covet are his cattle, male and female slaves, his wife, and others. Are we really to see as moral any rule that identifies well over half of humanity as worthy of nothing more than to be the property of others?

Now consider what is perhaps the most important and most often overlooked idea within these Ten Commandments, and that is the logical outcome if we actually enforce them. Not only is it not illegal to be disrespectful of your parents (wrong in many cases, but not illegal) or to work on the Sabbath, worship other gods, make graven images, blaspheme, covet or commit adultery; but if we follow through with what the Bible tells us to do when these commandments are violated and kill the violator, then we are actually breaking the law by doing what the Bible tells us to do.

Death is called for in the Bible for worshiping other gods (Deuteronomy 17:1–5), making graven images (Deuteronomy 27:1–5), blaspheming (Leviticus 24:16), working on the Sabbath (Exodus 31:14), failure to honor your parents (Deuteronomy 21:18–21), adultery (Leviticus 20:10), and so forth. So not only are the Ten Commandments most definitely not the basis for our legal system, but to follow them fully could result in *you* walking the green mile! I read a post on the internet recently where someone joked about a game in which the participants take turns actually doing what is directed in the Bible. The last one to go to jail wins. I don't think this would be too far from accurate.

Friends of religion often deny this last claim, which only makes it clear they've never actually read the Bible no matter how vociferously they insist they have. What must we do if someone is caught working on the Sabbath? Kill them, of course. Your child learns of a new religion that she finds interesting and tries to tell you about the merits of praying to the Hindu god Ganesh? Kill her too. "All this killing for minor offenses is just Old Testament law that we no longer follow," Christians often say. "Jesus came to change all that," we often hear. But it is not until the New Testament and gentle Jesus that we actually find that there are some things we might do for which we can never be forgiven no matter how much we pray for salvation. Seems you can do almost anything and it can still be made right simply by asking Jesus to forgive you, but remember that if you blaspheme against the Holy Spirit, then you are damned—no hope of reprieve (Matthew 12:32, Mark 3:29). Perpetual torture for something as simple as speaking words against something for which there is no evidence seems another fail for biblical notions of justice.

Fortunately, an honest, skeptical, evaluation reveals no reason to turn to ancient superstitious writings as a source of justice any more than for morality, family values (discussed next), historical verisimilitude, or treatment of women. Even believers have long taken a position of selective compliance with those portions of the Bible that are in keeping with our human moral intuitions while silently rejecting the blatant injustice found throughout. It seems there is good reason to conclude that biblical justice is a creation of men, imperfect as we evolved to be, in a very different time and place than where we today find ourselves.

The Bible on Family Values ("Leave Your Families if You Love Me," Says Jesus)

> If any one comes to me and does not hate his own father and mother and wife and children and brothers and sisters, yes, and even his own life, he cannot be my disciple.
>
> —Jesus, Luke 14:26

One of the great things about living in a free society is that one is free to live as their conscience directs, just so long as their beliefs and resultant actions are benign and not harmful to others. If you want to go to church or not, either choice is perfectly acceptable; and if your choice is to attend, it does not matter which church or denomination you choose, just as it does not matter how you spend your time should your decision be to opt out of religious activities. As Thomas Jefferson said long ago, "But it does me no injury for my neighbor to say there are twenty gods or no God. It neither picks my pocket nor breaks my leg."

Unfortunately, there are a great many people, some of them very influential lobbyists and even elected officials, who feel they are empowered by God to tell others, who may not share their religious views, how to live; and nowhere is this more obvious that in family relationships. Some feel they have been given a monopoly on, of all things, family values, and that God in the Bible reveals this monopoly to them.

In the United States, messages espousing the necessity of Christian family values to our society are so much a part of daily life they are hardly ever called into question. It seems that the area of family values has been ceded to religion as under its sole purview, leaving the church as the final arbiter on what constitutes good (or bad) family values. In America, to say someone is a good Christian or that he is a good family man seems to be transposable characterizations. This is not just informal influence over private family matters. Influential organizations such as the Family Research Council, headquartered in Washington, DC, hold great sway over legislation in this country. They influence decisions made in government that affect all citizens, and it is their position that they do so based on family values rooted in the Christian religion.

This idea of Christian-based family values is a centerpiece of American politics. Sam Harris, points out, "Fifty-seven percent of Americans think that one must believe in God to have good values and to be moral, and sixty-nine percent want a president who is guided by 'strong religious beliefs'" (Harris, *The Moral Landscape: How Science Can Determine Human Values*, 2010). This position is difficult to defend as there is no reason at all to believe that religious beliefs convey any traits we would desire in our political leaders.

Do values matter? Of course they do. Are Christians good people with values that should be emulated? Often yes, sometimes no; but this is true with any group. The majority of Christians are indeed good and decent people. This is not in question. What is in question is the source of this goodness. It is entirely possible that many Christians cling so tightly to religion because they are good people seeking a way to manifest that goodness, and since they've been told that being a Christian is a good thing, this is where they land. They are almost certainly not good people because they are Christians, and it has already been demonstrated that they could not be consistently good people if they literally followed the Bible.

Even when considering one of the most famous biblical examples of what might be considered family values, the commandment to honor thy father and mother, there is more than meets the eye. Who could take issue with honoring your parents, at least so long as they are worthy of being honored? Of course, I would not suggest honoring a father or mother who abused their children. Under most normal circumstances, however, surely, it is a good idea to honor one's father and mother as was stated in the section on biblical justice. However, as also pointed out in the previous section, if you carry out this commandment to its full realization, the punishment for the child who fails to honor his parents is grossly out of proportion to the offense committed. In Deuteronomy 21:18–21, we read:

> If a man have a stubborn and rebellious son, which will not obey the voice of his father, or the voice of his mother, and that, when they have chastened him, will not hearken unto them: Then shall his father and his mother lay hold on him, and bring him out unto the elders of his city, and unto the gate of his place; And they shall say unto the elders of his city, This our son is stubborn and rebellious, he will not obey our voice; he is a glutton, and a drunkard. And all the men of his

city shall stone him with stones, that he die: so
shalt thou put evil away from among you; and all
Israel shall hear, and fear.

Killing children, even insubordinate ones, seems a bit out of
character for a good family man.

The Bible gets so much so wrong that it is nearly impossible
to address these shortcomings without covering the same ground in
multiple places. Slavery and misogyny are just two examples that were
already addressed but must again be touched upon here in the discussion of family values. I hope I will be forgiven the brief redundancy.

When not sanctioning the killing of children, it seems the Bible
is clearing the way for other dangers to be visited upon society's most
helpless. While most of those who read these words would agree
that adults should ensure the safety of defenseless children, the Bible
makes provisions for purchasing child slaves (Leviticus 25:44–46),
just so long as they are not of your own race. The importance of
families staying together apparently only applies if you were lucky
enough to have been born into the *right* race. Could it be that with
the Bible as our moral compass racism is also a good family value?
Fortunately, the evolved moral intuitions of today see the selling of
children into slavery, regardless of race, as an abomination. Racism in
the Bible will be addressed shortly.

The Bible directs us to beat our children (Proverbs 23:13), but
to be fair, the next verse points out that the reason you beat the child
is so he won't go to hell. Surely, God could have created us such
that there might be a way to keep our children out of hell that does
not require that we beat them. Perhaps it is fitting that children be
beaten, however. They are not, after all, the blessing that some today
might think. The bearing of children is a curse as seen in Genesis
3:16; a verse, by the way, that also makes the woman subservient to
man (another good family value, perhaps?).

Remember from the discussion on biblical morality that many
religious people see the willingness of Abraham to tie his own son
down and slaughter him with a knife (Genesis 22:1–12) to be
among the most beautiful stories in the Bible because it demonstrates

Abraham's devotion to God. Some Christians argue that this was just one of those bad Old Testament stories that was changed by the New Testament. They forget, never knew, or ignore, that this story is cited in the New Testament as a virtuous act (Hebrews 11:17). Christians are not alone on this count. The feast of Eid in Islam commemorates Abraham's willingness to slaughter Ishmael (different son, same story), and this is one of Islam's most important celebrations.

While many theists excuse the story of Abraham as merely a test, as God in his infinite mercy and justice sent an angel to stop Abraham just before, he actually disemboweled his son. This excuse doesn't go very far in light of the fact that Jephthah actually did slaughter his own daughter as part of a deal struck with God in Judges 11:30–39. For God's help in securing an important military victory, Jephthah promised God that upon his return home, he would offer the first thing to come from his house as a sacrifice to God. As it turns out, the first thing to come out of Jephthah's house was his daughter. The excuse that God stopped Abraham just short of killing his son (therefore it wasn't a bad thing) is also morally repugnant in that there would certainly have been permanent emotional scars that resulted from knowing that your father was willing to butcher you because the voices in his head told him to. Family values, it seems, are complicated matters.

It seems doubtful that the Family Research Council would see polygamy as an example of good family values, but where do they get this idea? The Bible indicates that having multiple wives is perfectly acceptable as far back as Genesis 4:19. Later in the book of Exodus (Exodus 2:7–11), we see not only sanction for polygamy but also what seems to be sexual slavery: "And if a man sell his daughter to be a maidservant, she shall not go out as the menservants do. If she please not her master, who hath betrothed her to himself, then shall he let her be redeemed: to sell her unto a strange nation he shall have no power, seeing he hath dealt deceitfully with her. And if he have betrothed her unto his son, he shall deal with her after the manner of daughters. If he take him another wife; her food, her raiment, and her duty of marriage, shall he not diminish. And if he do not these three unto her, then shall she go out free without money." Making the case that taking more than one wife is a solid example of family values is hard enough, but can anyone reading this really accept selling a daughter into slavery, apparently for sexual purposes, as a family value worthy of emulation?

God's destruction of the city of Sodom has been alluded to a few times already in this book because of what it might tell us about gender equality. What can this story teach us about family values? Remember that the killing of all men, women, and children except for Lot and his family was God's judgment for, among other things, the attempted rape of two angels. The innocent children of this town died, but Lot, who offered up his own daughters to be raped (Genesis 19:5–8) in place of the angels, got to leave with his family. It would seem to most of us today a better example of family values might be to risk your own life defending one's daughters from the threat of rape than offering them up for that end.

Family values in this one righteous family are quite interesting, actually. Later, after escaping the destruction of their city, Lot's daughters apparently got their father drunk and had sex with him on two successive nights (Jerry, Jerry, Jerry![23]). Not the sort of family most today would want theirs modeled after. It is also important to consider that Lot was seen as the innocent victim in this case of incestuous date rape (Genesis 19:30–36).

While the story of Lot and his Jerry Springeresque family is an ancient Bible story, it is replete with relevant corollaries in the political and religious discourse of today. The already-mentioned example of Todd Akin and the concept of "legitimate rape" not leading to pregnancy is as ignorant of human reproduction as the story of Lot's youngest daughter lying with him to get pregnant when he was passed out from drinking too much wine. Maybe Lot was just a better, more manly man that I am, but I am pretty sure I couldn't get a woman pregnant if I was passed out drunk. Also, the idea that Lot was the innocent victim of incest is eerily familiar in the story from Friar Benedict Groeschel, who claimed that in some Catholic sex

---

[23] My apologies to those who may be too young (or too cultured) to not get the Jerry Springer reference.

abuse cases, the priests were victims of teens who seduced the priests (Bennett-Smith 2012).

Respect for and protection of one's wife also seems to somehow rate low on the scale of biblical family values. Abraham offered up his wife to the Pharaoh to ensure his own safety. Genesis 12:12–16 reads, "Therefore it shall come to pass, when the Egyptians shall see thee, that they shall say, This is his wife: and they will kill me, but they will save thee alive. Say, I pray thee, thou art my sister: that it may be well with me for thy sake; and my soul shall live because of thee. And it came to pass, that, when Abram was come into Egypt, the Egyptians beheld the woman that she was very fair. The princes also of Pharaoh saw her, and commended her before Pharaoh: and the woman was taken into Pharaoh's house. And he entreated Abram well for her sake: and he had sheep, and oxen, and he asses, and menservants, and maidservants, and she asses, and camels."

It seems Abraham's lie about his wife was more upsetting to the Pharaoh's family values than to Abraham's. Genesis 12:18–20 reads, "And Pharaoh called Abram and said, What is this that thou hast done unto me? Why didst thou not tell me that she was thy wife? Why saidst thou, She is my sister? so I might have taken her to me to wife: now therefore behold thy wife, take her, and go thy way. And Pharaoh commanded his men concerning him: and they sent him away, and his wife, and all that he had."

Editorial note here in case anyone is confused about the use of Abram and Abraham. This is actually not a typo and is the same person. In Genesis 17:5, we read, "Neither shall thy name any more be called Abram, but thy name shall be Abraham; for a father of many nations have I made thee."

The Bible on Racism (God Loves Everyone—Who Looks Like Me)

The doom of Ham has been branded on the form and features of his African descendants.

The hand of fate has united his color and destiny.
Man cannot separate what god hath joined.
—James Henry Hammond,
US Senator, 1857–1860

Having spent considerable time and effort so far critiquing the Bible, it is important to stress what should be an obvious point— value judgments are kept at a minimum, and I am sticking with the biblical examples to the extent practicable. Misogyny, slavery, injustice, genocide, and various moral ambiguities have not been projected onto the Bible, simply pulled from its pages. If these things were not there for all to see, then they could not be quoted. It is a bit tedious, pedantic even, to continually list chapter and verse after so many examples of these things which most of us today would consider bad things in the Good Book but necessary in this sort of discussion.

What other mixed moral messages might we be getting from the Bible? Racial equality, perhaps? I am approaching this from the presupposition that racism is, quite simply, not a good thing. Clearly, if anyone disagrees with this point, then what follows will not make much sense to him or her. There are some who truly do believe that racism is not a bad thing and that we should recognize one race as superior to others. Interestingly, it is rarely someone else's race that is superior, but our own, in much the same way it is rarely one's own religion that doesn't make sense but someone else's. Anyone who lacks the moral clarity to see that hatred of another human being because they happen to be the wrong ethnicity is not likely to have the cognitive ability to have read this far anyway, so let us continue without them.

Does the Bible sanction racism? Among the myriad problems encountered while discussing race in the Bible is that even breathtakingly obvious racism is often given a free pass because the Bible is supposed to be good. For example, the Bible states in the Old Testament that the Jews are God's chosen people, in some parts of the New Testament that Jesus claims to have been sent to minister only to the Jewish people (Matthew 15:24), yet we are to believe that none of this is racist in any way.

The idea that one race is now or has ever been favored over all others is racist by definition; saying it was God's choice does not make it somehow okay. If similar claims were made by a member of the Ku Klux Klan or Aryan Nation—that the white race is God's chosen (such claims have often been made by the way) and that Jesus came only to minister to the white man—how could this be seen as anything other than a vulgar and lucid example of racist ideology? It could not. But the Bible gets a free pass on this. Many Christians don't even acknowledge these parts of the Bible, and besides, God works in mysterious ways, so when he said it then, he had a good reason so we need to look for his underlying message and not just what was said. It's like being told, "Do what I meant, not what I said!" The truly awkward part of all this for biblical literalists is that there have been and continue to be a great many devoutly racist and jingoistic people who use the Bible as justification for their claims to racial or national superiority when the Bible was never even addressing them or their nation.

Other than the Jews being God's chosen people, what might we find in the Bible that could be seen as justification for racism? Quite a lot as it turns out. The Bible tells us the emergence of dark-skinned people after the great flood is the result of a curse placed on Canaan by Noah (Genesis 9:20–27). This curse was not for something Canaan did but for something done by Ham (Canaan's father and Noah's son). It seems that Noah went a bit far with the post-flood libation and passed out naked. Ham saw his father in this state and did certain things, some of which are open to speculation, which angered Noah. So the curse was issued. Never mind the injustice of putting a curse on Canaan (and all his descendants) for something his father did. This is the biblical justification for thousands of years of belief that Africans are a cursed people. If you happen to be a Christian and are angered by this, don't write me to complain—bring it up with your church. Despite how ridiculous we may find this thinking today, this has been the majority consensus among Christians for most of the history of Christianity.

It is worth noting that science has proven conclusively that modern humans first appeared in Africa, from which we spread out to populate the planet. This is one of many examples of the Bible getting it exactly wrong. According to the Bible, the dark-skinned Africans resulted from the curse of Ham long after God created what we must presume to be a much-lighter-skinned Adam and Eve. We now know that we all came out of Africa. We are all Africans. There may be no clearer example of modern societal morality, norms, and mores being out of synch with the Bible than our views on racism in the West today versus what the Bible has promulgated and was once almost universally accepted. The words in the Bible did not change. Our morality on this issue evolved as a result of human intellect and experience, not divine sanction.

The Bible Versus Science (Science Wins Every Time—It's a Scientific Fact!)

> You could give Aristotle a tutorial. And you could thrill him to the core of his being... Such is the privilege of living after Newton, Darwin, Einstein, Planck, Watson, Crick and their colleagues.
> —Richard Dawkins

> There is a cult of ignorance in the United States, and there has always been. The strain of anti-intellectualism has been a constant thread winding its way through our political and cultural life, nurtured by the false notion that democracy means that "my ignorance is just as good as your knowledge."
> —Isaac Asimov

This part of this book should not have to be written. You should not need to read it. But in the most technologically advanced nation on earth (for now at least), we have a very strange situation, indeed. It seems that alongside the decoded human genome, nanotechnology, global positioning systems of unbelievable accuracy (enabled by our understanding of the physical laws that govern the universe), we also have a populace who is largely ignorant of basic scientific facts and as a result is often distrustful of science and the scientific method.

In twenty-first-century America, it seems that 42 percent of us believe that life has existed in its current form since the earth was created (Masci 2007). This is in spite of the fact that evolution is not only a proven fact. The theory is in the specifics of how it happens, not that it does happen. Modern medicine and biology make sense only in light of our understanding of evolution. We also live in an America, unique in our nation's history because of its prominence, where an anti-science posture almost seems a prerequisite to being seriously considered for high office with leaders like Mitt Romney,[24] John Boehner,[25] and Michelle Bachman[26] arguing against the scientific consensus on issues such as climate change, evolution, and the efficacy and necessity of vaccines. This is a dangerous change from the long and proud tradition of scientific literacy in our national discourse.

Recall the earlier discussion of the scientific method as a way of knowing. Consider again the history of rational thought and the eventual scientific revolution, which has been a one-way pushing back of ignorance, always at the expense of religious dogma. Consider also what has already been shown of the unreliable nature

---

[24] Mitt Romney stated in 2011 that "my view is that we don't know what's causing climate change on this planet, and the idea of spending trillions and trillions of dollars to try and reduce CO_2 emissions is not the right course for us."

[25] Boehner has argued for the teaching of creationism in science classrooms. This, in spite of the fact that there is not only no evidence for creation, it isn't even a science.

[26] It is hard to know where to start with Bachman. Just one gem from Bachman was her insistence that young girls were being forced to have an injection that caused mental retardation. This injection, the human papillomavirus vaccine, is only known to do one thing: reduce the risk of contracting HPV, a known cause of cervical cancer, and there is no known link to mental retardation.

of the Bible in the first part of this chapter. Is it not then a cause for concern that so many of us feel that the Bible is a more reliable source of knowledge than science? To be fair, this is not limited to religious dogma. Rational interrogation of the natural world has pushed back unsupported dogma of all sorts, but the relation to superstition (and religion is superstitious by definition) is unique. Religious beliefs are unique in that they claim divine sanction and are therefore unassailable. You can't argue with God after all. Religious beliefs are consequently distinctively tenacious, and the only cure is the careful and consistent application of rational evidence and reason.

Those of us who argue for the veracity of science over religious dogma are often lambasted with challenges to science such as "Science is not the only way of knowing things." True, science is not the only way of knowing, but it is the most consistently reliable by orders of magnitude and without question. There is not a single example of knowledge that we now enjoy for which the Bible is a more reliable source than is science. If you look at the converse of this statement, we could grow old talking about the nearly inexhaustible list of things for which science provides better explanations than does the Bible.

A frequent challenge to science from the religious set is, "Scientists are always changing their minds!" It never ceases to amaze, amuse, and sometimes even frustrate me that some people see this as a weakness of the scientific method rather than perhaps its greatest strength. The fact that scientists are so ready to accept a better explanation for natural phenomena (and all real phenomena are natural) than the ones they previously held is what has allowed our exponential growth in knowledge since the advent of the modern scientific method. Isaac Asimov commented on this brilliantly:

> The young specialist in English Lit... lectured me severely on the fact that in every century people have thought they understood the Universe at last, and in every century they were proved to be wrong. It follows that the one thing we can

say about our modern "knowledge" is that it is wrong.

My answer to him was, "When people thought the Earth was flat, they were wrong. When people thought the Earth was spherical they were wrong. But if you think that thinking the Earth is spherical is just as wrong as thinking the Earth is flat, then your view is wronger than both of them put together."

It is enlightening to consider just a few examples of what the Bible tells us and juxtapose those ideas with what scientific knowledge has to say on the same issues. An organization calling itself Clarifying Christianity has posted on the internet a page with the claim, "The Bible is not a science book, yet it is scientifically accurate. We are not aware of *any* scientific evidence that contradicts the Bible." Yet the Bible tells of things such as the Genesis creation myth, a six-thousand-year-old earth, a geocentric universe, people who lived for hundreds of years, and many other things which science directly and irrefutably contradicts. The notion of a young earth and young universe on the order of some six thousand years old was briefly addressed and refuted already, but now let's unpack that belief of a young earth and compare it to science for perspective on just how the Bible got it exactly wrong and science has provided much more eloquent, satisfying, and most importantly, correct answers.

How is this age of the universe arrived at from reading the Bible? It's quite simple (and simplistic) really. It is by taking the genealogies found in the book of Genesis primarily that Church of Ireland Bishop James Ussher concluded that God created the earth on Sunday, October 23, 4004 BC. Yeah, no kidding, and that is still believed by a great many today. Don't believe me? Just have a go at telling the average Evangelical Christian the truth about the age of the earth and see what you get. While they may pull up short of saying the earth is around six thousand years old, you will very likely get some sort of excuse for how the earth can't really be billions of years old.

Scientific evidence, on the other hand, has proven that the earth is over 4.5 billion years old and the universe itself around 13.7 billion years old. This means that if one takes the literal interpretation of the Genesis creation myth, then science must not only be wrong but wrong by many orders of magnitude. Science has estimated (based upon very reliable evidence) the universe is about 2,283,333 times older than what is claimed by young earth creationist groups such as Answers in Genesis, sponsor of the Creation Museum and the Ark Encounter, both in the state of Kentucky. This is like estimating the distance from Washington, DC, to Singapore (where I sit as I write these words) is actually about 22.3 feet rather than the actual 51,025,920 feet, or 9,664 miles. Being wrong to this degree is like saying that an average human hair is actually 187 meters (just over 613 feet) in diameter. It is as wrong as saying that the current fastest man in the world at the time of this writing, Usain Bolt, can actually run 63,933,324 miles per hour. I hope my point is sufficiently made. Young earth creationists are not just wrong; they are monumentally, stupefyingly, breathtakingly, embarrassingly, and unforgivably wrong, and they are wrong because they rely on a literal interpretation of the Bible while ignoring better sources of information that are demonstrably correct. To willfully be this wrong truly is indefensible as there is undeniable proof that their position is simply not tenable. Rather than simply admitting this incongruence between science and religion, folks like the Answers in Genesis crowd often simply lie about what the science actually says.

Among the myriad problems with views held by young earth creationists is that archaeological evidence exists for human civilization prior to the creation of the universe itself if God really did create the cosmos only about six thousand years ago. According to a humorous article from *The Onion*, "Members of the earth's earliest known civilization, the Sumerians, looked on in shock and confusion some 6,000 years ago as God, the Lord Almighty, created heaven and Earth" (*The Onion* 2009). Funny articles aside, science is clear on the age of the earth. This presents the young earth creationist with another dilemma (number 14). Either God did not create the universe about six thousand years ago (in which case the Bible is wrong) or he did it but planted false evidence of a very old universe just to confuse us. Seriously, the nerve of God planting evidence that agriculture came about a full seventeen millennia before, and even beer 3,500 years before, the universe. Not all theists, of course, believe the Bible is the verbatim word of God that should be taken literally. Many do, however, and to say, "We are not aware of *any* scientific evidence that contradicts the Bible," only admits that you are stupendously ignorant of either science or the Bible or most likely both.

The Bible tells us in Psalm 93:1, Psalm 96:10, Psalm 104:5, 1 Chronicles 16:30, Ecclesiastes 1:5, and perhaps other places that Copernicus, Galileo, Einstein, and every working scientist alive today were and is dead wrong in believing the Earth is not firmly at the center of the universe. Yes, according to the Bible, the Earth does not move (which it does), but the rest of the universe does (which is actually true), and the universe moves around the Earth (which is wronger than wrong). Science has shown us conclusively that the Earth moves about the Sun, along with the rest of the solar system. Our solar system itself rotates on an arm of a run-of-the-mill spiral galaxy, about two-thirds of the way out from the galactic center, around a supermassive black hole. Our sun and a couple of hundred billion other suns (and associated solar systems) make up our galaxy. Our galaxy is itself just one of hundreds of billions of galaxies.

The Bible-based belief, now mostly dispensed with, that Earth is at the center of the cosmos and the (still widely held) belief in a young Earth are easy to understand when one assumes that scientifically illiterate men who only had personal observation to draw from wrote the Bible. It makes no sense at all, however, when assuming that the omniscient creator of the universe, who would presumably have known better, wrote this magic book. To argue that a six-thousand-year-old Earth is at the center of a six-thousand-year-old universe is not only one of the most incredibly wrong ideas anyone ever had; it is perhaps the greatest single example of hypocrisy when claiming that Christianity is a religion of humility. Imagine the hubris involved in believing that the countless billions of stars, indescribable vastness, and astonishing age of the universe were all created just for us.

Remember that the order of creation in Genesis is also contradicted by science. When I was still a believer in God but no longer a biblical literalist, I believed that perhaps arguing that a day for God might be billions of years for us could salvage the Genesis creation myth. That too did not survive scrutiny. God created light before he created light-producing things like the Sun and other stars (Genesis 1:3–17). He created plants on the third day, but the Sun, a prerequisite for photosynthesis on Earth, on the fourth day. Genesis also tells us that God placed the Moon there to rule the night (Genesis 1:16), but the Moon spends a considerable portion of its time hidden in the daylight and does not even come out at night, seemingly in defiance of God. This is due to the fact that the Moon orbits Earth in what we perceive as the twenty-nine-day synodic period (actually twenty-seven days to make the full orbit). This is what gives the appearance that the moon has phases, allows us to sometimes see it during the daytime, and sometimes not see it at night.

The Bible tells us that Noah created a single boat that was only somewhere between four hundred and five hundred feet long but was still able to hold between two to fourteen of each animal species on the planet. The number of animals actually gets a bit confusing because contrary to all the cute Sunday school depictions and "common knowledge," there were not two of every animal on the Ark. Depending on the type of animal, they went into the Ark by twos or by sevens. Must we really address this claim? Okay, we must.

According to Genesis 6:15, the Ark was to be three hundred cubits long by fifty cubits wide and thirty cubits high. The exact length of a cubit is not precisely known but is widely taken to be about the length of an average adult male's forearm. Consider that there are currently estimated to be nine hundred thousand species of insects on the planet (prepared by the Department of Systematic Biology, Entomology Section, National Museum of Natural History). If there were even a fraction of this number of insects during biblical times, and we have every reason to believe there were, then insects alone would have overcrowded the ark. Many literalists argue this was not a problem because Noah only took two of each *kind* of animal (so one dog kind, one bird kind, etc.). Never mind that this "kind classification" is zoologically meaningless and not accepted seriously by any biologists actually working in biology, or for biological reasons, it also must by definition accept evolution (the very thing they argue against). While arguing that evolution is a lie, they also argue these few "kinds" that were on the Ark evolved into the diversity of life we now see. It should be considered also that evolution would have to work far more quickly and efficiently in this view than how biologists actually understand it to work. If this "animal kind" story were true, then from a very few "kinds" of animals only a few thousand years ago we would have the current evolved diversity of life on our planet.

Also consider that the amount of water necessary to cover the highest peak of Mount Everest by fifteen cubits (Genesis 7:19–20) would have likely sent the earth careening out of its orbit due to the incredible change in mass. I suppose an omnipotent god could have held Earth in orbit if he wanted to, but this would violate what science tells us about how the universe works, and remember the claim that science does not contradict the Bible. Consider also what happened when the year-long global flood was over and the waters subsided; what did the herbivores eat? And the carnivores? Fortunately, most rational human beings don't take this story literally. There really is nothing about the Noahic flood myth that is not contradicted by scientific understanding. Never mind what all the thriving cultures in places like Iraq, Egypt, China, Korea, India, and others where people were diligently going about their business completely ignoring this global flood event.

Apparently, the laws of planetary motion are something else we can throw out if the Bible is our guide. It seems Copernicus, Galileo, and Newton were not correct in their ideas as the Sun not only moves around the Earth and not the other way around; the Sun can stop dead in its tracks on its way around the Earth so that a battle could continue in daylight (Joshua 10:12–13). Science has clearly ruled out this possibility. Where the Bible tells us the Sun goes round the Earth and it can stop in its orbit then start again on its way, science not only tells us the geocentric model is wrong; it tells us with amazing accuracy how the Moon orbits the Earth and the Earth orbits the Sun along with other heavenly (no pun intended) bodies. We understand the movements of the planets with such amazing accuracy. In fact, we can predict that there will be five solar eclipses each year in 2206, 2709, 2774, 2839, and 2904 (I'll stop there); and remember that on July 16, 2186, there will be a solar eclipse that will last for seven minutes and twenty-nine seconds (Natuional Aeronautics and Space Administration 2009). This will be the longest solar eclipse in five thousand years. We know this with great certainty because we now understand so much more about science and so much more about how the Bible got matters of science completely wrong.

Some argue that according to the Bible pi is 3 (1 Kings 7:23). According to science, it is approximately 3.14159265. This might not seem like much of an error, but it is considerable, especially for a book that some claim to be more accurate and reliable than any knowledge obtained by human efforts. I will offer the caveat that I am not convinced that this passage is actually arguing for the measure of pi and offer this example only for consideration because some Christians argue that it actually does argue for this (while omitting that the Bible got it wrong if measuring pi was the intent). It is interesting that I have heard apologists argue that the calculation for pi is exactly what the passage from 1 Kings is talking about, and they then went on to argue that this is amazing in its accuracy. This is not a reasonable position.

According to Psalms 38:3 and other places in the Bible, disease is caused by God's anger. Thanks to science, we now have a superb understanding of the germ theory of disease. And isn't it "miraculous" and wonderful that we do? If the Bible and notions of an angry god causing disease were all we had to go on, then prayer would be our only recourse for health care. Thanks to our greater understanding of such things as germ theory, the importance of improved sanitation, the development of improved antibiotics and vaccinations, we now live longer, healthier, and more productive lives than at any time in human history despite what the Bible says about people having once lived hundreds of years.

Americans tend to have high regard for scientific achievement or the benefits of science, but we are also a highly religious society, and here we have a considerable dilemma (number 15). When a significant percentage of our population literally follows such guidance as offered in Proverbs 3:5 to ignore human (scientific) understanding but follow the Lord (biblical understanding which is demonstrably wrong on so many topics) instead, this is a perfect recipe for ignorance. We are doomed to remain ignorant if Ecclesiastes 3:11 is any indication—apparently, we cannot begin to understand the things that God created, so we should not even try.

It should be clear that if there is a god, no human being alive can truly know what it is he wants or expects from us. On the other hand, we have science, and while it is far from perfect, it is the best way humans have yet developed for distinguishing truth from fiction, good ideas from bad, and for ensuring the future prosperity and survival of our species. Where religion gave us an angry god shaking the earth, science gave us plate tectonics. Religion gave us demonic possession and exorcism; science gave us an understanding of neurological disorders and effective treatment. Religion gave us the Genesis creation myth; science gave us cosmology and a wonderfully accurate understanding of the diversity and interconnected nature of all the various species on earth. Where God gave us cancer, HIV, and AIDS (if God is real and he is in control), science has managed to cure a little girl's leukemia using a modified HIV virus (Grady 2012). As Michael Specter stated in his book *Denialism*, "There is at least one compelling reason that the scientific method has come to shape our notion of progress and modern life. It works" (Specter 2009). It is unfortunate that so many seem unable to distinguish between what works and what they wish were true.

The Bible on Jesus (There's a Jesus for Every Occasion)

This, the last section of the chapter that focuses directly on the Bible, segues into the next chapter that specifically addresses Christian apologetics. Discussing the nature of Jesus reveals interesting implications on the veracity of the Bible. This also lays bare noteworthy considerations as it applies to counter-apologetics. These two lines of inquiry lead to this being an appropriate transitional topic between the discussions of the Bible and apologetics. In dealing with the Bible on Jesus, there is unavoidable redundancy and overlap. I endeavor to avoid repeating myself where possible and at least ensure relevance where repetition is necessary.

As with so many topics covered in this book, there was a personal story that led me to seriously consider the nature of Jesus. "You can forget about all that bad stuff in the Old Testament. Jesus came and changed all that" was a challenge issued directly to me at a very high-level conference of senior government leaders. I have mentioned this notion already but bring it up again here because if I had not spoken up when I did, it appears that a very significant failure of imagination and understanding may have been missed. This is significant because as an Army lieutenant colonel, I was one of the most junior people in the room. A point that I will revisit in the closing of this book is that all too often, important decisions that affect us all are made while giving deference–by–default to religious considerations, often due to ignorance of the facts.

The exchange resulted after one of the conference participants opined that Islam couldn't be a moderate religion the way Judaism and Christianity are today. This, went the allegation, was because of the nature of Quranic writings. Basically, this person argued, even if individual Muslims may be moderate, the violent nature of the Quran wouldn't allow the Islamic religion to be moderate. I asked if the same could not be said of the Christian Bible and that while most Christians are actually peace-loving folks, the Bible actually has more sanction for violent acts that does the Quran. In fairness, the Bible is a bigger book, and as a percentage of its total pages, less of it is violent than the Quran. But the raw number of violent acts is higher in the Bible than the Quran, and the real point of my observation was to draw attention to the hypocrisy of a Christian calling the Quran a violent book (at the risk of being accused of committing a tu quoque fallacy). After a pregnant pause, I was told, "Oh, you must be talking about the Old Testament." I asked for a point of clarification or relevance. "We don't rely on the Old Testament. Jesus changed all that" was the reply from another conference participant. While this point is hotly debated, there is definitely an argument to be made that what we know of Jesus from the New Testament does not in any way negate the Old Testament. In fact, quite the opposite may be true. Just one example is from Matthew 5:17–18: "Think not that I am come to destroy the law, or the prophets: I am not come to destroy, but to fulfill. For verily I say unto you, Till heaven and earth pass, one jot or one tittle shall in no wise pass from the law, till all be fulfilled." This passage will be addressed again in the discussion of the nature (or not) of Peaceful Jesus.

In case it is not yet obvious, there are a host of problems with the view that the Old Testament is somehow not relevant, a view by the way which an Air Force chaplain who happened to be at this same conference also shared. First, and this is a follow-up point I made at the conference in question, without Old Testament prophesies (which Jews normally feel Christians have misinterpreted), there is no basis for stating that Jesus is the Messiah who answered the prophesies. Many Christians are quite fond of stating how many Old Testament prophesies Jesus fulfilled, but you simply can't do this and also discount the Old Testament as irrelevant. It is the Old Testament itself that Christians look to for the "street cred" they believe Jesus has for answering these Old Testament prophesies. To put it simply, no Old Testament, no coming Messiah.

This matter of Old Testament relevancy also brings up an important point about why Jesus was even necessary. Recall that I addressed the issue of drive-by proselytization in chapter 1 and will again in the discussion of the argument from morality in chapter 4. Admittedly, this is one of those areas where redundancy becomes a problem. For purposes of this particular point, I will only add that at the very core of the Jesus narrative is that he came to save us from the mark of original sin. Without the original sin and fall from grace in Genesis, there is no need of the saving grace of Jesus—probably the most important single belief in Christian dogma. All this ground-work comes from the Old Testament. Either the Old Testament matters or it is to be discarded. Herein lies Christian dilemma 16. If you wish to rely on the Old Testament when convenient, you must embrace it when it is embarrassing. You simply cannot use it as the entire foundational justification for and eventual coming of Jesus and then discount it when reminded of the unsavory bits. À la carte religion does not work.

The belief that Jesus made right all the Old Testament wrongs does not hold up well to scrutiny, and this is a problem for Christians. Jesus is said to be the perfect, sinless Son of God—God himself even. And where there were acts of violence, slavery, rape, genocide, and other injustices in the Old Testament, Jesus was all about peace, love, and harmony according to many Christians. To borrow a common phrase from New Testament scholar Bart Ehrman, however, "It depends on which Gospel you read." Or to be more specific, *which part* of which Gospel you read. It seems that perhaps one of the most fascinating facts about the biblical Jesus is that he did not seem to be one person but several.

Even famously atheist scientists and authors such as Richard Dawkins and Sam Harris sometimes speak in favor of the historical Jesus (while still doubting his divinity, of course). Dawkins wrote an article titled "Atheists for Jesus" (2006) discussing his view that Jesus was a moral philosopher ahead of his time in many ways. Sam Harris even said, "I love Jesus," when asked in an interview why he hates Jesus. Harris did add the caveat that he at least loves one of the Jesuses that he reads about, pointing out there are other less-savory characterizations of Christ in the Bible as well.

It is interesting to consider that while some atheist writers and scholars praise Jesus not as God but as a moral philosopher ahead of his time, many theists reject this position almost violently. C. S. Lewis, one of the most prominent of Christian apologists, said of this idea that Jesus might be anything other than God: "A man who was merely a man and said the sort of things Jesus said would not be a great moral teacher. He would either be a lunatic—on a level with the man who says he is a poached egg—or else he would be the Devil of hell... But let us not come up with any patronising non-sense about His being a great human teacher" (Lewis 1952).

So what are we to think of Jesus based on the words of the Bible? As it turns out, Jesus wasn't always so pleasant, and at times when Christ was quoted as saying nice things, those things were not necessarily new or unique to Christ. Was he a man? Was he divine?

And if so, when did he become divine? Is he on the same level as God? Is he actually God himself?[27] None of this is really clear, and nothing that I write here should be controversial; it is all in the Bible for anyone who cares to read it.

As we are talking here about the biblical nature of Jesus Christ, consider now what we think we know about him and how we think we know it. Hardly a day goes by that I don't hear something amazing about Jesus. No matter what your troubles, no worries, friend, just turn to Jesus Christ for the answers. You need not even fear death itself because Jesus died for our sins so that you will live forever with him in heaven. But what do you really know about him? Here's an idea, the next time you go to church, ask the most knowledgeable person you know there to tell you every single detail they know about the greatest man who ever lived, and also ask how they know this to be true. Don't worry, it won't take that long. Trust me, I've tried it. Better yet, don't trust me and really do try it yourself.

How We Think We Know What We Think We Know about Jesus

Before going into specifics of the nature of Jesus, his sayings, and his actions, it is important to understand how this knowledge comes to us. Juxtapose the absolute certainty with which many Christians express the "fact" that Jesus Christ was who he claimed to be (who someone claimed to be is a very interesting source of evidence by the way, and it's not that clear what Jesus claimed in any event) with what the majority of New Testament scholars agree on about our knowledge of Christ, and you will see a great disparity. There are many reasons to challenge anyone claiming knowledge of Jesus as certain.

---

[27] I realize I am changing from past to present tense here mid-thought, but there is a reason. If Jesus was a historical person, then he *was* so in the past. If Christians are correct and Jesus is the divine Son of God, then he *is* such now.

The earliest stories that specifically address the birth, life, death, and resurrection of Jesus Christ in any detail at all are the Gospels of Matthew, Mark, Luke, and John; this is not in debate. The writings of Paul come a bit earlier, but in the writings of Paul, there is only about a paragraph (and a short one at that) that specifically addresses the actual Jesus and not just teachings attributed to him. From 1 Corinthians 15: "That Christ died for our sins according to the scriptures; And that he was buried, and that he rose again the third day according to the scriptures: And that he was seen of Cephas, then of the twelve: After that, he was seen of above five hundred brethren at once; of whom the greater part remain unto this present, but some are fallen asleep. After that, he was seen of James; then of all the apostles. And last of all he was seen of me also, as of one born out of due time." Most of what Paul tells of Jesus was clearly secondhand and/ or claims of postmortem appearances. The significance of which is that the most prolific writer and most important figure in the establishment of the church, Paul, admits he never met Jesus (at least not until after he was dead[28]) nor did anyone else upon whom Paul bases this report. It is all secondhand (or worse) information.

If Jesus really did the things claimed in the Bible, these are likely the most important things ever to occur in human history. To borrow another quote from C. S. Lewis, "Christianity, if false, is of no importance, and if true, of infinite importance. The only thing it cannot be is moderately important." While I quote Lewis again because something worthwhile can be gleaned from what he had to say, he was also wrong in his hyperbole. Christianity is of importance even if false because it is the world's leading religion and so much of the world's resources are consumed by it. So many decisions are made based on belief in it, and this is so in spite of the fact that there is no good evidence that it is true.

When considering the influence, both historically and today, of Christianity, it is interesting then that there is not a single surviving report about Jesus contemporaneous with his life and ministry. Not

---

[28] If my sarcasm isn't readily apparent in the printed word, I don't believe anyone has met anyone else after either of those individuals have died.

one. Even if Jesus was not actually divine and was merely a trouble-making apocalyptic preacher who made just a bit too much of a nuisance of himself with the Jewish and Roman authorities, we should expect to find mention of him in the records kept by the authorities of the time. But it wasn't until 112 CE that we have any recorded mention of Jesus in any non-Christian source (Ehrman B. D. 2009). This really does leave us with little choice but to stick with the first four books of the New Testament, the Gospels, for what we think we know about Jesus.

Are there good reasons to believe the Gospel accounts are a true and accurate retelling of the events in the life of Jesus, or are there reasons to question the historical verisimilitude of all that is written in the Gospels? Historians try to ascertain what is most likely to have occurred based upon the available evidence. This becomes problematic when discussing biblical claims of miraculous events that are in direct contravention of what we know about how the world works. Miracles are, after all, the least likely things to have actually happened. This is why they are called "miracles." Otherwise, they would be mundane events, not miraculous in nature. By the very definition of what we would consider a miracle, they would be pretty much impossible to establish as historical facts. For this reason, the truth-value of supernatural claims will not be addressed here. Claims of miracles simply aren't worth taken seriously enough to write about. The focus here will be on things that could actually be proven (or disproven), at least to a reasonable degree.

Let's begin with the nature of the Gospel stories. One issue that many find surprising is that the Gospel accounts are not eyewitness accounts. The consensus among New Testament scholars is that the men who wrote the Gospel accounts not only were not really Matthew, Mark, Luke, and John; they likely never met Jesus. The followers of Jesus were predominantly illiterate Aramaic speakers whereas Greek speakers, most likely well-educated Greek speakers (Ehrman B. D. 2009), wrote the Gospels.

Christian apologists often point out that the Gospels are the earliest written accounts of the life of Jesus. They do this in order to support the veracity of the Gospel claims, the thinking being that the closer to the event being discussed, the more reliable the account. This is actually not helpful to the Christian, however. According to the *Oxford Guide to the Bible*, edited by Bruce M. Metzger and Michael De. Coogan, Mark was the first of the four Gospels. We know that Mark was written no earlier than about 70 CE. Consider that not only was Mark apparently not written until decades after the death of Christ, the earliest record we have of the authenticity of Mark being referenced as the author of the Gospel that bears his name came from the Bishop of Hierapolis, Papias, some sixty years after it was written down (Metzger and Coogan 1993). Now, if I am wrong in my disbelief, then I freely admit that the birth of Christ, his life, death, and resurrection, was perhaps the greatest event since the creation (again, if true) of mankind. Why then was the earliest known record of his life only written down forty years after his death and the earliest attribution of that authorship not until another sixty years had passed?

Think about this brothers and sisters because this is truly profound when you consider the implications. The earliest record of anyone attributing the first Gospel to Mark was in 130 CE. They are attributing to Mark something that was written about Jesus forty years after he died, and worse still, this was written by someone who probably never even met Jesus or saw the events he described. This is the best evidence we have for what we think we know about Jesus.

To put this into context (and yes, I am beating a dead horse here a bit), imagine then someone in 1993 said he had heard that a man named Ted wrote an account in 1933 of the life of Benjamin Harrison, who died in 1893. Ted, who never met President Harrison, wrote of him forty years after Harrison's death, and nobody mentioned that Ted was the author of the Harrison account for another sixty years. This might not seem that strange—*yet*. You might argue that modern biographical accounts are often written about people long dead by those who never met the person being written about. True, but there is a key difference between the Ted who wrote about Benjamin Harrison and the Mark who is claimed to have written the Gospel account of Jesus. There are detailed records about Harrison contemporaneous with his life, from a variety of sources, both from people who liked and did not like Harrison. Then to bring our comparison even closer to reality, let's suppose that Ted attributes to President Harrison qualities that no human has ever been proven to possess, like the ability to raise the dead, walk on water, or turn water into wine, and yes, even come back to life after being dead for three days. This is why so little credence or attention is paid here to the miracle claims. As a final complication, assume we also learn that it wasn't really Ted who penned the Harrison narrative. We only call the author Ted, and we really have no idea who really wrote it.

Even if we were to totally ignore the dearth and untimeliness of written accounts of the life and times of Jesus Christ (something Christians seem to be able to do with great alacrity), there are other problems with this story just as troubling. Remember that the very reasons so many believe Jesus to be the Messiah are on shaky ground. Among the prophecies his arrival reportedly fulfilled is that the messiah would be a descendant of David. We are told in Romans 1:3 and Acts 2:30 that Jesus was a descendant of David, but it was shown earlier in this chapter that the only evidence given for this is tremendously bad evidence, the horribly conflicting genealogies.

As it turns out, the genealogies not matching is far from the only problem with asserting that Jesus fulfilled the prophecy of the long-awaited messiah. In fact, there is very little about Jesus that even remotely resembles what one would expect from a reading of the Old Testament. Consider just one example from religious scholar Reza Aslan in response to the notion that Jesus fulfilled Old Testament prophecies that the Messiah would die and be resurrected: "Nowhere is any such thing written. Not in the Law of Moses. Not in the prophets. Not in the Psalms. In the entire history of Jewish thought, there is not a single line of scripture that says the Messiah is to suffer, die, and rise again on the third day" (Aslan 2013).

Moving on from the lack of reliable historical information about Jesus, what can we glean about Jesus from the information we do have? What of the different characterizations of Jesus found in the Gospels? Just one excerpt from Bart Ehrman's book *Jesus, Interrupted* shows how wildly different are the perspectives one can read in the Bible: "Was Jesus in doubt and despair on the way to the cross (Mark) or calm and in control (Luke)? Did Jesus's death provide an atonement for sin (Mark and Paul) or not (Luke)? Did Jesus perform signs to prove who he was (John) or did he refuse to do so (Matthew)? Must Jesus's followers keep the law if they are to enter the Kingdom (Matthew) or absolutely not (Paul)?" (Ehrman B. D. 2009). Perhaps the most fascinating aspect of religious conviction I see in most Christians goes back to the second Christian dilemma I pointed out. It is not simply that they believe but that they believe with such deep conviction and such specificity in things for which there is no evidence, and often they believe most strongly in the things for which the evidence is least and most contradictory.

Having sufficiently, even if tersely, addressed how we think we know what we think we know about Jesus, let's look at some of the actual claims about his life and character, and even touch only briefly on his alleged divinity (not if it is true or not but what the Bible actually says about it).

Peaceful Jesus?

Is it a fair characterization to call Jesus the Prince of Peace? I am skeptical of this representation, at least if we are going *sola scriptura*. For example, we are instructed to love our neighbors as ourselves in Matthew 23:39. Sounds like great advice. So great, in fact, it had apparently been thought of long before Jesus's birth. The same advice was given in Leviticus 19:18 (that's the Old Testament folks—before Jesus). This does not take away from the goodness of the message of loving our neighbors; it just did not originate with Jesus. It is also interesting (and confusing) that this beautiful sentiment from Jesus is found, pre-Jesus, in the same book of the Bible (Leviticus) that sanctions killing for such acts as homosexuality (20:13), children cursing their parents (20:9), adultery (20:10), and fornication (21:9) just to name a few—but I digress.

While there are peaceful teachings attributed to Jesus, there are also teachings of Jesus that are less peaceful. Previously, I mentioned that in the Bible Jesus said, "Think not that I am come to send peace on earth: I came not to send peace, but a sword" (Matthew 10:34), and also, "But those mine enemies, which would not that I should reign over them, bring hither, and slay them before me" (Luke 19:27). Do these last two examples mean that Jesus was a terrible person? Not conclusively. As already demonstrated, we don't even know for sure who wrote these things about Jesus and can't be certain he said any of the things ascribed to him. But it does give something to consider when told that Jesus is the Prince of Peace and that this is a Bible-based belief.

Just for fun, I often quote these two lines, attributed to Jesus in the Bible, when I am told that Islam is a violent religion because the Quran is violent or that Mohammed was violent (both may be completely fair conclusions). When I quote these lines in this context, however, I pretend they were uttered by Mohammed and recorded in the Quran. I also sometimes say it was Ganesh, Hanuman, Shiva, or Vishnu and that it was quoted in some Vedic writing or another. It is interesting how quickly so many Christians will jump on this as a textbook example of their conviction that Islam, unlike Christianity, is violent, only to turn around and try to equivocate their way out of it when I reveal it was actually Jesus's words. I have even tried to defend Mohammed from my Christian friends while they think these words were from Mohammed, using the same apologetic techniques of "Well, in context, it isn't as bad as it sounds." It is rather humorous to see the about-face that is done when they realize it was the words of Jesus and not Mohammed! "Oh, but what Jesus meant was..." or literally, "You are taking that out of context!" immediately after I tried to use the same defense when they thought this came from the Quran or Hindu writings.

When someone is convicted of a violent crime, there may be considerations that could lessen the severity of the sentence a judge may hand down. Was the accused acting in self-defense? Was it a crime of passion? Conversely, if a violent act was premeditated, it may be considered more egregious and result in a harsher sentence. If someone goes home to retrieve a weapon before acting out then they had time to consider their actions. Well, remember the story about Jesus losing his temper in the temple and turning over the tables of the moneychangers? While this story is very well known, most Christians either don't know or care insufficiently that it was not a temporary lapse of judgment or loss of temper. It was, at least according to John 2–15, a premeditated act of violence: "And when he had made a scourge of small cords, he drove them all out of the temple, and the sheep, and the oxen; and poured out the changers' money, and overthrew the tables." Remember that a "scourge" is the same sort of weapon used to rip the flesh from Jesus during the passion narrative. This was clearly a premeditated act of considerable violence.

Divine Jesus?

While it wasn't clear from the very beginning of Christianity, it now seems a solid feature of Christian orthodoxy that Jesus is part of the Holy Trinity, one and the same with God the Father and the Holy Spirit. But where is the Holy Trinity spelled out in the Bible? It is not—at least not clearly. The concept of the Holy Trinity is something that apparently developed along with the growing consensus (in the Christian community) that Jesus was more than just God's chosen Messiah.

A reading of the Gospels reveals only passing reference to the "Father and the Son and the Holy Spirit" language that we today associate with the Trinity. And even that can be interpreted in other ways. There are other attempts to retrofit verbiage in the Bible as a description of the Father, Son, and Holy Spirit; but these attempts are unconvincing. It would seem that something as important and also so hard to comprehend as the triune nature of the Christian god would have been explained just a bit better if it were a fully developed concept during Jesus's time. It was not, however, until the Council of Nicaea in 325 CE that the issue of Christ's divinity and oneness with the Trinity (if that math even makes sense) was decided. This last point bears repeating! If you were a follower of Christ in the first three centuries after his death, it is not at all clear that you would believe in the concept of a Trinity or even that Jesus was, in fact, divine. The divinity of Christ, coequal with God the Father and the Holy Spirit took centuries to become a codified dogma of the Church. Some believed it before then to be sure, but the issue wasn't settled until three centuries after the death of Christ. Any clearly evident and well-established "truth" does not need to be settled in committee three hundred years after the fact.

A convenient facet of this last point is that one not even need refer to an in-depth study of early Christian practices to see the divine nature of Jesus evolve over time. A simple reading of the Gospels, with an understanding of when they were written, yields some interesting insight on this matter. In the first Gospel to be written, Mark, Jesus was apparently a man like any other. Well, not exactly like any other. He was very special in that God had chosen him for a very special purpose, but there is no mention of Jesus being divine or born of a virgin, and any amazing feats attributed to him seemed to be the result of God working through him, just as he had done through others in the past and since. Be careful in your reading on this point. In the first Gospel to appear in the modern Bible, Matthew, Jesus is indeed claimed to have been born of a virgin. Mathew was not, however, the first to be written; it only appears first in the New Testament. Later, the Gospel of Luke also tells us that Mary was a virgin when she gave birth to Jesus. The virgin birth is not mentioned in John's Gospel, but John does go further than the first three Gospels and identifies Jesus as being co-equal with God and takes his divinity all the way back to the beginning where Jesus was with God when the universe was created.

What must be believed if one is to subscribe to Christian dogma is that God's message is so important that he sent us the Bible, and his son to die on the cross but not quite important enough to be clear in the meaning of either it seems. What the Bible has to tell us about the nature, sayings, and actions of Jesus Christ is very much like what it has to tell us about morality, family values, the role of women in society, and a host of other important issues. It is left to the human intellect and moral intuitions to determine which parts are worthy of our attention and which are better not adhered to. It is little wonder that the core beliefs held dear by friends of religion vary so greatly from age to age and among different groups even today.

The simple fact is that those who subscribe to the notion that the Bible is God's special book almost never deal with it honestly. Perhaps if more people who claim the Bible as a great source of moral guidance and evidence of God's goodness actually read it, then there would be no need to quote from it here. There is great incongruence here that cannot be ignored. Either the Bible is God's inerrant word—and slavery, genocide, etc. are good and moral things—or these things that are seen by almost everyone today as evil really are evil and the Bible is not to be reliably consulted on issues of right and wrong.

There are, of course, other options. Perhaps the Bible is, in fact, God's word, but God is not so good after all, and he commands us to do evil things. There is also the option that is most in keeping with the available evidence and the one adopted by most skeptics—God is probably not real, and this book was written by men (without divine inspiration or guidance), perhaps well-intentioned men doing the best they could with the information available to them at the time, but men just the same. I subscribe to this last option.

CHAPTER 4

Refutations of Christian Apologetics (and Other Good Reasons for Rejecting Bad Ideas)

Nothing dies harder than a bad idea.

—Julia Cameron

The only sure weapon against bad ideas is better ideas.

—Alfred Whitney Griswold

A Grain of Salt, a Kernel of Truth, and a Seed of Doubt

About the time I decided to begin writing this book, I attended my first Christian apologetics conference. I was amazed at the skill with which the apologists were able to spin half-truths, pseudo-science, charisma, faulty logic, and persuasive elocution into what sounded, on the surface at least, almost reasonable. Many attendees were swayed by passionate oratory and assertions peppered with terms like, "It therefore logically follows," in spite of the fact that the conclusions usually did not therefore logically follow. The syllogisms (more on syllogisms in a moment) often did not consist of valid premises, so in spite of assertions to the contrary, the conclusions were not logically sound. Human language is a very powerful and beautiful, if imperfect, thing. Words have meanings—often very precise meanings—and just saying something logically follows does not make it true.

If you walk into such events already a believer, you can't help but walk away with a renewed sense of confidence in your preconceived notions. After all, these speakers have made a living out of

174

reinforcing each other's sophistries; it is their profession. There are graduate degree programs in this field, after all, so one would expect them to be able to present their case well—even if it is a bad case. I am not vouching for the educational quality of these institutions that offer degrees in apologetics, but one can definitely learn to present a cogent argument, even for a bad position, after several years of focused practice.

Anyone who has ever witnessed a court case has seen what I'm talking about. Even if a defendant is 100 percent guilty of multiple crimes, if he can get a really good attorney it is possible he may get off completely. Even if justice prevails and he is convicted, many may still be impressed by the attorney's ability to spin zero evidence into a surprisingly solid defense. It behooves us all, however, to practice sound critical thinking, not just in religious discussions and court cases but also in everyday life. When observing a religious debate or discussion (or debate on any topic for that matter), challenge your assumptions and listen with a skeptical ear—to both sides. Recall from the chapter 1 discussion on the nature of religious arguments that this was one of the things that lead to my deconversion. Any idea that is worthy of belief should be able to withstand the same rigors as competing claims without recourse to creative redefinitions, shifting the burden of proof or moving the goal posts midgame. I will argue this is exactly what religious apologists do—beginning with sneaky syllogisms.

We've all heard people say things like, "From premise A and premise B, we can logically believe C," but many are not aware of the power of the syllogism for both proving a valid point as well as for misleading if used incorrectly. I realize at this point it might seem a pointless tangent to veer off into talk of syllogistic logic so abruptly, but it is necessary. It is difficult to have a discussion of any depth on apologetics or, more importantly here, counter-apologetics, without a basic understanding of one of the most common tools of the trade—the syllogism.

Without going into too much detail, the type of syllogism we are talking about is a statement consisting of a major premise, a minor premise, and a conclusion. A syllogism might look something like this: All humans are mortal. All theists are human. Therefore, all theists are mortal. As we will see in later discussions of the various apologetic arguments, this logic tool is often misused in such a way that it seems a conclusion may actually logically follow from given major and minor premises when in fact this is not the case—often because either the major premise or minor premise (or both) is not valid.

As many apologetic arguments make truth claim about reality, a point should be made here on the nature of reality before proceeding. No matter how wrong the apologist may be in his or her conclusions on such things as the nature and origins of the universe, reality is quite strange and hard to grasp. It is the difficulty in understanding reality that apologists often use to persuade their audience. Theists often tell me that it is just too hard to accept that the universe just came into existence by itself, so God must have done it. I readily accept that the brute fact of the cosmos's existence is damnably hard to accept. I confess, "It just happened, or it's always been here all on its own" is just about as hard to accept (even to atheists like myself) as "God did it." In fact, I'd almost be willing to say that both ideas seem impossible were it not for the fact that one of the two (or some variation of one of these) must be true, or else this book would not exist and you would not exist to read it.

Clearly, either the universe just happened on its own, it has always been here, or something (God perhaps) caused it to happen. An important difference in these assertions is that if you go with "God did it," then you have all your work still ahead of you because you've only dodged the "where did it come from" question by inserting God, and any being powerful enough to create a universe is even harder to explain than the universe itself. If all things require a creator, then what created God? This difficulty is one of the things apologists rely on to put forth their arguments. Don't make it too easy for them. We must look beyond the way things seem and go with the evidence because often things simply are not as they might seem on the surface.

To make my point that reality can in fact be strange, indeed, let's consider the example of the speed of light. If you are among those who feel you must turn to religion for wonder and mystery, you clearly have never tried to look into Einstein's universe. To those already familiar with the constancy of the speed of light, often depicted simply as *C* and how light travels at the same velocity regardless of your speed or direction of travel, also called your inertial frame of reference, I beg your indulgence. Perhaps a restroom break? A nice stretch maybe? Have a ham sandwich? Rejoin us on the discussion of the Cosmological Argument.

To illustrate where I am going, think about what happens if you throw a baseball to a friend at sixty miles per hour and there is a second friend standing between you (off center, please, so as to avoid concussive injury and lawsuit). What happens? The baseball travels away from you, toward friend number 1 and past friend number 2 at sixty miles per hour. Now add a second ball to this game. You and friend one each throw a ball simultaneously toward each other at 60 miles per hour. Now, what is different here (aside from the fact that you and your friend should go join the circus if you can do this without hurting each other)? From your inertial frame of reference, each ball is traveling at sixty miles an hour, albeit in different directions. The same thing is seen from the inertial frames of reference of each of your friends. But for the baseballs, there is a difference. If baseballs could perceive such things, each ball would see each of you three bipedal primates and the Earth moving at sixty miles per hour relative to itself. However, each baseball would see another baseball moving at 120 miles per hour relative to itself due to the combined velocity of sixty miles per hour for each ball moving in opposite directions. This is why, incidentally, head-on automobile collisions are so devastating. The force is a result not of one car moving at, say, fifty miles per hour, but a combined speed of fifty miles per hour plus the speed of the other car, or one hundred miles per hour if the other car is also traveling at fifty miles per hour.

So what does any of this have to do with the high price of yak meat in Mongolia? Simply this: If you assume that because this tendency of velocity to depend on your inertial frame of reference means it is always true for all things, just because it is always true when you actually see it on human scales of perception, then you are wrong. You are not only wrong; you are lost. No really, you are physically lost. At least if you depend on the modern marvel of satellite navigation, you are lost, because GPS navigation only works because some very smart people know that there is a very important exception to what we see every time we drive or throw baseballs, and they have adjusted the applicable calculations accordingly. This is because the velocity of light is exempted from this concept we have been discussing and it has a constant velocity of 186,242 miles per second regardless of your inertial frame of reference.

Two questions are likely in the minds of many at this point, both questions beginning with "What the hell...." First, "What the hell is he talking about?" and second, "What the hell does any of this have to do theistic apologetics or yak meat?" What I am talking about with the constancy of the speed of light is this: consider that you are driving your car toward me in my car traveling toward you. We each have very special cars that will travel at half the speed of light (somebody get GM on the phone!). We each turn on our headlights. Oh, did I mention there is a hitchhiker standing beside the road midway between us with his towel? The hitchhiker's name is Arthur Dent. If you don't get the reference, stop reading this book for now, run out and buy Douglas Adams's five-part trilogy beginning with *The Hitchhiker's Guide to the Galaxy*. It's a far better read anyway. I say this without any fear of contradiction.

Now, if light behaved in the way we would expect based upon all our personal observations and the previous baseball example, the light would leave each of us at 186,242 miles per second (which is, like, way faster than a Corvette!), and the light from each car would pass the hitchhiker at 289,363 miles per second because that is the speed at which the light is leaving our cars, plus the speed of each car, each traveling at 93,121 miles per second. Likewise, most would logically expect the light from your car to pass me at 372,484 miles per second, or twice the speed of light since we are travelling toward each other at a combined speed of light, and the light is leaving you, toward me, and me toward you, at the speed of light. Oh, and our light photons/waves would be expected to pass each other at 558,726 miles per second. Trust me, this is as hard as my math gets, so don't be frightened away.

Counterintuitively, our conclusions (for those of us with such conclusions) of speeds anything other than 186,242 miles per second for all concerned are wrong. No matter how counterintuitive it may seem, the light from your car would leave you, pass the hitchhiker, pass the light from my car, and pass me at 186,242 miles per second in each case. The speed of light is 299,792 kilometers per second (hey, I got tired of typing 186,242 miles!) regardless of your inertial frame of reference. Why this occurs is a fascinating story unto itself, but to explain it here would take my already lengthy tangent too far afield. But strange as this fact is, it is still a fact. Don't believe it? Don't think it matters even if it is true? Well, if the great Americans at the Second Space Operations Squadron at Schriever Air Force Base in Colorado didn't take this fact into consideration, our GPS navigation systems would not work. Hence, you would not only be wrong, you would (I'll say it again) be lost.

As for the question "What the hell does this have to do with apologetics?" I have admittedly gone a long way around to make a simple point, but it was necessary to offer a convincing example of things not being as they clearly seem, with the added bonus of showing we don't need superstition to see wonder and mystery all around us. When apologists posit that the universe must have had a cause, they attempt to do so because that may seem a logical assumption based on our *normal* observations. After all, how many things do you see just jumping off tables without any reason? Not many. They fall off tables because they are pushed off. But as we have just seen with the speed of light, not only can appearances be deceiving; they can be unbelievably yet demonstrably wrong.

As we saw in the previous chapter, there is no good reason to assume the Bible is a reliable source of information on any of the topics addressed (or any others frankly). Now let us consider if the field of apologetics fairs any better at explaining the strange world of reality. As each of the following apologetic arguments is addressed, I will show why they are unconvincing and worse than unconvincing, even immoral at times. At the end of the chapter, I will come full circle and conclude what I've started here and show how apologetics, by its very nature, is worse than simply wrong; it is among the most intellectually dishonest pursuits of which I am aware.

The Cosmological Argument (A Kalam-itous Rationalization)

The cosmological argument has been around for a very long time, and as apologetic arguments go, it has an impressive pedigree. Versions of this argument can be traced to Plato and Aristotle, with significant contributions from Muslim and Christian philosophers such as al-Ghazali and St. Thomas Aquinas. In simplest terms, all proponents of the cosmological argument have asserted that the cosmos could not exist without something having caused its existence, hence the name cosmological argument. This cause of the universe is normally understood to be a god. Apologists often then add a level of complexity by asserting that somehow the god who created the universe conveniently happens to be their particular god. This is a completely unjustified non sequitur. I would argue there are actually three "nested" non sequiturs here: the first being that the universe actually needs a cause, the second being that if the universe had a cause, that cause must be a god which did itself not need a cause, the third being that this god must be any particular god, such as the Christian god.

In its most basic form, the contemporary cosmological argument (the Kalam Cosmological Argument) may take the form of a simple syllogism:

- Major premise: whatever begins to exist had a cause.
- Minor premise: the universe began to exist.
- Conclusion: therefore, the universe had a cause (and that cause is God).

There are, of course, variations and nuances, but this is a common form of the argument as it is popularly used today, and it is this syllogism on which I will focus.

This syllogism suffers from flaws that should stop the cosmological argument in its tracks were it not for the nature of religious
belief and argumentation. Unlike rational discourse, which proceeds
from evidence to conclusions, religious belief starts with the conclusion (God, my god, is real) and seeks evidence to support the conclusion while ignoring any and all evidence that refutes the conclusion.
For this reason, the cosmological argument keeps turning up like a
bad penny.

Like many apologetic arguments, this one is not only unconvincing, it is detrimental to rational thought and actually detracts
from the sum of human knowledge. Before moving on to a deeper
discourse on this detriment to rational thought, however, let's deal
with the syllogism.

The major premise is a bare assertion fallacy—there is simply no
way of knowing that whatever begins to exist has a cause, and merely
asserting it as true does not make it so. In fact, this disagrees with
our best understanding of how the universe actually works. With
cosmologists as our only experts on the true nature and origin of the
universe, is it not amazing to consider that among the proponents of
the cosmological argument, there is not a leading cosmologist among
them? There is a reason for this—theologians have a terrible track
record at cosmology! In all the leading textbooks as well as books
for the lay audience, written by leading cosmologists, not a single
one turns to God as the reason for the universe. Scientists simply do
not take the cosmological argument seriously for a host of very good
reasons. While there are a very few cosmologists who actually do
believe in some sort of higher power, even those few who do believe
in a god do not turn to that god to explain the workings of the universe—because they understand how the universe works and the god
hypothesis is not needed for that understanding. If a god is real, he or
she created the universe in just such a way that turning to god as an
explanation for cosmic origins adds nothing to our understanding.

The minor premise also rests upon a bare assertion fallacy.
Contrary to the wishes of Christian apologists, big bang cosmology
does not make creation, ex nihilo (from nothing), by the Judeo-
Christian god, a fait accompli. True, according to our best under-

standing, the current, observable universe did begin about 13.7 billion years ago in the big bang. This does not mean, however, that our current observable universe is all there is or ever was. In fact, there may be a multiverse made up of countless other universes. Consider also that the big bang theory does not propose creation ex nihilo but rather that everything in our universe was, at one point in the distant past, in one infinitely dense singularity in which all the laws of nature, time, and space as we currently understand them did not apply. For more on this, see books by Stephen Hawking and Leonard Mlodinow, Victor Stenger, Brian Greene, Alexander Vilenkin, and a great many others (none of whom resort to a god as the first cause).

Remember that apologists often seek only evidence that supports their beliefs while ignoring evidence that mitigates against their beliefs. We see in the cosmological argument and its supporters a shining example of this. Science supports a beginning to the universe? Great! The Bible said so, and science supports the biblical view? Not so fast. Remember that the Bible tells us God created the universe six thousand years (or so) ago in six 24-hour days. Big bang cosmology tells us the current observable universe, which is not necessarily the ultimate beginning of everything, started almost 14 billion years ago, with the Earth not being formed until almost 10 billion years later, which means the Bible is off by a factor of 2,353,333 (or so). That only partial *apparent* correlation is embraced while the gross discrepancy is ignored is quite telling.

The first part of this syllogism's conclusion (therefore, the universe had a cause) could be considered sound were it not for the two invalid premises. Sure, *if* it were true that anything which came into existence must have a cause and *if* it were also true that the universe did, in fact, begin to exist (*and* before and outside of that there is and never has been anything else), *then* it could be said that the universe had a cause. This still in no way even hints that this cause might be the god of Abraham (or any other particular god). This really amounts to a cosmological argument for a cause, not an argument for any particular god and not a very convincing argument at that.

Perhaps the biggest failing of this argument is that it raises but does not address the question of where the first cause (God) came from. Anything with the ability to create a universe from nothing would, it seems reasonable to assume, be far more powerful and complex than anything found in the universe itself. If this cause of the universe did not itself have a cause, then it must have either been around forever or came into being uncaused. It is amazing that theists see an eternal or uncaused universe as impossible yet an eternal, uncaused, more powerful and complex creator god as perfectly normal and something that needs no explanation at all.

Admittedly, believing that the universe could either have always been here or could have come into being without assistance is enough to give you a brain cramp. Neither answer is easy to accept, regardless of which option is ultimately true. The philosopher Daniel C. Dennett made a similar point when talking about things that are hard to grasp using the example of possible life on other planets. We are either the only life in the incredibly vast universe or we are not, he pointed out. Either possibility is difficult to imagine, but one of the two possibilities must be true. In the same way, comprehending an uncaused universe, eternal or not, is not easy. How is it any less difficult, however, to imagine an even more unlikely and harder to explain entity (God) exists, uncaused, and that He created the universe? The insertion of the god hypothesis into cosmology explains nothing and introduces greater complexity, against which Occam's razor greatly mitigates.

Even when I was a Christian child attending a Christian school and before I even knew what a syllogism was, I knew this was a problem for this argument for God. Clearly, if the assumption is that everything that exists had to be caused by something else to exist, then God also must have had a cause. This does not deter the apologist, however. Special pleading is invoked at several points in an attempt to bolster this argument. The first example of which is in the wording of the major premise. Rather than say "anything which exists had a cause," the wording has been carefully modified so as to exclude God from this rule. "Everything that *begins* to exist must have a cause" gets around this because then it is gratuitously assumed that God is the only thing that didn't begin to exist because he has always been here. There is, of course, no reason at all to believe this beyond wishful thinking—it is simply asserted.

Special rules are also sometimes used to distinguish between that which is contingent, or something that exists but has the potential to not exist, and that which is necessary, or something that exists and cannot not exist. God, according to many supporters of the cosmological argument, is a *necessary* being and must have existed eternally outside of time and space due to his very nature. Everything else, on the other hand, is contingent and is finite in time and space. Again, no evidence is provided; this is simply asserted. Consider now that this is exactly the kind of explanation one could be expected to construct only if you begin from the presupposition that God is real and you need a way to explain his existence. There is no evidence for this position, simply a desire that it be true.

This argument is not only unconvincing, it is detrimental to our understanding of how things work in that the god hypothesis is only turned to when we have given up looking for answers and at that point discovery stops. The great thinkers of the past, such as Ptolemy, Galileo, Copernicus, and Newton, who were, like virtually everyone back them, religious (at least in their public proclamations), did not turn to God as an explanation for those things they understood, only those things for which they did not understand. As our knowledge increases, we turn to God for fewer answers relating to cosmic origins (or anything else).

The Teleology of Unintelligent Design (Who Put the Amusement Park Next to the Waste Treatment Facility?)

> Design must be proved before a designer can be inferred.
>
> —Percy Bysshe Shelley

The teleological argument, or argument that there is design inherent in the universe and therefore a designer, has been around for a very long time. Even the great classical Greek philosophers argued that the appearance of design in the human body can't be mere chance and must have been directed by some creator (they just thought it was a different creator than do Christians). It is easy to see why this assumption was made. If we do not delve too deeply, it does seem that our design is just a bit too convenient. After all, aren't we perfectly suited to our environment? As we will see, however, this apparently intelligent design does not hold up well to scrutiny, especially in light of our modern understanding of cosmology and evolution.

In simplest terms, the argument from design goes something like this: The universe and everything in it—the earth, nature, life—is all too complex and orderly to have simply happened by sheer random chance, without a guiding hand. It is clear, goes the argument; this was all done with some purpose and conscious design. This design implies a designer; and the designer, of course, is God (conveniently again, the particular god of the apologist making the argument). This argument shares much with the cosmological argument just discussed. The basic rationale is the same as are the inherent flaws.

As with other apologias, there are different versions of arguments from design, all equally flawed. At times, arguments for design may even sink to the level of criminality. In part III (chapter 5) of this book, I will refer to the court case *Tammy Kitzmiller, et al. v. Dover Area School District, et al.* In the decision of this case, Judge John E. Jones opined at one point, "The citizens of the Dover area were poorly served by the members of the Board who voted for the ID[29] Policy. It is ironic that several of these individuals, who so staunchly and proudly touted their religious convictions in public, would time and again lie to cover their tracks and disguise the real purpose behind the ID Policy." Much of this lying to promote a religious view was done under oath.

In refuting the teleological argument, I will focus on two aspects of arguments from teleology—the historical argument from appar-

---

[29] Intelligent design.

ent design in nature and the more modern "fine-tuning argument." First, let us take a look at the general claim of design in nature.

The design argument was perhaps most famously put forth in 1802 by William Paley (1743–1805). Paley argued that if you were to find a watch lying on the ground, you would be led, by the complexity of its inner workings and apparent purpose (telling time), to conclude that it was designed by some intelligent designer and didn't "just happen." This analogy is then applied to the universe generally and to us humans specifically to infer a designer in these cases as well. In the absence of better evidence, this was once seen as a persuasive argument, even impressing Charles Darwin himself at one point. It was the same Darwin, along with Alfred Russell Wallace and others, who utterly destroyed Paley's conclusion by demonstrating how the complexity of life on Earth actually came to be—without the need of a conscious designer.

The first problem with the design argument is that (just like the cosmological argument) it leads all but the most incurious to the question, "Who designed the designer?" A central claim of the design argument is that complex things cannot simply exist without the influence of a designer. However, the designer must be far more complex than his creation, and proponents of this argument have no reservations about the designer existing without his own designer. This fatal flaw demonstrates a troubling aspect of how apologists fail to adequately apply reason. Clearly, anyone intelligent enough to concoct such elaborate arguments should see the inherent flaws, but they are content to ignore these flaws because they challenge the apologists' desired conclusions.

There is also the problem that complexity, apparent order, and beauty do not automatically prove design is involved. Neither does the *appearance* that we might have been created with a purpose, such as the ability to better cope with our surroundings. We have two eyes, which is great for hunting since it gives us stereoscopic vision.[30]

---

[30] I should point out that I am well aware of the gross generalization I am making here in talking specifically about humans and other predators. The two forward-facing eyes give stereoscopic vision to most predators, while non-pred-

The same is true for two ears and being able to hear what direction a sound is coming from, but many people live just fine with only one of either. In fact, while it is not preferred, you can live without eyes or ears. Helen Keller was quite productive without the senses of sight and hearing. Likewise, you can live so well with just one kidney that people often give up one for a loved one who badly needs it, but you were born with two. Two lungs? You can get by with only one. The list goes on.

Even if we allow the premise that there is design in nature, the designer comes out appearing somewhat inept. Having pointed out that we often have two of certain organs, there are other things in the human body that we absolutely cannot live without, and often we have only one of these. The brain, heart, and liver come to mind. Also, if we were actually created by an intelligent designer, how do we explain the appendix? The appendix is an artifice left over from a time when we had not yet learned to cook our meat, but the appendix is no longer needed. Only a designer who was quite flawed would have made some of the engineering mistakes seen in the human body. The fact is that evolution through natural selection is the only concept that explains the complexity of life here on earth as well as all the "design flaws" we see in our physiology (bad backs, holes in our eyesight, and the recurrent laryngeal nerve just to name a few). No designer is needed. In fact, life is exactly as it would be expected if and only if there were no intelligent designer, and we are the result of evolution.

It is no exaggeration to say that almost all the species that have ever existed have gone extinct. We almost became the late great human species ourselves about one hundred thousand years ago. In fact, we came so near extinction that our gene pool shows signs of this when compared to most other species alive today. According to Francis Collins and Craig Venter, human beings are 99.9 percent identical at the level of our DNA (Fullwiley 2008). The shallowness of our gene pool owing to the fact that the human population at

---

atory animals often have eyes more to the sides of their head to provide a more panoramic view, which facilitates seeing approaching predators.

the time we spread outside Africa was as low as about ten thousand humans. Would a truly intelligent designer, one who is all-powerful, create life, the universe, and everything such that most of the species that have ever existed would become extinct?

How about the universe itself; does it really appear to be the work of an intelligent creator? Most who believe this never really consider the immensity of the universe. There are as many as four times more stars in the Milky Way galaxy than the number of all the people who have ever lived. And there are as many other galaxies outside the Milky Way as there are stars in our own galaxy. Then consider that the nearest star to us (other than our own Sun) is so far away that if we could travel at the speed of light (you remember, 186,242 miles per second regardless of your inertial frame of reference), it would still take us over four years to get to it. At this same speed, it would take us one hundred thousand years to get from one side of our galaxy to the other. Consider also that in all the vast space between Earth and the other side of our galaxy or between galaxies, the environment is absolutely deadly to human life. Again, this is how a universe designed specifically for us would most likely *not* look. It does, however, look exactly as we might expect a product of natural processes (without us in mind) to appear. Modern cosmology offers far more satisfying explanations for the origin, formation, and nature of the cosmos than does the argument from design.

Percy Bysshe Shelley wrote long ago, "Design must be proved before a designer can be inferred." Design has never been proven, yet apologists go on to argue that a designer must be real, as if the *assertion* that there is design makes it so. It is also instructive to consider what Shelley said next, "The matter in controversy is the existence of design in the Universe, and it is not permitted to assume the contested premises and thence infer the matter in dispute." He makes a great point here, one that is all too often overlooked. A major flaw in the design argument is the premise that design has been already established. It has not. Shelley continues, "Insidiously to employ the words contrivance, design, and adaptation before these circumstances are made apparent in the Universe, thence justly inferring a contriver is a popular sophism against which it behooves us to be watchful."

The point here being that apologists gloss over the fact that there is no compelling reason to believe the universe and everything in it was actually designed and then proceed to assert there must therefore be a designer. Well, of course, if there actually is design there must be a designer. The design has not, however, been established.

Finally, even if we were to grant the premises put forward by advocates of the design argument—namely, that there is too much complexity in the universe to have happened by chance and there must have been a designer—another claim is often made without any compelling reason ever being given, that the designer is the god of the person making the argument. If we must assume a god did it, then any god would work just fine. Proponents of this argument almost universally make illogical multiple leaps of faith that since all that we see must have been designed, it must have been God that did the designing, and it "therefore follows" that it is *their* god.

The fine-tuning argument, another form of teleology, holds a unique position among apologetic approaches. It is widely regarded as an argument that causes even some skeptics to take pause and consider its implications, namely the amazing coincidences (or intentional fine-tuning if the theists are correct) of the physical constants of the universe. These constants are things such as the force of gravity, the strength of the strong nuclear force, the weak nuclear force, and so on. These finely tuned constants are such that to change them even slightly would result in a universe in which life could not exist, or so goes the argument. As with any other apologetic argument, there are different versions of the fine-tuning argument and different apologists who offer it in slightly different ways but it normally offers a syllogism something like this, again offered by William Lane Craig (Craig W. L., *Theistic Critiques Of Atheism*):

1. The apparent fine-tuning of the universe is due to physical necessity, chance, or design.
2. This fine-tuning is not due to physical necessity or chance.
3. Therefore, it logically follows that it is due to design.

Remember that many apologists have mastered the misuse of the syllogism, delivered in a forceful voice and confident tone, such that almost anything they say sounds reasonable, at least until you actually consider it for a moment. The importance of this is hard to overstate. It is very easy to be led astray by a cleverly articulated yet unsound syllogism. The problem with conclusion (3) above, for example, is that there is no evidence that premise 2 is valid. Even if we allow that number 1 is valid, we have no evidence at all that this apparent fine-tuning is not due to physical necessity or chance as claimed in number 2.

Proponents of the fine-tuning argument offer a list of constants that must each be individually fine-tuned so that life here in this universe can exist. The assertion is then made that if any of these were stronger or weaker than they are then undesired (for the formation of life), conditions would exist. Such problems as hydrogen would not form, for example, or no elements heavier than helium would ever form. As my point here is not to argue for the fine-tuning argument, all the specifics of this approach will not be listed, but suffice it to say, it can get a bit long, complex, and frankly tedious.

How does a Christian apologist know that it is not from physical necessity or chance that constants are as they are when the greatest physicists alive today cannot make the same assertion? There are a number of theories that account for this apparent fine-tuning, but there is no consensus. After all, we only have this universe in which we live as a guide, so how can we know that this is not the only way that the constants *could* work out? It bears repeating that, contrary to the repeated proclamations of apologists, the inability of science to say conclusively why something occurs does not mean by extension that God did it. Perhaps physical necessity or chance really are the only options, perhaps not. Perhaps some of the constants discussed are due to physical necessity, some to chance—we simply do not know.

We see in the fine-tuning argument a clear example of why I call apologetics one of the most intellectually dishonest fields of human endeavor of which I know. A key feature of this intellectual dishonesty is the use of what I call "scientific language." This is the use of scientific jargon to decidedly nonscientific ends. We see this time and time again when apologists quote scientific findings, either out of context or simply misstated, such that the scientific language sounds as if it supports the existence of God. This in spite of the fact that an overwhelming majority of elite physicists (who come up with the scientific findings) do not believe in God, and even among those who do believe in God, almost none agree that this scientific data is evidence of God.

A textbook example of this is seen in the *Wall Street Journal* opinion piece by Eric Metaxas, "Science Increasingly Makes the Case for God" (Metaxas 2014). In this article, squarely refuted by prominent physicist Lawrence Krauss (Krauss L. M. 2015), Metaxas repeatedly makes reference to huge numbers, long odds, and selective quotes from famous scientists such as Fred Hoyle and Paul Davies, all pointing to how science has now made the case for God. The only problem is that none of the conclusions of the article are even remotely valid. To offer just one example of his misuse of science (scientifical language), Metaxas invokes the fine-tuning argument both for life on earth as well as for the creation of the universe itself while displaying either ignorance of or insufficient care for our current understanding of the physical constants of the universe. Where, for example, Metaxas states that all the variables are either completely random or the result of some intelligent guiding hand (God), Krauss points out the flaw in this thinking: "An even more severe problem in Metaxas's argument is the assumption of randomness, namely that physical processes do not naturally drive a system toward a certain state. This is the most common error among those who argue that, given the complexity of life on Earth, evolution is as implausible as a tornado ravaging a junkyard and producing a 747." Metaxas uses scientifical language in his *WSJ* opinion piece, whereas Lawrence Krauss uses actual science in his to greatly different effect. Could it be that Metaxas is correct in his belief that God is real and Krauss is mistaken to be an atheist? Sure, it's possible, but the evidence, especially the scientific evidence, does not support that position. To argue otherwise is simply dishonest on Metaxas's part.

Six Reasons Why This Argument Is Unconvincing

First and foremost, the fine-tuning argument shares the same Achilles' heel from which all apologetic arguments suffer. Specifically, the invocation of God as the explanation does not do what an explanation is supposed to do—*explain things*. All it does is move one step away from the thing needing to be explained. Consider the following example: We don't know how Johnnie Walker got the alcohol in this Blue Label Scotch I'm sipping at this moment, and we need an explanation, so we decide that a nearsighted gnome named Norm put it there. We then go about proclaiming that we now understand how the alcohol gets into Scotch—Norm did it.

Now, it is highly unlikely that any Christian apologists are going to accept this Norm hypothesis, but it is also highly unlikely they can formulate a meaningful difference between the Norm hypothesis and the god hypothesis. Both are bare assertions that are offered without evidence, and neither provides explanation. If our answer is "Norm did it," then we still must explain where Norm came from, how Norm did it, how the Norm hypothesis makes testable predictions, and how Norm is falsifiable (and how an omnipotent gnome can be nearsighted in the first place, but that's a different story).

Second, even if we allow that a god did the fine-tuning, we are still challenged with why this god would choose to go about creation in the way he did. How can one fail to wonder why he took so long to work his magic and why he created so much superfluous fluff in the cosmos—this superfluous fluff is all the additional stuff in the universe that is not necessary to our communion with God. If the universe was created and fine-tuned for us, then why create such a vast cosmos.

Consider also that the most important thing (for purposes of Christian theology) that God created (man) only just arrived very recently in cosmological time. A generous estimation of our existence as a species puts the first modern humans on the scene no more than about 250,000 years ago, but the universe is very nearly 14 billion years old. To put that into context, if the age of the universe were represented as the distance from New York to Los Angeles, our time as a species would be 2.76 inches. Or consider if you've ever run a 10K foot race, and that distance represents the age of our universe. By comparison, humanity's time here could be represented by the thickness of a single dollar bill—that's thickness, not width or length!

So not only was virtually all the time since the beginning of the universe spent without humans in it, humans only inhabit an unbelievably infinitesimal fraction of the observable universe. Now that we are here, most of the universe is absolutely deadly to us. This is a very strange situation for a place that was supposedly fine-tuned just for us. This situation again is *exactly* what we would expect if the naturalistic explanation is correct and exactly *not* what we would expect from a special act of creation by God.

Third, many who argue for the fine-tuning of the universe grossly overstate their case. It is often put forth that if you change the constants in the universe only very slightly (and then proceed to offer excruciatingly large numbers to impress upon the listener how fine the tuning actually is), then human life would not be possible. This may actually be true, but it may also not be true; we don't really know this. That is also not to say that another type of life would not be possible. It is very easy to fall into the anthropomorphic trap of seeing that we could not live in a different kind of universe as proof that this universe was made just perfectly for us rather than to simply realize that we evolved to suit our environment. If the universe had looked differently, we would have evolved differently. Yes, it is true that there are many possible eventualities for the universe in which conditions would preclude life of any type, but the fact that we can engage in this debate means that in at least one universe (this one), conditions did in fact favor the development of (somewhat) intelligent life.

This anthropomorphic way of seeing the universe as created for us rather than that we evolved in the universe we have is illustrated brilliantly by Douglas Adams:

> This is rather as if you imagine a puddle waking
> up one morning and thinking, "This is an inter-
> esting world I find myself in—an interesting hole
> I find myself in—fits me rather neatly, doesn't it?

In fact it fits me staggeringly well, must have been made to have me in it!" This is such a powerful idea that as the sun rises in the sky and the air heats up and as, gradually, the puddle gets smaller and smaller, frantically hanging on to the notion that everything's going to be alright, because this world was meant to have him in it, was built to have him in it; so the moment he disappears catches him rather by surprise. I think this may be something we need to be on the watch out for. (Adams 2002)

Fourth, while far from a brute fact, there is the possibility argued by some physicists and cosmologists that ours is only one of a possible infinity of other universes, each one having different dimensions and constants that are tuned differently than the one in which you are currently reading these words. Given enough universes (and an infinity is a very large number indeed), then it is an almost certainty that these constants exist in the right combination in at least some of these universes. Research recently conducted by Fred Adams of the University of Michigan in Ann Arbor indicates that life-sustaining universes might be far more likely than apologists like to imagine (Brooks 2008).

Fifth, if the universe is in fact fine-tuned for anything, it seems fine-tuned not for human life but rather for the creation of the superfluous fluff discussed a few paragraphs back. Fluff such as dark matter and dark energy seems to be what the universe is fine-tuned for, not us. Consider that we are all made of atoms (and yes, we could get technical and talk about quarks, etc., but let's keep this simple). And not only we humans are made of atoms, but so is everything else in the observable universe. Yet scientists now believe that less than 5 percent of the universe is actually made up of atoms. The rest seems to consist of dark matter (23 percent) and dark energy (72 percent) (NASA 2012). If the personal god to which the Abrahamic tradition subscribes is responsible for this, should we expect the universe to be this way? Most likely, the universe would be far more like the geocentric biblical universe if this God were real.

Sixth, and perhaps most importantly, if there really is an all-powerful creator god, then the constants in the universe are completely irrelevant anyway. If it was his plan that life-forms are to be created in his image, then he can do it with the constants being arranged any way he likes. He would not be limited to only one set of constants since he created the constants in the first place. He created whatever significance the constants may have in this cosmos. The point being that apologists are wasting their time arguing that the unique arrangement of these constants proves the god hypothesis. If God is real, the constants are irrelevant.

Betting against Pascal (I'll Take Those Odds!)

"What if you are wrong?" This question is a favorite of true believers and is normally accompanied with the warning that if God is real and you believe, then you get eternal reward, but if you don't believe, then the punishment will be total and eternal. The reasoning continues, if God is not real and you believe, then you lose nothing. You just die the same as the unbelievers, but you still live a good life (with the implication often being that somehow you won't live a good life if you don't believe). The safe bet is to believe since the believer risks nothing but the nonbeliever risks everything. The person asking the "what if you are wrong" question is often not aware that this is actually a quite old and often-used argument for professing a belief in God known as Pascal's wager.

In *Pensées*, a collection of apologetic writings by French mathematician and philosopher Blaise Pascal (1623–1662), Pascal argued the basic premises of his famous wager. They are as follows: God cannot be proven by human reason. There are only two possible answers to the question of God's existence—God is real or he is not (you must wager on one of these two answers). And finally, since the reward or punishment is so great, the wise bet is to profess belief in

God. The thinking also assumes that even if God is not real, you still live a good life if you believe, so no harm done.

On the surface, this may seem a persuasive argument, especially to someone already predisposed to a belief in God; and certainly, many find it a compelling proposition. To those trying to persuade others to believe, it is sometimes a favorite tool and is often presented as a fait accompli to which no defense is possible. The problem is that this argument is not only rationally flawed, it is also morally questionable once you evaluate its implications.

Pascal's wager is a bad bet resting on a false dichotomy that assumes there are only two possible answers to the God question—either the Christian god is real or there is no God at all. There is, however, no reason at all to be limited to these two choices. If the Jewish notion of God is true, there is no eternal hell as Christians understand it, and Jesus was actually a deeply confused apocalyptic preacher rather than the son of God and God himself. In this case, both the Christian and atheist are wrong, but neither actually goes to hell forever. If, on the other hand, the Muslim is right, and Mohammed was Allah's final prophet who delivered the final truth of God's message, then it is blasphemy to worship Jesus, who was a prophet, not the son of God and certainly not God himself. Jesus did not die on a cross and was not resurrected. If Islam has it right, then we are all judged by our actions. We essentially have to earn our way into heaven, and believing alone is not enough (especially if you believe Jesus is actually God) to ensure salvation. By considering only the other two monotheistic Abrahamic traditions serious challenges are presented to Pascal's argument, and this is without invoking all the other concepts of God held by so many, let alone the conclusions of naturalism which has proven so much more successful than any religion in explaining the world around us.

Pascal's wager is actually just as compelling for any god ever imagined by man as it is for the Christian god. When challenged by a student from Liberty University with the question "What if you are wrong?" Richard Dawkins replied, "What if you are wrong about the great juju at the bottom of the sea?" The simplest answer to what many theists see as a checkmate (what if you are wrong?) is quite simply "What if you are the one who is wrong?" A Hindu, a Sikh, a follower of Thor for that matter can ask, "What if you are wrong?" just as effectively as can a Christian. Just like the cosmological and teleological arguments and so many others, Pascal's wager is simply a very weak argument for some sort of higher power we might call God. It is in no way an argument for the particular god claimed by a single religion.

Having addressed the false dichotomy and other rational inadequacies of Pascal's wager, let's look at its moral failings, which are significant. One of the most compelling problems with this view is the belief in infinite torture for a simple rational conclusion based on evidence. Keep in mind that nonbelief in God is not an act of willing insubordination but rather a conclusion arrived at based on an honest evaluation of the available evidence. It is difficult then to conclude this is the just and fair judgment of a loving creator. It is difficult to imagine a more unjust and immoral act than to subject someone to eternal, infinite torture for finite sins, especially if the sin being punished is the simple act of using human reason to arrive at a conclusion that seems most likely to you based upon the available evidence. This is a concept addressed in other parts of this book, for different reasons, so I will leave the discussion of eternal torture for now.

If we are to follow Pascal's approbation, we should *profess* a belief in God just in case he is real. A point often missed by believers is that this is not actually an argument for the *existence* of God but rather an argument for *professing a belief* in God. If you are professing a belief just to hedge your bets, as opposed to a sincere conviction born of compelling evidence, you are being disingenuous. It is safe to assume that any supreme deity capable of knowing what you're thinking all the time would be well aware of this insincerity. Does it not stand to reason that God would judge us just a bit more leniently for being honest with him and ourselves and admit our doubts rather than to lie about a belief we don't really have?

What of the claim that there is no harm done by belief in God, even if this belief turns out to be unfounded? Pascal argued that even if God is not real, you still lead a more moral life than if you do not.

Even if the Christian is completely wrong and there really is no God, what does it hurt to believe? Quite a lot in some cases.

Many of us are missing out on so many things in life because religious dictates forbid them. In many cases, believers hurt themselves and others by obeying perceived religious obligations. Something as simple as condom use, which the Catholic Church tells us is a bad thing, can greatly ease human suffering by reducing diseases such as AIDS and minimizing the likelihood of unwanted pregnancies. There is a direct relationship between increased human suffering and church teachings in this case. Then there are social issues such as same-sex marriage, in which religious beliefs lead to a denial of equal rights to large segments of society. To take the issue of homosexuality to the extreme of religious belief, who among us has not seen the news coverage of members of the Westborough Baptist Church with proclamations of "God hates fags"? As repugnant as this message is and fortunately rejected by most Christians, it is not without biblical sanction. If God is real and the Bible truly is his message, then the Westboro folks have gotten it exactly right as according to Leviticus 20:13: "If a man also lie with mankind, as he lieth with a woman, both of them have committed an abomination: they shall surely be put to death; their blood shall be upon them." If God is not real, then we are told to kill large segments of our population because of a superstition.

These are just a few of the countless examples of things that are detrimental to human well-being that are arbitrarily imposed on us as a result of religious beliefs. Many more will be addressed in chapter 6. This does not mean that no good is done by the faithful. It is, however, worth considering the words of Steven Weinberg on religious belief: "With or without it you would have good people doing good things and evil people doing evil things. But for good people to do evil things, that takes religion." So stop asking, "What if the atheist is wrong?" The important question is "What if the *theist* is wrong?" The most enduring argument for killing gays, rape victims, and insubordinate children, withholding funding for stem cell research, arguing that condoms are evil, etc., is that God is real and these are things that he has deemed to be good or bad. The evidence does not support the argument that there is no harm done if we believe in God even if he is not real.

A Bad Bet, a False Witness, and an Immoral Decision

Upon critical evaluation, Pascal's wager is left wanting on all fronts. It is an argument not for the existence of God (especially not for a particular god) but rather for a *profession* of belief that is based upon a false dichotomy and multiple false premises. This argument makes claims that are not only unsupported by evidence but are often actually refuted by the evidence. Pascal's wager is not a safe bet.

The Ontological Argument (The Worst Argument in Existence for Existence)

Perhaps the most bizarre of all the major apologetic arguments is the ontological argument. It is so bizarre, in fact, that even many apologists today shy away from it. It was even rejected by none other than Saint Thomas Aquinas. When a man who famously said, "To one who has faith, no explanation is necessary. To one without faith, no explanation is possible" (how's that for shutting down your brain?), this says a lot about the strength of an argument

In simplest terms, this argument states that God must exist if we can conceive of him as something that is greater than anything else we can imagine, because to exist in reality is greater than to exist in the imagination.

For our purposes, this argument can be traced to Anselm of Canterbury (1033–1109). In Proslogion (Anselm, 1998), Anselm proposed that if we conceive of "that which a greater cannot be thought," then this maximally great entity (by definition God) exists in our mind. However, it must also exist in reality because to exist in reality as well as the mind is greater than to exist in the mind alone. This maximal greatness of omnipotence, omniscience, omnibenevolence, and so forth must then be real. We are conceiving of ultimate perfection, and it is "more perfect" to be real than to exist only in the imagination. In this way, it is an a priori argument for God that rests on human reason and presuppositions alone. God is self-evident by virtue of the fact that we can imagine his greatness, and to exist in reality is greater than to be imagined to exist. If you find that confusing, I don't blame you. A huge amount of special pleading is required to argue that God must be real because he is the greatest thing we can imagine (a bare assertion with no supporting evidence), and to exist in reality is greater than to exist only in the mind. Simply imagining that the god of the Bible himself had a creator and that creator had a creator easily refutes this. There are two things already imagined that are greater than God. I think I just got an aneurysm trying to wrap my synapses around that.

As this argument is based on reasoning alone, it is also of a nature that reasoning and intuition alone is enough to refute it. David Hume refuted it thusly, "Whatever we conceive as existent, we can also conceive as non-existent. There is no being, whose non-existence implies a contradiction. Consequently there is no being, whose existence is demonstrable" (Hume, *Dialogues Concerning Natural Religion*).

Another common weakness this argument shares with other apologetic attempts is the nonspecific nature of the argument. It seems that if one simply replaces the god of Abraham with any other god, the argument holds just as steadily. We do not propose (and it is doubtful St. Anselm would have proposed) this means the other conceived concepts of gods are therefore real simply because we can imagine them. In this way, the ontological argues for the existence of a god and then makes a blind leap from "a god" to *the* god that the apologist happens to believe in. Why not Norm the Nearsighted Gnome?

Some rationalists use the previously mentioned device of the invisible pink unicorn to illustrate the flaws in such arguments. The invisible pink unicorn is an imaginary deity whose power and perfection is demonstrated by the fact that it can be both invisible and pink at the same time. This is truly an amazing feat. You can imagine this omnipotent unicorn just as well as you can conceive of the god of Abraham. In fact, I even get a strange sort of mental image of a translucent pink unicorn every time I hear the term "invisible pink unicorn." (Yeah, I know that isn't the same as invisible, but I can't form a coherent mental picture of the Holy Trinity either!) Cleary, for the invisible pink unicorn to exist in reality would be greater than to simply exist in my admittedly limited imagination, but this does not make it real in any way.

In what surely must rank among the greatest logical hypocrisies in history, Anselm basically argued that a skeptic who argues against the evidence for God is making a logical contradiction. According to Anselm, "The fool said in his heart, 'there is no God.' But certainly that same fool, having heard what I just said, 'something greater than cannot be thought,' understands what he heard, and what he understands is in his thought… but [it] cannot exist only in thought, for if it exists only in thought it could also be thought of as existing in reality as well, which is greater." Alselm asserts not only is God real because you can conceive of his perfection and greatness, but also it is illogical to think otherwise. This is so logically flawed I am not even sure how to classify it. Special pleading? Bare assertion fallacy? Circular logic? Maybe this is some sort of illogical amalgamation of intellectual dishonesty? Special circular bare pleading, perhaps?

This argument falls short for a number of other reasons. It is a fallacy to state that something exists in the mind. When you conceive of something in the mind, then you have an idea of that thing in your mind, not the actual thing. Your mind exists, not the thing of which your mind is thinking. Even if you are thinking about something real, that thing does not exist in your mind; it exists (separate from your mind) whether you think of it or not, and your thinking of it has no impact at all on its reality. The thought of a real object is still just a thought, no different that if you think of an imaginary thing. Just as when you take a photograph of a horse, then you have a photograph of a horse, not an actual horse. In much the same way, when you think about a horse, you have an idea of a horse, not an actual horse. We can conceive of all manner of perfect (and imperfect) things, but this does not make them things that actually exist.

Another critical flaw of this argument deals with the perceived perfection of God. If the only evidence we have attesting to God's character is the Bible and if the Bible accurately describes God's character, then there are good reasons to question the perfection of God. The Bible is replete with examples of God not only failing to prevent or condemn but actually commanding imperfect acts. With this as a frame of reference, it is quite easy to conceive of a being of far greater perfection than the God Saint Anselm had in mind when putting forth his ontological proof of God. So the final challenge to the ontological argument is that when conceiving of the greatest, most perfect thing, there are reasons to challenge the assumption that the thing imagined would be the god of the Bible.

The Argument from Minimal Facts (and Even More Minimal Evidence!)

The minimal facts argument, or minimal facts approach, is perhaps the most recent of the various apologias on offer that attempt to prove the existence not just of a god but of the god of Abraham and even more specifically, a divine Jesus Christ. A unique feature of this argument is that it claims to not really be focused on proving that God is real as a preconceived matter of faith but rather to seek the most reasonable explanation for a set of "facts" that are "agreed upon by a majority of scholars." The most likely explanation for these facts, according to the argument, is that God resurrected Jesus after the crucifixion. It is almost as if the proof of God was just an accidental outcome of seeking a rational explanation for the historical facts upon which all these scholars agree. But there's more to the story.

This argument is attributed primarily to Dr. Gary Habermas, and as already stated, it rests upon the idea that a majority of scholars agree on a set of facts; both the scholars and the facts are chosen from the literature by Habermas. The number of facts varies, but for the purposes of this discussion, a list of twelve are used that Habermas provided in an interview in 2008. These facts are as follows:

- Jesus died due to crucifixion.
- He was buried.

- His disciples doubted and despaired after Jesus died.
- The tomb in which Jesus was buried was discovered empty a few days later.
- The disciples had real experiences that they believed were real appearances of the risen Jesus.
- These appearances turned their lives around to the point they would be willing to put themselves in harm's way for their beliefs.
- This Gospel message was preached in Jerusalem.
- This Gospel of the deity, death, and resurrection of Jesus was the center of their proclamations.
- The Church was founded on these teachings.
- Their day of worship was Sunday (a strange thing for Jews).
- James (Jesus's brother who had been skeptical of the divinity of Jesus) was converted when he believed he saw the risen Jesus.
- Paul, who had persecuted Christians, also converted after a vision of the resurrected Christ.

Habermas claims these are facts agreed upon by the majority of scholars, even those who are skeptical of the divinity of Jesus, including some atheists and agnostics. He claims to have arrived at this conclusion by surveying writings in English, French, and German from about 1970 to present from scholars all along the spectrum, from atheist to evangelical; and he admits only those "facts" into his argument that are agreed upon by the overwhelming majority of those who have written scholarly works on these issues. After establishing his criteria for accepting his list of facts, the conclusion then is that the most compelling explanation for these facts is the bodily resurrection of Jesus Christ.

This argument is far from convincing for a host of reasons. Even the use of the word *fact* is troublesome. Few if any of the issues that Dr. Habermas discusses would rise to any reasonable definition of what most would consider a fact. What Habermas calls facts are beliefs common to friends of religion but not facts by any conventional understanding. It is not even a *fact* that Jesus Christ ever even existed in the first place, so it is difficult to see how any intellectually honest person can put forth these other claims as facts. Is there good reason to believe a person named Jesus did in fact live and preach in Judea about two thousand years ago? Maybe, but this is ultimately debatable. When you consider the lack of any written record of his life here on earth until decades after his death (and even then the accounts were written by people who never met Jesus, who spoke a different language than Jesus and his disciples, who likely lived in a different country, yet normally had a vested interest in propagating the Jesus narrative), it is a stretch to declare even mundane human aspects of his life as actual facts. To assert that miraculous claims about the life of Jesus are facts would require exponentially more evidence than has ever been provided.

For example, writing on what was said about Jesus in non-Christian sources, Craig A. Evans offers: "Non-Christian sources in which reference is made to Jesus fall into three basic categories: (1) dubious sources, (2) sources of minimal value, and (3) important sources." The nature of source types 1 and 2 is self-evidence enough that I need not address them here. Feel free to consult Evans's full account for his entire explanation. But what of the "important sources"? According to Evans, "Only two sources qualify for the third category." He is talking here of Tacitus and Josephus. Josephus didn't capture his account of Christ until about sixty years after the death of Jesus, and the scholarly consensus seems to be that at least part of Josephus's writings consists of later forgeries. Tacitus, on the other hand, wrote about "a most mischievous superstition," referring to the followers of Christ, almost ninety years after the reported crucifixion. According to Evans, "Only a modicum of helpful information about the historical Jesus can be gleaned from non-Christian sources. But what is gleaned is not unimportant" (Evans 1994).

When we consider the nature of all written accounts of the life of Jesus, all of Habermas's "facts" are, by extension, dubious to say the least. Some of these "facts" even work against Habermas's argument so clearly they can all be rebutted in this single paragraph. That Jesus died and was buried (if true) proves nothing at all other than he was human. We will all die and be buried (or cremated etc.). That

Jesus was crucified further provides very convincing evidence not of Jesus's divinity but rather that he was indeed *not* divine. His own followers were shocked by this turn of events and certainly did not expect it. The belief that Jesus died is often used by non-Christian theists when debating Christians, by asking, "How can a god die?" That his disciples doubted and despaired after Jesus died does not support the divinity argument in my mind. The "fact" that Jesus's own brother, James, was skeptical of Jesus's divinity during Jesus's entire life is also quite telling. Surely, if Jesus was indeed divine, his own brother of all people would have picked up on this little detail.

The empty tomb is one of the key "facts" used as proof of the resurrection of Jesus. Is there a rational person alive today who would not see a problem with this assertion if made about any religious figure other than the one central to one's own beliefs? There is nothing historically compelling whatsoever about the claim of an empty tomb. This is *theologically* important to Christians but not convincing to legitimate historians. Christians don't even know where this tomb was. Many Christians today believe the Church of the Holy Sepulcher to be the site of both the crucifixion and burial of Jesus, but this idea only dates back to about the fourth century and was identified as such by Helen, the mother of Emperor Constantine, after she had been dispatched by her son to establish churches on sites of importance in the life of Jesus.

Did the early Christians not see the importance of such a place? Why did they not immediately begin to show deep veneration for this very special site? Why is there not a church located at this site that dates back to the time immediately after Christ's death and resurrection? In fairness, I would accept that there was a very brief period in Christian history soon after the death of Jesus that Christians were actually a persecuted minority, and this might have made establishing an actual Church difficult. But claims of Christians being a persecuted minority have always been greatly exaggerated. Any time a Christian bewails their eternal plight as a persecuted minority remind them that Christianity has been the dominant religion in the Western World for about 1,700 years and in the entire world for much of that time. Whatever brief period of persecution Christians may have endured would not preclude veneration of this holy site of some sort very soon after the life of Jesus.

The only "fact" about the empty tomb is that there is no evidence for its existence outside of the Bible, and as chapter 3 shows quite clearly, the Bible is not very reliable on most claims. We simply do not know there was an empty tomb. We know there are Gospel accounts of an empty tomb. Accounts that differ wildly on such specifics as who found the empty tomb, what was found there, what was done about what was found there, whether there was an angel there at the empty tomb, and other key points. These are all important details upon which the Gospel writers did not agree. A final point on the empty tomb that is important to consider is that Habermas himself admits nearly a third of his experts, most of whom are Christians, do not agree it is a fact. Clearly, to go about presupposing a number of "facts" about an empty tomb that is not itself established, even among true believers, is premature.

That the Gospel message was preached in Jerusalem; the Gospel of the deity, death, and resurrection of Jesus was the center of their proclamations; and that the Church was founded on these teachings are really not that different from the claims of many other religions aside from the specifics of who we are talking about within the specific religion of Christianity. Most religions are spread in a certain area initially, based upon proclamations of and about a charismatic leader.

What of the claim that the Church was founded on these teachings? The falsity of this statement alone should be enough to refute the minimal facts argument. Even a cursory study of the New Testament reveals that the Church was not only, or even primarily, founded upon the teachings of Jesus. Just consider that the alleged teachings of James, the brother of Jesus, was much more in keeping with what is attributed to Jesus than what Paul taught, yet only one book attributed to James made it into the New Testament whereas Paul is by far the most important writer of the New Testament, and Paul's teachings seem very different from many of James or even of Jesus. It is true that many New Testament scholars question if Paul actually wrote all the books attributed to him, but the point here stands that it is not entirely valid to say the Church was founded on Jesus's teachings.

Their day of worship was Sunday. So what? I've heard a few justifications of just why I should find this interesting, but I really don't even think it warrants further comment.

"The disciples had real experiences that they believed were real appearances of the risen Jesus." Really? How exactly do we know this with enough confidence to call it a fact? It is interesting that most people who are willing to call this a fact would not hesitate to call in a psychiatrist if someone today claimed to see postmortem appearances of Elvis (or even Jesus).

"These appearances turned their lives around to the point they would be willing to put themselves in harm's way for their beliefs." The same could be said for every radical Muslim terrorist or World War II Japanese Kamikaze pilot who was willing to use the airplane he was piloting as a weapon and to die for his conception of god in the process. Christians don't find this convincing for Islam or Shinto religious truth claims, why should we find it convincing for the claims of Christianity?

Finally, that "Paul, who had persecuted Christians, also converted after a vision of the resurrected Christ" is problematic for several reasons. We know this was the same Paul who sought to popularize this new religion. While I can't prove that Paul was less than honest, he certainly had every motivation to present the story in such a way that it would support his ends. People embellish stories, present them in a certain light, and even fabricate stories out of whole cloth in order to further their goals. This happens all the time. It is not miraculous or difficult to understand. The question I ask myself and encourage you to consider is this: What is more likely to have occurred; that Paul was either mistaken in his understanding of the facts and perhaps even reported his story less than honestly or that a resurrected son of God, who is also God himself, had magically appeared to Paul after having been killed and asked him to help spread the good word? I know which one I find most feasible.

I also find Habermas's use of expert scholarship to establish facts troubling. It is interesting to note that, with rare exception,

Habermas says his list of scholars is restricted to those with terminal degrees in fields directly relating to theological studies. The reason this is interesting is that it is relatively rare that a non-theist would dedicate the time and effort to obtaining a doctoral degree in such fields. So the number of non-Christians in Habermas's study is sure to be very small, indeed. One of the most troubling features of this argument is found when one simply asks for a list of the "scholars" used to arrive at the conclusions of this argument. I personally asked Dr. Habermas for this list and was told that these sources can be found in the literature but was given no specific answers. By comparison, if anyone wanted to know what experts I talked to in preparing to write this book, I would be more than happy to provide a list with little effort. I have also discussed this issue with Dr. Richard Carrier, who had the same results when asking Dr. Habermas for a list of his "scholars" who agree on these "facts."

The first time I heard this argument used, I knew something didn't quite feel right but without assuming the apologist who was using it had simply lied about the number of scholars or some other detail I couldn't quite put my finger on it. I felt like Bertrand Russell when commenting on the ontological argument, "The argument does not, to a modern mind, seem very convincing, but it is easier to feel convinced that it must be fallacious than it is to find out precisely where the fallacy lies" (Russell, *A History of Western Philosophy*, 1945).

I wanted to get the thoughts of an actual historian, so I consulted the aforementioned Dr. Richard Carrier, who has a PhD in ancient history from Columbia University, to share his take on these claims. According to Carrier:

> Almost all of Habermas's claims are uncontroversial [that Jesus was crucified and died is indeed agreed upon by almost everyone. So what? That has nothing to do with whether he rose from the dead. Almost everyone agrees believers claimed to see Jesus, but most now in fact believe this was in hallucinations or dreams, exactly like the book

of Revelation. So it is disingenuous to use that stat as an argument "for" the resurrection].

His only controversial claim, that 75% agree there was an empty tomb discovered, is invalid. His own remarks entail that it is not 75% of scholars, but 75% of scholars who have published articles arguing specifically for or against the empty tomb (he never gives an actual count that I know of). But those who publish on a specific issue do not represent a random sample, but could very well represent a biased sample, and so there is no way to assess the actual percentage of relevant scholars. You need a scientifically controlled randomized poll of verified experts. He hasn't done that.

For example, suppose 75% actually oppose an empty tomb, and then those who want to oppose what was actually a general consensus against an empty tomb would feel more motivated to submit those defenses for publication, especially given the readiness with which such defenses would be accepted by the plethora of religious journals. Whereas someone who wanted to defend the existence of Atlantis would have a harder time finding a kind reception—and yet even then I would not be surprised if there were more articles in print defending Atlantis than attacking it, simply because those who don't believe in it don't think it worth their time to debunk, or regard one or two good debunking articles as sufficient to close the case. Only the believers see the continual writing of such papers as worthwhile, precisely because the majority remains set against them no matter how many papers keep getting written.

The most unsatisfying part of the Habermas argument is his conclusion: that the best explanation for all these "facts" is that Jesus rose from the dead. A series of events two thousand years ago that was not historically documented to any significant degree all come together to be best explained by something that has never happened any other time in the history of our species. These claims are asserted as facts in spite of the *actual fact* that human beings have a long history of lying about what they see, of actually believing they see things that the rest of us know to not be there, and most of all, the long history of naturalism offering better explanations than those attributed to supernatural causes. I find it unconvincing that the most likely explanation for these stories is that someone who had been killed (someone who might not have ever even existed) came back to life and appeared to his friends but did so in such a confusing, self-contradictory, and poorly documented way. It is more reasonable that an intellectually honest person should arrive at a different conclusion. Even concluding "I don't know" is far more intellectually honest than to conclude the laws of nature have been suspended in this case.

The previously mentioned New Testament scholar and historian, Professor Bart D. Ehrman, has made two important points on the nature of discussions such as this. First, that historians are not in the business of explaining, with certainty, what definitely happened (i.e., facts). They are in the business of explaining what was most likely to have occurred based upon the evidence we have available. In some cases, we can be very certain. Was John F. Kennedy assassinated in Texas? Well, we can say with a very high degree of certainty that he was based on living eyewitnesses, video of it happening, and no contradictory evidence. Can we be equally sure that Julius Caesar was assassinated by a group of conspirators lead by Brutus and Longinus? No. But it seems most likely that this happened based upon available evidence, no contradictory evidence, and this is the kind of thing that has often happened throughout history. Second, that miracles are, by definition, the least likely things to have occurred; otherwise, they would not be miraculous. Therefore, a historian can never arrive at the explanation that something is best explained by the occurrence of a miracle.

Another concern with this approach is that it only accepts those "facts" that are agreed upon by the majority of scholars which support Habermas's conclusions. A clear majority of biblical scholars also agree that we don't even know who wrote the Gospels and that many parts of the Bible are forgeries, but these facts are not taken into consideration by Habermas in his minimal facts argument. Surely, the irreconcilable contradictions in the Gospel accounts alone should moderate the degree to which we can comfortably refer to any of these events as facts. One thing that would help give this argument just a small amount of credibility would be if the same results (agreement on the same set of "facts") could be obtained no matter who selected the group of experts. This is not the case, however.

I just did not feel the academic rigor was where it should be on this argument, and I also wanted the historian's view, so I posed two more questions to Dr. Richard Carrier:

Q: Are there other ways you feel Dr. Habermas's data may not be up to expected academic standards?

A: There are many others. For example, I know firsthand that many relevant experts are not interested in defending any position on the empty tomb because they believe the argument is unresolvable for lack of data. Someone who thought that is not going to write papers on it, since such papers would say nothing except that there was nothing to say, and it is rare for someone who doesn't care to be motivated to debunk someone who does. If in fact most scholars don't regard the issue as solvable and therefore never publish on it (and I'm sure this is the case), then this would hugely skew the results of the Habermas survey (as that is only of what actually got published). But someone who is agnostic is still not a believer in the empty tomb. Therefore, they cannot be counted among those who argue for or conclude there was an empty tomb. Notably, Habermas never counts agnostics. He never even mentions them in his statistics. That alone entails his statistic is invalid, as already it is excluding an entire segment of the sampled population (probably in fact the vast majority of the expert population).

Therefore, that 75 percent statistic is completely useless. It's only worse that Habermas evidently counted even non-experts in his paper survey. (Many names he does reveal in JSHJ are not qualified to derive reliable conclusions in the matter, like Richard Swinburne; hence his "study" did not distinguish, say, professors of ancient history from professors of philosophy who can't even read Greek or even, so far as we know, distinguishing them from entirely unaccredited Christian apologists.) He used no evident standard of qualification: every author was counted as equal to every other. It's even worse that 25 percent of experts disagreeing is by definition *the absence* of a consensus, and thus even his bogus statistic is logically irrelevant to the needs of his argument.

Q: Any other relevant points about this particular apologetic argument that you feel should be shared?

A: For me, the real last nail in the coffin, Habermas says "most" of the scholars he counted on the pro side "hold that the Gospels probably would not have dubbed [women] as the chief witnesses unless they actually did attest to this event" which apart from being incorrect (not a single Gospel identifies any woman as its source, much less "chief" source. We merely "presume" this because the story puts them there, but that becomes a circular argument, as all the Gospels after Mark have men verify the fact, while Mark says no one even reported the fact, not even the women!) is based on incorrect claims about the ancient world. (Women's testimony was fully trusted, as even Habermas admits in the very same paragraph. See my complete discussion of this in chapter 11 of *Not the Impossible Faith*). If even Habermas admits "most" of his 75 percent are relying on an *invalid argument*, then even if the count really were 75 percent (and for all the reasons above, it can't possibly be that, or anywhere near that), it's wholly invalid because "most" of those scholars are thereby in fact *wrong* (by Habermas's own inadvertent admission). Thus, you can't cite them in defense of the fact. Yet he does!

Like so many other apologetic arguments, this attempt is worse than simply wrong because of its intellectual dishonesty. Habermas seems like a very decent man in the interview from which the specifics of his minimal facts approach are taken as well as in later personal correspondence between him and myself. The conclusion, however, that all these events (which are not facts) somehow point to the resurrection of Jesus is just not convincing. In fact, one of the scholars that Dr. Habermas quotes, Robert M. Price, said of such attempts, "What evangelical apologists are still trying to show… is that their version of the resurrection was the most compatible with accepting all the details of the Gospel Easter narratives as true and non-negotiable… [D]efenders of the resurrection assume that their opponents agree with them that all the details are true, that only the punch line is in question. What they somehow do not see is that to argue thus is like arguing that the Emerald City of Oz must actually exist since, otherwise, where would the Yellow Brick Road lead?… We simply have no reason to assume that anything an ancient narrative tells us is true" (Price 2010).

As part of the research for this book, I have been in correspondence with Dr. Habermas and have asked for clarification and specifics on his argument. I feel it is important to point out a couple of outcomes of our discussions. First, Dr. Habermas seems to be, as stated earlier, a kind and decent man, and I appreciate him taking the time to correspond with me. He was also far more forthcoming about the limitations of his argument than any of those I have heard use his minimal facts approach in the past. Specifically, he stated, "Of course I realize that tracking scholars across a spectrum of views does not 'prove' anything about the events themselves. Therefore, and this is very frequently missed, what I am doing here is more of stating my methodology than that of demonstrating any 'proven foundation.' But I think knowing the scholarly 'lay of the land' is a good starting place for a discussion of the key issues related to Jesus' death and resurrection. After all, if even skeptical scholars agree with a basic outline of data, then that is a fair 'common ground' approach to the major questions."

I include this additional information not as a critique of Habermas but rather to his credit. In this correspondence at least, he is far more honest about the nature of the evidence he presents than many apologists who present the argument as more than it actually is.

The Argument from Morality (Not Just Logically Wrong, Morally Indefensible!)

> The objections to religion are of two sorts—intellectual and moral. The intellectual objection is that there is no reason to suppose any religion true; the moral objection is that religious precepts date from a time when men were more cruel than they are and therefore tend to perpetuate inhumanities which the moral conscience of the age would otherwise outgrow.
>
> —Bertrand Russell

One of the hardest pro-God arguments for some skeptics to deal with is the argument from morality. Make no mistake; this is not because religion does a better job of explaining morality or provides a sounder basis on which to rest moral or ethical decisions than rational inquiry does, but rather it may be because this is one area in which science has been largely willing to bow out and concede it has nothing to offer. One challenge of morality vis-à-vis the debate between religion and naturalism lies in the perception that science does not easily and convincingly offer strikingly clear and parsimonious explanations for morality. Science does this incredibly well for so many of the other facets of the human experience that it seems (to some) a failure of science's explanatory power when answers don't come easily on issues of morality, or those answers don't seem as tangible for morality as for so many other things. As is so often the case, however, once we actually find out what science actually can teach us about morality—what actually constitutes moral behavior, the evolutionary origins of morality, and how morality is moderated by human reason and intellect—we may become much more confident in the scientific position on this issue.

Somehow "We evolved to be moral" may seem to fall flat for many, and this is an area in which the "god of the gaps," addressed in the chapter 2 discussion on epistemology, is a common feature. An inability (real or perceived) of science to explain if there is universal objective morality and where this morality would come from is appealed to by some as a de facto proof of God. After all, goes the argument, if there is no God, where could morality possibly come from?

In its most basic form, the argument from morality can take the form of yet another simple syllogism:

- Major premise: Without a divine lawgiver (God), there can be no objective law (morality).
- Minor premise: There *is* objective morality.
- Conclusion: Therefore, God *is* real.

As with most apologetic arguments, there are variations and nuances, but as with the other arguments, this is a common form. This syllogism, like those before it, should be put to rest before getting to the more philosophically sublime problems of this argument.

The major premise is a bare assertion. There simply is no way of knowing that objective morality can only exist is if there is in fact a particular god. When Christians use this argument, they are clearly arguing for the existence of their particular god, and even if *a* god were necessary for objective morality to exist, who is to say this necessary god is not Zeus or Odin? It does not logically follow that if *a* god is necessary for the existence of objective morality, then it must be the god of Abraham. As I pointed out in the discussion of the cosmological argument, cosmologists are the only experts we have on the origin of the universe (contrary to the wishes of creationists), and the scholarly consensus among cosmologists is that a god is not necessary for the existence of the universe. The laws of nature as we understand them are the only explanation we have for the origin of the universe. While scientists do not yet (and may never) have a comprehensive understanding of how the universe began, science provides a great many answers with respect to cosmology where religion provides none. Nature's physical laws work just fine—sans god hypothesis. The existence of morality, just as the existence of the cosmos, has perfectly logical explanations that are found in nature—explanations that, by the way, are actually quite easy to understand as we shall see later.

The minor premise is also a bare assertion and is stated without evidence. It is not at all clear that morality is objective in the way it is meant by theists who invoke this argument. The position often taken up by theists is that morality is either objective, absolute, universal, and eternal (from God) or completely up to each individual's preferences, and each individual can do as he or she wishes. This is a terribly shortsighted and unimaginative position to take. In his book *The God Debates*, Dr. John Shook suggests, "An objective moral truth is made true by the natural fact that a society of people share a common culture which includes that accepted truth among its social rules. An objective truth is still relative to people, but not to any individual person." Shook compares this to laws. Laws are accepted by a society, and society may change that law, but individuals can't just arbitrarily decide it does not apply to them. Clearly, with two invalid premises, the conclusion should be looked at skeptically.

Now that we've dispensed with the most obvious failings of this argument, we are free to have a serious discussion on the nature of morality to include a critique of the idea that morality somehow comes from religion in general and the Bible specifically, which should be abundantly clear from the chapter 3 discussions where the Bible stands (or at least does not clearly stand against) on a host of moral issues. As already stated in other parts of this book, I will try to avoid excessive redundancy, and I have already addressed biblical morality in chapter 3. I feel compelled, however, to risk some repetition here as morality is used so often as an evidence of God's existence in spite of the myriad moral miscues resident within the Bible.

A writer often referred to as a source of inspiration and wisdom by believers is C. S. Lewis, whom I have referenced a couple of times already. A gifted writer, Lewis nonetheless offers the same illogical conclusions and gratuitous assertions in his defense of belief in God that I have come to expect of religious apologetics. In *Mere Christianity*, Lewis early on makes the same claim as many other theists, namely that there is a *common* morality (they would call it a *higher* morality), shared by all of us, and this is only true because it was given to us by God. "Think of a country," Lewis wrote, "where people were admired for running away in battle or where a man felt proud of double-crossing all the people who had been kindest to him" (Lewis 1952). Agreed, this is difficult to envision, but in no way is this so because the tendency against this sort of behavior is God-given. This is true because it is hard to imagine a society that would long flourish if such were the norm and not the exception. As we will see, there is far less reason to believe this would violate divine sanction than that it defies evolutionary theory.

What Is Morality?

A theist deferring to the Bible as a source of morality may value prohibitions against certain sexual acts and perhaps dietary restrictions or other things that God told us not to do or commanded us to do in the Bible. But these are things that most rational people would not normally consider moral issues were it not for scriptural sanction, and even then, only followers of that particular religion would agree on the morality of the practice in question. For purposes of this discussion, rather than scripture, let's rely on a widely accepted and uncontroversial conception of morality which can be accepted by believers and skeptics alike—behavior which increases well-being or decreases suffering to the greatest number of sentient beings. I feel secure in doing this without much fear of contradiction as religious people already do it by ignoring the bad parts of the Bible and emphasizing the good parts that even secular people would have no issue with.

This might seem an issue of semantics, but it is more than that. If we are restricted solely to biblical definitions of morality and accept it as indeed being the divine words of the creator of the universe, then we will have a view of morality greatly incongruous with what most of us value today. There are a plethora of behaviors that few people today would consider immoral but are not only prohibited in the Bible, but which actually carry the death penalty. Likewise, there are a number of acts that are biblically sanctioned, either expressly or implicitly, that almost no one today considers acts of morality and often in fact would be illegal in most modern societies.

In *The Brothers Karamazov*, Fyodor Dostoevsky is widely believed to have written (though I don't think *exactly* wrote but did imply), "If there is no God, then everything is permitted."[31] This is an often referred to aphorism by apologists attempting to make the point that only if there is a divine magistrate can we have true objective right and wrong. Without a god making the rules for us, so goes this thinking, we should feel free to rape and pillage to our heart's content. This ignores the fact that those of us who don't believe in God do actually rape and pillage just as much as we want; it just happens that we don't want to do this and don't need God to tell us not to. We also have law enforcement in place for those rare individuals who actually do want to go about raping.

Upon closer scrutiny, the assertion that morality is God-given simply does not hold up well. Why do we assume an act to be moral or immoral? Benjamin Franklin once said, "Sin is not hurtful because it is forbidden, but it is forbidden because it is hurtful… Nor is a duty beneficial because it is commanded, but it is commanded because it is beneficial." Two thousand years earlier, Plato made the same point in a slightly different way. In Plato's dialogue *Euthyphro*, Socrates

---

[31] I have often heard this line quoted from Dostoyevsky's *Brothers Karamazov*, but as best I can discern, this is a case of famous quotes never uttered, like "Alas poor Yorik, I knew him well" or "Pride goeth before a fall." So often quoted as to be almost household terms but all incorrect. In Dostoyevsky, the closest quote I can find to the one so often offered is "If there's no immortality of the soul, then there's no virtue, and everything is lawful." Of course, when you account for translation and the "sameness" of intent, the quotes are close enough for purposes of our discussion here. By the way, the two other correct quotes are "Alas, poor Yorik! I knew him, Horatio" from *Hamlet* and "Pride goeth before destruction, and a haughty spirit before a fall" from Proverbs 16:18.

poses the question to Euthyphro, "Is the pious loved by the gods because it is pious, or is it pious because it is loved by the gods?" This is exactly the sort of thing we should ask about morality within the context of religion. Does God forbid things because they are wrong, or are they wrong because he forbids them? And conversely, are acts of goodness deemed good because God commanded them, or did he command them because of their goodness?

No matter how this is answered, it poses serious challenges to the argument from morality as an evidence of God. If God commands an act because it is good, then the concept of goodness exists independent of God's mandate. It was already good, and that is why he commanded it. This raises the question of the need of God on moral issues since he didn't determine what is good but only commanded that we do what was already good. One might contend that this is a specious argument, and since God created everything and set the laws of nature and of the universe in place, then right and wrong does not exist independent of him but rather *because* of him. This line of reasoning would indicate that God commands things, and that is why those things are good. If it is true that the only reason things are good is because God said so, then truly anything *is* permissible. Anything *is* good, just so long as God *decides* it is permissible and good.

There is no truly objective morality under this last view; morality is dependent upon the caprices of a whimsical God. If this is true, then we really must adhere to the Ten Commandments, and we should not cherry-pick as we do currently. If you work on the Sabbath, then you *should* be killed. God commanded it, so it must not only be done; it *must* be moral to do so no matter what our current concept of morality might indicate. Not because working on the Sabbath is inherently evil but because God commanded that you not work on the Sabbath. Therefore, it is evil by holy decree and not open to interpretation.

If this is God's word, then either God directed us to do immoral things or these things were not immoral at one time but are now immoral. This is a huge problem for the theists who believe that God's book provides objective morality. If the morality changes from good to bad just because God said so, then it is not objective at all but subject to God's whims. If these acts were objectively immoral, then God at times commanded men to do immoral acts, and wouldn't that make God immoral?

Morality Is Older Than Religion (Maybe Even Older Than Humans)

It could be argued that moral behavior is not necessarily limited to humans. Not only do we see acts that could be considered "moral" in other primates today, we see evidence of it in our various ancestor species.

Ardipithecus ramidus, or *Ardi*, lived about 4.4 million years ago; long before *Homo sapiens* walked the earth and by extension, long before we created God in our image. Ardi teaches us interesting lessons about where we came from and how our ancestors lived? This beautiful *transitional species* (something that young earth creationists claim does not exist!) shows us that our ancestors were bipedal a lot further back than we had previously suspected for example. Also, based upon the fossil evidence found alongside Ardi, it appears that she (I refer to Ardi in the feminine because the most complete fossil yet found of this species was of a female) lived in a heavily wooded area, not open savanna as previously thought about our earliest hominid ancestors. A brief tangent here but an important aspect of the scientific method is demonstrated here. When evidence was found that indicated our belief that our earliest ancestors must have become bipedal on the open savanna may have been wrong, the reaction was not to resort to apologetics to explain away the "seemingly contravening" evidence. We changed our thinking on this particular matter to better suit where the evidence was pointing.

Ardi's evolution has important implications for why it is that she walked upright. Was it that this allowed for gathering and transporting of food across a larger area that could be brought back to a mate, using the arms now freed from the burden of walking on all fours? Perhaps this allowed Ardi to better provide for others. For the purposes of our discussion on morality, however, the most important thing we learned from Ardi is not how she might have gathered food but that she was almost certainly cared for by others of her kind.

Ardipithecus ramidus probably exercised what we today call altruism. They apparently looked out for each other. The team that worked so hard to bring us an understanding of this distant ancestor made some fascinating discoveries that show this to be true. Among the surprises found in the fossil record was a very clear and specific pathology in the bones of one of her feet demonstrating that she suffered from a significant infection that would have made it all but impossible for her to walk. This in itself is of no consequence, but this pathology also demonstrated that her crippling condition had healed. We know this because bone had grown over the previously infected area. It is extremely unlikely that this could have happened unless others of her kind cared for her when she was unable to walk and gather her own food.

While at least partially speculative, I don't think it wildly so to imagine that others who cared for her also protected her against predation. If this happened to any of us today—if we were incapacitated for some reason and others had to care for us until we could again care for ourselves—how would we describe the actions of our caregivers? I think goodness comes to mind. Morality, perhaps? Or at least the early stirrings of a nascent morality that could have grown, evolved, into what we today have to help us discern right from wrong.

Much more recent than Ardi but still ancient by our standards, the Neanderthals practiced what may have been the earliest stirrings of a religious impulse. According to Jerry Coyne, "Some skeletons bear traces of the pigment ochre, and were accompanied by 'grave goods' such as animal bones and tools. This suggests that Neanderthals ceremonially buried their dead: perhaps the first inkling of human religion" (Coyne, *Why Evolution Is True*, 2009). Clearly, there was some degree of caring for each other among the Neanderthals that necessitated burial rituals. And this was about twenty thousand years before the earliest writings of what has come to be the Bible. It hardly seems we needed divine sanction to begin caring for each other, and I am at a loss to imagine any truly moral act that does not have compassion and caring at its core.

I have often asked my theist friends if they really believe that our morality comes from God, and the answer is always an emphatic yes. Tomorrow I might be surprised with a "Maybe" or (heaven forbid) a "Not really," but so far, it has been a mind-numbingly consistent yes. Where the conversation gets more interesting, at least with those willing to have the discussion, is when you peel back the onion a bit to see what's underneath and ask about the implications of this belief. How, for example, was this morality communicated to us upright descendants of ape-like ancestors? Did it come in the form of Jesus? Was it much further back? Maybe with the (rock) hard-copy of the Ten Commandments brought by Moses from on high we finally had a way of knowing right from not quite right. The examples are rarely that solid. It is normally a vague, general love of everyone—something we have just fine without religion.

What of those societies that never had the benefit of scripture? How about the ancient Chinese, for example? There was a flourishing civilization in China at a time when those to whom God's word was revealed were almost entirely illiterate. It seemed that in much the same way super-advanced aliens apparently always visit remote areas largely populated by the least cosmopolite segments of society, God avoided the more learned and advanced civilizations of two to four thousand years ago, preferring instead to reveal himself to the Bronze Age equivalent of Alabama trailer parks. Okay, so it might not seem terribly sensitive of me to make fun of the good people who live in Alabama trailer parks, but as I spent much of my early life living in Alabama trailer parks, I hope I will be forgiven.

As it turns out, divine revelation seems to be the explanation for morality least in accordance with all available evidence. Naturalistic evolutionary explanations are much more satisfying and in keeping with the information we have at our disposal. Are the naturalistic explanations perfect in every detail? Of course not. However, warts and all, the naturalistic approach is the option with by far the greatest explanatory power. It is the only explanation with the advantage that it actually works.

Morality from the Bible

> I form the light, and create darkness: I make peace, and create evil: I the LORD do all these things.
>
> —Isaiah 45:7

Science's inability to offer a complete and perfect explanation for the origin, existence, and nature of morality does not, by default, equate to an argument in favor of a divine sanction for morality. In fact, the morality argument brings up one of the greatest "own goals" scored by religion against itself. The claim that morality somehow is an arrow in the theists' quiver is revealed to be a terribly weak claim, indeed, if one simply reads the Good Book.

As demonstrated in the previous chapter, the Bible is morally ambiguous at best, downright repugnant in places, and certainly not a source of moral guidance for an enlightened people. It has been shown that the Bible stands exactly on the wrong side of a number of moral issues. I must admit to a failure of creativity at this point. I have enumerated a number of these moral failings, such as slavery, misogyny, genocide, justice, racism, human sacrifice, and rape, a number of times already. These are crystal-clear issues of right and wrong that the Bible gets exactly wrong so many times it is hard to not frequently revisit them. If the Bible is the only way we have of knowing God's moral nature and it is an accurate depiction of God, then truly to argue that our notions of morality come from God is shown to be a vacuous claim, and it fails to answer why most Christians are actually really good people (most of the time).

What Happens When We Accept Apologetics, and Why Apologetic Arguments Are Worse than Wrong

In every single apologetic argument with which I have ever been presented, I see a couple of basic features. First, they are unconvincing to anyone not already predisposed to belief in that particular god. In this way, they are more retention tools than recruiting tools. Apologetic arguments are not effective for bring in new converts. They are, however, great excuses for those who desperately want to believe but really see no good reason to do so beyond wishful thinking. Second, they are *extremely* intellectually dishonest. The only way intelligent people can truly believe any of these arguments is to accept a willing suspension of disbelief in spite of mountains of evidence to the contrary. One of the ways this intellectual dishonesty is manifested is in a sort of lazy algebraic reversal in which the conclusion is placed at the front of the problem rather than at the end. Evidence is not evaluated against counter-evidence in order to determine what is most likely true. The conclusion is assumed, and then evidence is gathered to support that conclusion while evidence against it is ignored or even suppressed.

The central thesis of this book, though it may not always be readily apparent, is an appeal to honesty in the terms of epistemic disquisition. These apologetic arguments (and many others not covered here) are not only unconvincing; they are detrimental to human reason. An example of the harm done to human reason and intellect is from William Lane Craig, who goes to great lengths to hijack science for his own ends. This is seen in his common practice of quote mining or using quotes that in no way support his position in such a way that it *appears* the quotes actually support his conclusions. Consider Craig's very frequent practice of quoting Dr. Alexander Vilenkin in such a way that it appears Vilenkin is actually arguing for the necessity of God in the creation of the Universe: "It is said that an argument is what convinces reasonable men and a proof is what it takes to convince even an unreasonable man. With the proof now in place, cosmologists can no longer hide behind the possibility of a past-eternal universe. There is no escape: they have to face the problem of a cosmic beginning." Taken within the context of Craig's overall cosmological argument, he is clearly implying that Vilenkin is somehow in agreement that the Christian god created the universe.

This is problematic for Craig, however, because in e-mail correspondence, I asked Dr. Vilenkin if this quote was meant to imply the existence of God. Dr. Vilenkin replied, "Dear Mr. Davis, here is a short answer: The quote is correct, but I do not think that cosmic beginning proves (or disproves) the existence of God." In light of this, it is clear that Dr. Vilenkin's words should not be used to support the existence (or nonexistence) of God, and to do so is less than honest. In fact, if you read Dr. Vilenkin's book (which I highly commend), from which the quoted passage is taken, it is clear that Vilenkin argues against a rush to judge cosmology as proof of God: "So, what do we make of a proof that the beginning is unavoidable? Is it a proof of the existence of God? This view would be far too simplistic" (Vilenkin 2006). Vilenkin later points out in chapter 17 how he believes the universe was the result of a tunneling event in which "a finite-sized universe filled with a false vacuum, pops out of nowhere (nucleosis) and immediately starts to inflate." Finally, he states, "If there was nothing before the universe popped out, then what could have caused the tunneling? Remarkably, the answer is that no cause is required." How is it anything other than intellectually dishonest to quote (selectively) Professor Vilenkin as if he supports your view that God created the universe?

One real shame of apologetics is not just that they are most likely wrong but that they give an excuse to stop thinking. Something seems complex, hard to comprehend, mysterious? Don't worry about it. God did it. If everyone down through history had been content with this attitude, as far too many seem to be today, we would still have a view of the universe in which the Earth was at the center of an unchanging universe, evil spirits causing mental illness, curses and sin causing disease; and we would have no idea that the complexity of life can be explained by evolution as opposed to a special act of creation six thousand years ago.

We accepted Ptolemy's geocentric view of the universe for 1,400 years. We did this not because better information was not to be had; we did it because we were mired in thinking that something had created the cosmos with us in mind and we *must* be at the center of that creation. The only reason we kept the Earth at the center of our cosmology for so long is because this belief was defended using the same techniques as those employed by apologists today. Even though better scientific thought was available to support a heliocentric view, religious people supported the Ptolemaic view because it was better suited to their vision of how God created the cosmos. Rather than following where the evidence led, resort was given to creative and at times even repressive ways of defending the popular view. When questions arose about the erratic movement of the planets (the word *planet* actually comes from the Greek word for *wanderer*) through the heavens in Ptolemy's day, the last thing considered was that we might not be at the center of the cosmos, so Ptolemy developed highly elaborate and ingenious (but wrong) erratic "wobbly orbits" that sought to explain planetary movement.

I have explained in part I why I initially stopped believing. In part II, I addressed the degree to which the Bible should be looked at skeptically and demonstrated the failings of extra-biblical arguments. In part III, I will try to make clear why this matters so much more than most people realize.

PART III

Why Preach about Unbelief?

CHAPTER 5

Okay, so If You Don't Believe in God, Why Preach about It? (The Intrinsic Value of Truth)

Reality provides us with facts so romantic that imagination itself could add nothing to them.
—Jules Verne

Perhaps the question I am most often asked when the subject of this book arises is this: If you don't believe in God, then why bother even talking about it? This question comes in various flavors and to varying degrees of passion. To some, it is simply an honest curiosity. To some who ask such questions of nonbelievers, such as Christian apologist Dinesh D'Souza, it is a more developed challenge. D'Souza argues that when atheists say they don't believe simply because there is no evidence that this isn't really true. According to D'Souza, "But if you think about it, this is an inadequate explanation, because if you truly believe that there is no proof for God, then you're not going to bother with the matter. You're just going to live your life as if God isn't there." D'Souza continues, "I don't believe in unicorns, so I just go about my life as if there are no unicorns. You'll notice that I haven't written any books called *The End of the Unicorn, Unicorns Are Not Great,* or *The Unicorn Delusion,* and I don't spend my time obsessing about unicorns. What I'm getting at is that you have these people out there who don't believe that God exists, but who are actively attempting to eliminate religion from society, setting up atheist video shows, and having atheist conferences. There has to be more going on here than mere unbelief" (Segelstein 2008).

D'Souza goes on to argue that among the true atheist motivations is a desire to remove the source of moral authority (God in

229

D'Souza's view) from the picture in order that we may be immoral with impunity. Quite frankly, this deeply misguided point of view is just one of a great many reasons that books of this nature and speaking out against religious dogma and discrimination are actually necessary. D'Souza, in saying why we shouldn't bother speaking out and dishonestly saying why we do, is actually perfectly demonstrating why we must. Surely, most of us would agree that any accusation of intrinsic immorality with a racial minority or women, perhaps, would draw near universal scorn in today's society, but we often fail to see this stereotyping and discrimination for what it is when directed at nonbelievers. We've so completely bought into this dogmatic religious view as a society that even the secular among us don't readily see what is so deeply wrong with arguments such as those offered by apologists like D'Souza. It is wrong to stereotype nonbelievers as immoral people who lie about why we profess unbelief in God. This is actually one of the reasons we feel compelled to speak out.

D'Souza's observation that it is the atheist who denies God's reality so that we may be immoral with impunity reveals a veritable perfect storm of hypocrisy, by the way. If I or any other atheist wishes to simply live our lives immorally, we need not deny God. We might simply follow D'Souza's example. He resigned his position as the president of King's College, a New York City Christian institution, after it was revealed that he was engaged to a woman twenty years his younger while not yet divorced from his wife (Gilgoff 2012). I personally consider this to be a personal matter between D'Souza and his wife (and his fiancée) and would not bring it up were it not for the fact that this is precisely the kind of thing that D'Souza accuses nonbelievers of wanting to do, and according to him, this is their true motivation for denying God. Apparently, this behavior can be carried out just fine while proclaiming belief in God.[32]

---

[32]   D'Souza was also charged with, and pleaded guilty to one felony count of making illegal campaign contributions. A conviction President Trump later pardoned. Again, belief in God does not prevent nefarious actions if D'Souza is our guide.

Think again of D'Souza's claim that his lack of belief in unicorns does not lead him to denounce unicorns or to write books about there being no unicorns. He simply behaves as if unicorns are not real. While this might sound like a valid and even witty observation to his compatriots, I don't see it as relevant to the argument. People who believe in unicorns, if there really are any such people, don't hold a great deal of political sway in this country. Contrary to a belief in unicorns, belief in an invisible, undetectable magic man who works in mysterious ways we can't hope to understand, is seen by many in our society as a necessary precondition to holding high political office. Not only is it a prerequisite to holding political office, it leads many to believe one is somehow worthy to offer guidance on how we should live, both as individuals and as a society. This necessary precondition is in place because God—this furtive, enigmatic, thaumaturge—is also a close personal friend, and friends of religion know exactly what he wants of each of us.

Belief in God, unlike belief in unicorns, all too often earns you admiration from those who see faith, especially in the extreme absence of evidence, as a noble trait worthy of emulation. Belief in unicorns would rightfully cause people to question your judgment, but belief in God, for some reason, does not. Sam Harris offered the observation about George W. Bush that "the President of the United States has claimed, on more than one occasion, to be in dialogue with God. If he said that he was talking to God through his hairdryer, this would precipitate a national emergency. I fail to see how the addition of a hairdryer makes the claim more ridiculous or offensive" (Harris, *Letter to a Christian Nation*, 2008). This is not a healthy state of affairs. The fact that Bush so openly professed his personal relationship with an invisible friend was, to a great many voters, his strongest quality.

The simple fact is that this discussion matters. In spite of zero reliable evidence that God is real, a great many people make decisions that affect all of us based upon their belief in that God. Legislation is routinely enacted by people who believe they know how the God wants us to behave, what he wants us to eat, on what days of the week, with whom we are to have sex and in what positions, and a great many other matters. This matters because believers vote and, through the power of that vote, often attempt to regulate the behavior of others.

Motivations

What of the skeptic, rationalist, or just run-of-the-mill nonbeliever? What are the other motivations for his beliefs or lack of belief if D'Souza and others like him are wrong? After all, while it is clear that D'Souza is wrong about why we admit to unbelief in God, what might motivate us to actually speak out about our unbelief other than the obvious and previously mentioned political necessity? Why not just remain silent in our unbelief? One may argue, for example, that the motivation is clear—to write books in favor of the skeptical perspective to make money (books like this one, for example). I have heard this charge leveled against others who have written such books. For anyone tempted to fall for this trap, I would commend to you a small experiment like the one I've just undertaken.[33]

Go to any fine bookstore, such as the national chain outlet in which I am sitting as I write this, and compare the volume of books that argue specifically for or against religion. With little effort and very quickly, I found nineteen bookracks, four of which had seven shelves each, fifteen of which had five shelves each, and each shelf contained approximately forty books of a pro-religious nature. So roughly 4,120 specifically religious volumes.[34] I then spent the next twenty minutes (a self-imposed time limit) looking for books spe-

---

[33] Again, this book was written over several years and in many places. This portion as originally written some time in 2010.

[34] Even though I did this admittedly very unscientific count personally, it still seems hard to believe as I reread my own words and numbers while doing a final edit on New Year's Day 2017. Just for a sanity check, I did a quick Web search for explicitly Christian books other than the Bible and found 3,297 volumes. The estimate of 4,120 I came up with during my quick count in the bookstore included the entire "religion and spirituality" section, without regard to specific religion or denomination.

cifically arguing for an atheist worldview. I found seven. Not seven aisles or seven book cases or even seven shelves. I found seven books. About the same number of books as I found, with very little effort, written by authors and pundits from Fox News Channel alone (like Ann Coulter, Glenn Beck, and Bill O'Reilly), who routinely argue against the skeptical perspective and in favor of conservative Christian beliefs.

Just out of curiosity, I decided to then look for books that, while not arguing specifically against theism, do present perfectly reasonable explanations, supported by evidence, for the workings of the universe which religion once claimed as its domain. I have heard it said of books like this that they do not argue against God, but they do make it possible to not believe in God or to not look to God as the only explanation for the things we see around us. These books on the physical sciences, mathematics, etc. took up a grand total of six bookcases of five shelves each, or approximately 1,200 books. So if my motive were simply to get published, it would appear my odds are far greater if I write a book on quantum mechanics, which I am ill equipped to do, or one promoting religion, which I am unwilling to do.

The Intrinsic Value of Truth

> Is it more probable that nature should go out of her course or that a man should tell a lie? We have never seen, in our time, nature go out of her course. But we have good reason to believe that millions of lies have been told in the same time. It is therefore at least millions to one that the reporter of a miracle tells a lie.
> —Thomas Paine, *The Age of Reason.*

As we learned in this most recent political season, some people apparently do not really care if something they believe is actually true or not. Rather, they care how that belief makes them feel. I am not normally one of those people. The truth matters—a lot. Not all issues or ideas carry equal importance, but even for the little things, I would rather know the truth. Robert Green Ingersoll was right to point out that "the more false we destroy the more room there will be for the true." If we allow the fallacious to go unchallenged, then we should not be surprised if the truth does not find its way into the light.

All great advances in any field of learning, all the great leaps forward that have contributed to human well-being have shared at least one important trait; lying at the core of the discovery was the pursuit of the truth. Can you imagine us ever having eradicated smallpox, reached the moon, invented high-speed microprocessors, or any of the myriad other scientific marvels which contribute to our enjoying the highest quality of life in human history if truth were merely an afterthought? Impossible. The simple fact is that on all matters, great and small, it is better to know the truth and recognize that which is false.

Even in situations in which the truth is inconvenient or disconcerting, it is better to distinguish truth and falsehood. If you go to the doctor and are tested for cancer, of course, you don't want to hear that you have cancer. If, however, you do indeed have cancer, this is exactly what you need to be told in order to pursue life-saving treatment and in the worst case make plans for your eventual demise.

"Lying for Absolute Truth" Should Be Challenged

Lying for the truth is a phrase I often use, so I should be very clear about what exactly I mean. Friends of religion are often so convinced of the value of their message that they justify playing fast and loose with the truth and rationalize this (even subconsciously) by believing it supports a "greater truth." This is a very Machiavellian approach to achieving "ultimate truth" by being less than completely honest to get there. This applies in two fairly distinct senses. The first is very straightforward and unambiguous. If you willingly and knowingly misrepresent the truth by professing something to be true that you know is actually not true, you are lying. This is normally not a good thing, though there are times when lying is actually not immoral. A time when a lie might actually be a moral act would be if, during the Nazi holocaust, a German was hiding a Jewish family in his attic. If the SS asked, "Are you hiding Jews in your attic?" of course, to lie is the most moral act. This is not, however, what I am talking about. What I am talking about here and within the context of this book is the common practice of presenting false information or avoiding intellectual honesty for the purpose of bolstering religious convictions. Granted this was a long explanation of what I mean by "lying for the truth," but as you will see at least one of those I challenge in this section has taken umbrage to my characterization, so I felt the clarification was necessary.

Blatant lies are not only those things expressly stated that you know are false. You can bear false witness perfectly well by making a statement that is technically true but by doing it in such a way that it distorts the reality—just so long as you do so knowingly and if your intent is to misrepresent the truth. An example of this is the previously discussed practice of quote mining or taking something that someone actually said but using it in such a context that it actually conveys a falsehood. I have been very clear that I do not believe in God, but I often say "Bless you" when someone sneezes or "thank God" when I hear about someone's good luck. These are figures of speech common to all Americans, and to quote me, out of context, as an attempt to make it seem like I really do believe in God is just as dishonest as any other lie even though you might be accurately quoting my words. In the legal profession this is known as making a true but misleading statement. This often happens when theists quote (correctly, but out of context) people like Albert Einstein or Stephen Hawking in such a way that it sounds as if they were expressing belief in a personal god. Both Einstein and Hawking repeatedly made their disbelief in a personal god perfectly clear.

The second use of the term *lying for the truth* has a less-harsh meaning but is still censorious in nature. In this sense of lying for the truth, what I am talking about is when someone doesn't really know for certain that what he or she is saying is untrue but only because they don't bother to know. This is not because the information isn't readily available but because they are willfully ignorant. To compound the impact of this willful ignorance, many go about proudly propagating this ignorance. To exist in this state of blissful ignorance yet state your position as established fact is still dishonest. This latter form of dishonesty may be the biggest single defining characteristic of religious apologetics of which I am aware. This appears to happen quite often in religious circles, and this willful ignorance is so extreme as to be hard to distinguish from lying outright. Just one example from the creation—evolution discussion is instructive. An often-heard critique from creationists is that if evolution is true, then there should be transitional fossils, yet there are none. A transitional fossil is simply a fossil that remains of a species that is somewhere between and exhibits characteristics of both its ancestor and descendant species.

To make the statement that there are no transitional fossils, however, requires stupidity (you simply cannot think), deep ignorance (you are terribly lacking for legitimate information), or blatant lying (you are saying something you know to be untrue). The simple fact is that we have such an incredible wealth of transitional fossils that it is difficult to imagine that any person denying their existence is not lying on some level. I suppose it is possible that some who claim the absence of transitional fossils actually do believe what they say, but only because they have made a conscious decision to ignore the overwhelming evidence in spite of the embarrassment of riches we have that proves them wrong. This intentional ignorance, in the presence of reliable evidence to the contrary, in the hands of a religious authority figure that should know better—a professional apologist, for example—really must be seen as a form of overt dishonesty. Denying the existence of transitional fossils is such a perfect example of the kind of dishonest I am talking about here that it will be revisited several more times in this book.

This dishonest tendency is not limited to discussions of transitional fossils, of course. Addressed here is a representative sample of things often told by true believers, stated as if they were irrefutably true yet are easily shown to be false. Certainly, this is not an all-inclusive list, but enough examples are given to make the point and to show that this really is an issue that matters. It matters enough that even if I had no other motivation at all for writing this book, this would be enough. As you read through the following examples, please consider why anyone would feel it necessary to so blatantly misrepresent the truth on these matters. Surely, if one's beliefs have a solid foundation, there is no need to resort to such dishonest tactics to bolster one's position. This is especially true if you claim, owing to your religion, a moral superiority and access to absolute truth. Remember also that often these liberties are taken with the truth because the friends of religion believe they are promoting a "more important truth." This, again, is why I call this "lying for the truth." Please understand that in no way do I believe it is really the "truth" that religious propagandists have on their side, merely their position that they are fighting for a "higher truth" often inaccessible to the rest of us.

The Lie: The United States Was Founded as a Christian Nation

Who among us has not heard the assertion from religious leaders, right-wing pundits, and politicians out there that America was, indeed, founded as a Christian nation? It is often stated as a simple fact that the United States not only *is* a Christian nation, it always has been—just as the Founding Fathers intended. There is a problem with this assertion, however. It simply isn't true. John Meacham writes in *American Gospel*, "The right's contention that we are a 'Christian nation' that has fallen from pure origins and can achieve redemption by some kind of return to Christian values is based on wishful thinking, not convincing historical argument" (Meacham 2006). The weight of historical consensus is overwhelmingly in support of Meacham's assertion. There truly is no honest way to interpret the evidence and arrive at the conclusion that the United States was founded as anything but a secular nation.

Contrary to the attempts at revisionist history, often by non-historians, the historical record actually speaks quite clearly for itself. One such revisionist pseudo-historian who attempted just such a rewrite is David Barton. I mention David Barton here because he is a textbook example of what is wrong with the special status we give religion in America (as well as a great example of "lying for the truth"). Barton is not a historian or constitutional scholar yet is often used as an authority by Christians who wish to argue that America was, indeed, founded as a Christian nation—again, just as the Founding Fathers intended. To be fair, I am also not a historian or constitutional scholar, but I offer two caveats here. First, if people pointed to me as an expert on either history or constitutional scholarship, I would be the first to set the record straight and recommend an actual expert. Second, I have the advantage of actually having the weight of evidence on my side and gladly hold my ideas up to the light of scrutiny.

Barton's position is worse than simply wrong because it is very easy to check his "facts" and find out they are simply not accurate. Legitimate historians have roundly debunked Barton. According to the *New York Times*, "Many professional historians dismiss Mr. Barton, whose academic degree is in Christian education from Oral Roberts University, as a biased amateur who cherry-picks quotes from history and the Bible" (Eckholm 2011).

The way that religion is insulated against honest criticism in our nation allows unscrupulous people like Barton to get away with intellectual dishonesty in a way that legitimate academics cannot. Because of this, it took a while for David Barton to be revealed as less than honest in his reporting of history. The Christian publisher Thomas Nelson has discontinued his bestselling book *The Jefferson Lies: Exposing the Myths You've Always Believed about Thomas Jefferson.* When Thomas Nelson did finally look into criticisms that this book might be less than honest, they agreed and issued the admission that "our conclusion was that the criticisms were correct. There were historical details—matters of fact, not matters of opinion, that were not supported at all" (Hu 2012).

In a book titled *The Jefferson Lies*, it is fascinating that even a Christian publisher would pull it from the shelves because "basic truths just were not there." Just as an interesting additional aside, Glenn Beck—poetic justice at its best—wrote the foreword for the book. How can it be seen as anything but blatant dishonesty when someone like Barton puts into writing such easily verifiable falsehoods?

America was not only the first constitutionally secular nation; it is a secular nation specifically because *that* is what the Founding Fathers intended. While it might be accurate to say that America is a nation largely made up of Christians, it is simply not accurate to say America is a Christian nation. To assert that America is a Christian nation because a majority of Americans are Christians is no different than to say that America is a Caucasian nation because a majority of Americans are white. According to the American Religious Identification Survey (ARIS), approximately 24 percent of Americans are non-Christian. Compare that with the percentage of our population that is between zero and fourteen years old (20 percent), Hispanic or Latino (16 percent), black (13 percent), sixty-five years or older (12 percent), and Asian (5 percent). When it comes to deciding if America is a Christian (or Caucasian or other label) nation, there is no such thing as majority rule.

I will focus here on just a few of the most salient problems with the assertion that America is a Christian nation and that the Founding Fathers intended that it be so. Specifically, our foundational documents may have been the most secular in world history. Many of the Founding Fathers were not Christians. Even if it were the case that our Founding Fathers intended the United States to be a Christian nation (and they didn't), it is wrong to assume we should *always* emulate the Founding Fathers' example. And separation of church and state protects Christians just as much as other religious people (and nonbelievers) and has been embraced by many Christians for much of American history because of this fact.

Foundational Documents

This really is a pretty simple matter. Not only is God not mentioned even once in the entire Constitution of the United States,
it is clear that the power of government emanates from "We the
people," not an imperceptible otherworldly autocrat. I am often
reminded that the Declaration of Independence mentions that all
men "are endowed by their Creator with certain unalienable Rights."
It is interesting to understand that just before this proclamation, the
Declaration of Independence talks about "the separate and equal station to which the Laws of Nature and of Nature's God entitle them."
While mention is given to some vague notion of a "Creator" and of
"Nature's God," this does not narrow down in any way which god
might be referred to here or if it is not just some poetic reference to
something mysterious which we don't understand, much in the way
that the clearly atheist Stephen Hawking talks about understanding
the mind of God when talking about cosmology and physics or how
the equally nonreligious Albert Einstein said that "God does not play
dice with the world." Only the most incurious person would not
wonder why a group of Founding Fathers who wanted to create a
Christian nation would not have been a bit more specific and make
at least one single reference to Jesus Christ in our Constitution.

Since the US Constitution was first adopted in September
1787, it has been modified many times. In 1791 the first ten amendments, the Bill of Rights, were adopted. Conspicuous in the first
of these amendments was the establishment clause, "Congress shall
make no law respecting an establishment of religion," which not only
does not mention a specific god or Jesus, it makes the formal recognition of such as the official state religion illegal in the United States.
Prior to the inclusion of the Bill of Rights, a similar sentiment was
expressed in Article VI, paragraph 3 of the Constitution. This is the
"No Religious Test Clause" and states in part, "No religious test shall
ever be required as a qualification to any office or public trust under
the United States." Since 1791, there have been an additional seventeen amendments to our constitution, and in all that time and all
the myriad opportunities to do so, our leaders have never explicitly

sanctioned Christianity as the official religion of the United States. Again, from Meacham's *American Gospel*, "Despite generations of subsequent efforts to amend the Constitution to include Jesus or to declare that America is a 'Christian nation,' no president across three centuries has made an even remotely serious attempt to do so" (Meacham 2006).

It is interesting that the Treaty of Tripoli, which was ratified unanimously by the US Senate and signed by President Adams in 1797, actually states explicitly in Article 11, "As the Government of the United States of America is not, in any sense, founded on the Christian religion."

The Founding Fathers Were Not Necessarily Christian

One of the most perplexing issues for me as an unbeliever is the penchant of many Christians to take ownership of any believer in any god as somehow being a champion for their (Christian) position. This ignores the gaping chasm between being a Christian and being a believer in Islam, Judaism, or even a belief in God that is not theistic in nature. It is entirely likely that most of the Founding Fathers would have answered yes to a direct question, "Do you believe in God?" If, however, you look a little more honestly and asked them if they believe in the supernatural claims about Jesus in the Bible, many of them would tell a very different story than you might expect. The fact is that deism, a belief that evidence and reason may be sufficient for belief in a god but which rejects the revelation and supernatural claims of religions such as Christianity, was widespread among our Founding Fathers.

In fact, many of our Founding Fathers were openly hostile toward much of Christian dogma. Thomas Paine, who was a vocal and controversial deist, when professing his faith, wrote, "I believe in one God, and no more; and I hope for happiness beyond this life. I believe in the equality of man and I believe that religious duties consist in doing justice, loving mercy, and endeavoring to make our fellow-creatures happy" (Paine 1796). While not necessarily on speaking terms with atheism, deism is also a far cry from theism, represented here by Christianity. The same Thomas Paine said of Christianity: "As to the Christian system of faith, it appears to me as a species of Atheism—a sort of religious denial of God. It professes to believe in a man rather than in God. It is a compound made up Chiefly of Manism with but little Deism, and is as near to Atheism as twilight is to darkness. It introduces between man and his Maker an opaque body, which it calls a Redeemer, as the moon introduces her opaque self between the earth and the sun, and it produces by this means a religious, or an irreligious eclipse of light. It has put the whole orbit of reason into shade" (Paine, 1796).

Our deistic Founding Fathers often saw a stark contradiction between the doctrines of the Bible and human reason. To believe in the miracles of the Bible is to believe that an all-powerful god, omnipotent and perfect, would need to repeatedly suspend the laws of nature—the same laws he had put in effect—in order to provide course corrections for his wayward creation. All this may actually be true. I can't prove it to be false, but it is not a reasonable position to take and not one most of our Founding Fathers would accept. When writing about the faiths of our Founding Fathers, David Holmes observed, "For Deists, the principle revelation for Christianity—the Bible—bore every sign of human counterfeiting or alteration, they saw the magnificent design of nature as revealing a Creator, or what Thomas Jefferson termed 'a superintending power'" (Holmes 2006). Thomas Jefferson even went so far as to make his own version of the New Testament by omitting all the references to miracles and the divinity of Jesus Christ and called it "The Life and Morals of Jesus of Nazareth."

Of Jefferson, Jon Meacham wrote, "Intellectually daring, Jefferson had little time for the intricacies of creeds, talk of miracles, and the familiar tenets of the faith that grew out of the life and, for believers, resurrection of Jesus" (Meacham 2006). And later, "As a man of science he believed in the primacy of rational observation, dismissing much of the supernatural as superstition." Thomas Jefferson actually had positions on Christianity that today would virtually guarantee he could not possibly be elected president of the

United States. On the issue of the Holy Trinity, Jefferson observed in a letter to Francis Adrian Van der Kemp in 1816, "Ridicule is the only weapon which can be used against unintelligible propositions. Ideas must be distinct before reason can act upon them; and no man ever had a distinct idea of the trinity. It is the mere Abracadabra of the mountebanks calling themselves the priests of Jesus."

Jefferson was far from alone in his rejection of a strict Christian theology. According to Holmes, "If census takers trained in Christian theology had set up broad categories in 1790 labeled 'Atheism,' 'Deism and Unitarianism,' 'Orthodox Protestantism,' 'Orthodox Roman Catholicism.' And 'Other,' and if they had interviewed Franklin, Washington, Adams, Jefferson, Madison, and Monroe, they would have undoubtedly have placed every one of those six Founding Fathers in some way under the category of 'Deism and Unitarianism'" (Holmes 2006).

True, the Founding Fathers often used the term God, but this should not in any way be confused with adherence to the Christian religion. Many of them were, indeed, deeply convicted true believers in Jesus Christ, but many were not. To make reference to God can mean many things and should always be considered in context. A perfect example is the use of the word God on the Jefferson Memorial. A true believer might find Jefferson's quote reassuring, "I have sworn upon the altar of God eternal hostility against every from of tyranny over the mind of man." After all, Jefferson is swearing to oppose tyranny, and who could have a problem with that? In context, however, we see that the tyranny that Jefferson has sworn to oppose is actually the clergy who oppose him:

> The returning good sense of our country threatens abortion to their hopes, and they believe that any portion of power confided to me, will be exerted in opposition to their schemes. And they believe rightly; for I have sworn upon the altar of God, eternal hostility against every form of tyranny over the mind of man. But this is all they have to fear from me.

The Founding Fathers Were Often Great but Never Perfect Men

I frankly grow weary of all the right-wing political talk of the greatness of America being tied directly to us behaving today just as the Founding Fathers intended. There was greatness among the Founding Fathers to be sure. The wisdom exercised by the men who founded this nation, however, was human wisdom and subject to all the weaknesses inherent in that humanity. Every time I hear someone defer to the argument from authority and insist that we should be a Christian nation because that is what the Founding Fathers intended, I can't help but wonder if we should also own slaves, not allow women to vote, or revert to the situation at the time of such great men as George Washington when some residents of the United States did not count as fully one person.[35]

On the matter of extending the vote to more Americans, Founding Father John Adams wrote to James Sullivan on May 26, 1776, "Depend upon it, Sir, it is dangerous to open so fruitful a source of controversy and altercation as would be opened by attempting to alter the qualifications of voters; there will be no end to it. New claims will arise; women will demand the vote; lads from 12 to 21 will think their rights not enough attended to; and every man who has not a farthing, will demand an equal voice with any other, in all acts of state. It tends to confound and destroy all distinctions, and prostrate all ranks to one common level." Surely, we should shudder at the horror of having all humans treated as if they are at one common level!

If we rely on the example of the Founding Fathers, only white male land owners over twenty-one years of age would have the right

---

[35] Actually, women were allowed to vote in some states at some times prior to the ratification of the 19th Amendment in 1920, but this was definitely the exception and not the rule. As for the three-fifths rule, article 1, section 2 of the Constitution, while never actually using the word *slave*, does identify the worth of free persons for purposes of apportionment and "three-fifths of all other persons"—all other persons in this case being slaves or indentured servants. This was changed with the 14th Amendment.

to vote (unless they are a Catholic, Jew, or Quaker, then they still couldn't vote), slavery would be common, and our forty-fourth president and his family would not only most certainly *not* have been our first family, they may each only be counted as three-fifths of free human beings. There is much to value and respect in what our Founding Fathers achieved and passed down to us, but we should not blindly defer, uncritically, to what it seems the Founding Fathers may have intended. We have learned much in the intervening years since the founding of our nation, and that too should be valued.

Separation of Church and State Protects Us All, Not Just the Atheists

Former US senator from Pennsylvania Rick Santorum while on the campaign trail for the Republican nomination for president stated, "I don't believe in an America where the separation of church and state are absolute," in an interview with George Stephanopoulos. "The idea that the church can have no influence or no involvement in the operation of the state is absolutely antithetical to the objectives and vision of our country... to say that people of faith have no role in the public square? You bet that makes me want to throw up."

Fortunately for us all, Santorum's understanding of American history or the nature of church-state separation is apparently no more accurate than that of the previously mentioned David Barton. The separation of church and state is, indeed, absolute, just as the Founding Fathers intended (and yes, if we determined they were wrong in this, we should change it, but they were not). It would be truly fascinating to see if Santorum, a Catholic, would state his case in this way if the separation of church and state were not actually an ingrained feature of our national identity. This separation was not, for the record, instituted to protect atheists but all of us. Thomas Jefferson used the term separation of church and state in a letter to the Danbury Connecticut Baptists in 1802 to assure them that their religious liberties would be protected against what was perceived as a threat of religious oppression from the Congregationalists of Danbury Connecticut:

> Believing with you that religion is a matter which lies solely between man and his God, that he owes account to none other for his faith or his worship, that the legislative powers of government reach actions only, and not opinions, I contemplate with sovereign reverence that act of the whole American people which declared that their legislature should "make no law respecting an establishment of religion, or prohibiting the free exercise thereof," thus building a wall of separation between church and State.

It is interesting to consider that not only was it one of our greatest Founding Fathers who is credited with the term "separation of church and state," he was actually closely mirroring a statement of Roger Williams, the founder of the first Baptist Church in America who, in 1644, talked about a "hedge or wall of separation between the gardens of the church and the wilderness of the world."

I can't help but wonder how eager political leaders like Rick Santorum would be to argue against this separation if Christianity were not such an overwhelming majority in the United States. If one counts Catholicism separate from Protestantism, as some do, then Islam is already the largest religion in the world (Rizzo 2008). What if this were the case for the United States? It is a near certainty that all the Christians who are speaking out against the separation of church and state would then find it a wonderful idea, lest the Muslim majority seek to impose sharia on our land.

The Lie: America Is in Crisis Because We Fell Away from Our Christian Foundations

Okay, this one will be short. It is quite simply an imaginary problem based upon a false premise, the falseness of the premise having been just demonstrated.

I hope that I have sufficiently validated that much of what we are often told about our Christian heritage is either untrue, out of context, or at the very least greatly exaggerated. America's deep religiosity is something that came long after our nation's founding. America was never founded as a Christian nation, but to the contrary, the unique, even unprecedented greatness of America was allowed to flourish largely because it was the first explicitly secular nation in history. Not only are we not in peril because we have fallen from our Christian roots, we have in reality fallen from our secular roots by adding such things as "under God" to the pledge and "in God we trust" to our money, both addressed in the next lie. This is the false premise upon which the imaginary problem is based.

The imaginary problem is that America is in some sort of unprecedented crisis. Could the economy be better? Sure. Would I personally be happier if my house were worth more or if more of my income were free to spend on scuba diving and paragliding in Bali rather than paying for groceries, health insurance and taxes? Of course. Make no mistake, however, we live in a time and place (as a species, not just here in America) in which our quality of life is unprecedentedly good. Forget all that talk from a select few fear mongers who say we are living in a society beset with sin and debauchery. If you remove the fact that we are more tolerant of gays, which is not really a moral issue anyway (being gay is not immoral, I mean; intolerance of gays is), our morality is far more sublime than at any point in our history. More people have the right to vote, speak freely, and live free from fear of violent death, starvation, or predation than at any time in human history. Quite simply, we are more moral, happy, and healthy that ever before. Period. QED.

The Half-Truth: Atheists Want to Take "Under God" from the Pledge (Where It Has Always Been)

I have often been asked if I want to take "under God" from the Pledge of Allegiance. For the uninitiated, questions like this are often far more than simple questions. They are often accusations. "You want to take 'under God' from the pledge?" carries with it quite a bit of additional baggage. You must somehow be un-American, a communist, lacking in any sense of patriotism to want to alter the pledge like that! After all, it's always been there. Right? Wrong.

There are two compelling reasons to remove the reference to God from the pledge, and only one of those reasons stem from my lack of belief in God. As an atheist, I don't feel that we should all make reference to a god we may not believe in just to show allegiance to our secular nation. As a fan of honest history, I want the God reference taken out of the pledge because of when and why it was inserted in the first place.

I certainly do not expect believers in a god or gods to make proclamations of unbelief just to please me. I also would never expect a member of one religious group to make proclamations of belief in the gods of religions other than their own. Why then should all Americans be required to recite "under God" in a pledge, especially after the words "one nation" and before "indivisible" when not all of us believe in a god and many others either don't believe in that particular god or at least don't see that god in the same way as those who pushed for insertion of "under God" in the first place. We are supposed to be one nation, indivisible, but have inserted one of the most divisive of all ideas right in the middle of the text.

Francis Bellamy wrote the original Pledge of Allegiance in 1892, and it did not contain any reference to God. When Congress adopted the pledge in 1942, the reference to God was still conspicuously absent (conspicuous in retrospect only, as no one seemed to miss it at the time). It was not until pressure from groups such as the Knights of Columbus (who began using "under God" in their recitations of the pledge in 1951) and others and several failed attempts that Congress passed and President Eisenhower signed into law the new version of the pledge in 1954.

While those who supported the altered version of the pledge were likely sincere religious believers, it is important to understand that factors other than religious piety really drove this decision. The addition of "under God" (just as the addition of "In God We Trust" to paper currency in 1957) was driven largely by the Cold War, anti-Communist fervor of the time. This change to the pledge was meant to draw more starkly a distinction between the patriotic (and God-fearing) Americans from those godless Communists in the Soviet Union.

Just an interesting side note here. In addition to penning the original pledge, Bellamy also commended a way of saluting during the pledge that is sometimes called the Bellamy salute. It has fallen out of favor as it looks remarkably like the Nazi salute.

The Lie: Even if God Is Not Real, Religion Is Still Good for Society

> Religion. It's given people hope in a world torn apart by religion.
>
> — Jon Stewart

> The so-called Christian nations are the most enlightened and progressive... but in spite of their religion, not because of it. The Church has opposed every innovation and discovery from the day of Galileo down to our own time, when the use of anesthetic in childbirth was regarded as a sin because it avoided the biblical curse pronounced against Eve. And every step in astronomy and geology ever taken has been opposed by bigotry and superstition. The Greeks surpassed us in artistic culture and in architecture five hundred years before Christian religion was born.
>
> —Mark Twain

Arguments for the importance of religion often go beyond belief in the Bible or the previously covered apologetic arguments for the existence of God. One argument is that religion is important even if God isn't real because of its positive effects on society and human well-being. When looking at data that demonstrates empirical measures of societal health, well-being, and happiness, however, there is often an inverse relationship with religiosity in given populations. It seems that often those societies that are most religious are also the least happy and healthy. Conversely, those societies which are the most happy and healthy are often the least religious. This is troubling when organizations such as the Family Research Council (discussed in chapter 3) has a stated position that "believing that God is the author of life, liberty and the family, FRC promotes the Judeo-Christian worldview as the basis for a just, free and stable society" (Paul 2007).

If there is a link between a nation's level of religiosity and its level of happiness, it is clearly not a consistently positive relationship. In multiple comparisons of religiosity and indicators of well-being, there seems to be a relationship in which as religiosity goes down, so do many negative indicators of societal well-being. Appendix C offers a series of tables that graphically depict the results of these comparisons. To illustrate these trends, I have plotted the data on a series of tables to provide the picture worth a thousand words. The results are quite interesting. I concede at the outset that not everyone will agree with my choice of criteria of human well-being necessarily. I don't even agree that some of these criteria are the best indicators of well-being, though some clearly are, but I chose these for a reason. As I am talking to a largely Christian audience, I include issues such as abortion because this is so widely seen as a moral issue and one of human well-being.

For example, when the United States is compared with other advanced nations, a measure of "religiosity" was taken from Gallup polling data designed to determine how respondents expressed their feeling that "religion is very important to my daily life." HIV and homicide rates were then taken from the United Nations Development Program's Human Development Index (http://hdr.undp.org/en/statistics/). Among nations such as Japan, Austria, Denmark, France, Switzerland, Norway, and Sweden, the United States is the most religious nation at 65 percent yet has the highest HIV infection rate and homicide rate of the nations considered. The least religious nation was Sweden (17 percent), which had one-third the HIV rate and less than 43 percent the homicide rate of the much more religious United States (table 1, appendix C). Let me make it abundantly clear that I am not making any judgment with respect to HIV infection rates in terms of morality. This disease is traumatic enough without the added stigma that often attends it. My only point being that HIV infection is clearly not good for the individual or society, and it is often more prevalent in the more religious societies, less prevalent in the less religious societies. If the theistic party line were valid, then one would expect God to ensure this is not the case.

It is even possible to look at areas of society where it would simply defy common sense to not expect a positive relationship between religion and societal benefits, and even here, the results can be surprising. Abortion rates are a prime example where we would expect fewer abortions in societies with higher religiosity. This is a divisive issue in the United States and is one in which a clear position is professed by those who are religious, and a much clearer delineation than with most other issues. However, when looking at a sample group of nations, there is no evidence that religiosity results in lower rates of abortion. Again, the US is the most religious nation considered yet has the highest rate of abortion in the comparison with 22.6 percent of pregnancies aborted. Denmark by comparison had a religiosity rate of 18 percent and an abortion rate of 19.1 percent (table 2, appendix C).

An important area for consideration with respect to well-being and societal health is happiness of the members of that society. According to Adrian White:

> The search for happiness is not new and neither is academic interest in the topic. In 1776 the American Declaration of Independence argued for 'certain inalienable Rights, that among these

are Life, Liberty and the Pursuit of Happiness'.
As such, nations have been formed on the basis of
the search for happiness, and this desire has been
put on a par with the right to life and the right
to freedom. (White, "Psychologist Produces the
First-Ever 'World Map of Happiness,'" 2006).

Adriane White used a number of factors, including life satisfaction, life expectancy, and ecological footprint to develop a scale
that measures overall satisfaction with life scale, or SWLS. White's
"World Map of Happiness," when compared to rates of religiosity,
shows that belief in God does not seem to translate into an increase
in happiness (table 3, appendix C). According to White, the happiest ten nations are, in descending order starting with happiest,
Denmark, Switzerland, Austria, Iceland, the Bahamas, Finland,
Sweden, Bhutan, Brunei, and Canada. When you overlay this with
the findings of Phil Zuckerman, in his book on contemporary rates
and patterns of atheism (Zuckerman 2005), you see that among
these ten happiest nations only the Bahamas, Bhutan, and Brunei
rank in the top fifty most religious nations on earth. But Bhutan is a
predominantly Buddhist nation, with no inherent belief in a superintending deity, and Brunei is officially Islamic and is a clear outlier
in this group.

Guy P. Harrison specifically looked at the work of White and
Zuckerman and pointed out, "Believers might be surprised to learn
that the three countries occupying the bottom of White's happiness
ranking are highly religious societies with virtually no atheists. They
are Democratic Republic of the Congo (ranked 176 in happiness),
Zimbabwe (177), and Burundi (178)" (Harrison, *50 Reasons People
Give for Believing in a God*, 2008). All three of these *very unhappy*
nations are highly religious. Is there reason to believe that they rank
so low on White's list simply because they are religious? The answer
is probably very complex and involves a host of considerations that
may or may not actually be directly related to religion. But remember, the question being asked is not specifically, "Does religion make

us unhappy?" but rather, "Is there reason to believe religion is good for society?"

Like religion itself, happiness is hard to quantify and to compare between groups. White's work in this area, while not perfect nor an exact science, does provide important data and measures that are very relevant to understanding the issue of religion and well-being. About White's contribution, Science Daily reported, "It can be argued that whilst these measures are not perfect, they are the best we have so far, and these are the measures that politicians are talking of using to measure the relative performance of each country" (Science Daily 2006).

When making these points, I have sometimes been accused of using an "apples and oranges" comparison. The argument is that the United States can't be compared fairly to nations like Denmark and Sweden because there are unique demographic and socioeconomic issues in the United States that do not apply in the other nations considered. To address this charge, I also looked at comparisons within the various states in my own country.

For indicators of well-being and religiosity within the US, Gallup data for religiosity was contrasted with six sub-indices of life evaluation, healthy behaviors, work environment, physical health, emotional health, and access to basic necessities, which taken together comprise a well-being index ranking.

When the ten most and ten least religious states are compared with the well-being index scores of those same states, clear trend lines again emerge. Just as was the case when comparing the United States against less-religions nations, the results show an inverse relationship between religiosity and well-being. The most religious state, determined by a poll that asked, "Is religion an important part of your daily life?" was Mississippi, which also had the lowest well-being index of all fifty states. Vermont, the least religious state, had the highest well-being index in the United States. The rest of the nation fell along trend lines along a commensurate continuum (expected based on these two examples) (table 4, appendix C).

While none of this proves conclusively that religious devotion results directly in increased societal ills, it does offer interesting and relevant evidence for consideration with respect to the importance we place on religious matters. This challenges the claim that societal well-being results from, or is dependent upon religious belief or practice. In fact, the opposite often seems to be the case. In multiple measures of human well-being, societal health, and even in indicators of "morality," the healthiest societies are most often those with the lowest rates of religiosity and the least healthy are most often those that are most religious. What is most likely at play here is that both well-being and lower rates of religiosity in most societies result from basic needs being met and a resulting sense of safety. Conversely, societal dis-ease may often result in manifestations of lower well-being and higher religiosity. Looking at the data in this way calls into question not only the claim that religious belief is good for society but also (again) that religion has any claim to moral authority.

The Lie: Evolution Is Only a Theory and Creation Science Should Be Given Equal Time (We Should Teach the Controversy)

Religious believers often argue that the moral and ethical foundation of a healthy society rests upon the belief in a higher power, a creator god. Unfortunately, a large number of religious adherents find belief in this higher power irreconcilable with the fact that we evolved from other life forms. For some, belief in both God and evolution is not only irreconcilable, it is considered immoral. The result is a denial, in spite of all evidence, in the validity of evolutionary theory.

This reluctance to accept evolution might only be an interesting observation if it were just a personal belief on the part of evolution deniers, but it is not just a personal belief. It influences legislation, education, and many other aspects of our daily lives, both public and private, for believers and unbelievers alike. All too often, very influential people, for purely religious reasons, either want to minimize the standing of evolution in our school curricula or argue for the biblical creation myth being given equal time. As explicit teaching

of creationism in public school science classes has been ruled uncon-
stitutional time and again, biblical literalists continually repackage
Christian creationism and rerelease it under titles like creation science or intelligent design while simultaneously trying every conceivable means to undermine the only valid scientific explanation for the
complexity of life on earth, namely evolution.

Numerous political leaders have weighed in on this issue, often
to the detriment of our educational system. Former House majority leader Tom DeLay commented that horrendous crimes like the
Columbine school shootings might be the result of teaching our
school children "that they are nothing but glorified apes who have
evolutionized [*sic*] out of some primordial soup of mud" (Paul 2007).
This is a refutation of evolution based upon religious or misguided
moral objections and an implicit assertion that creation should be
taught in place of evolution at worst or alongside evolution at best.
And lest we think this is a position unique to conservatives, there
is no shortage of liberal politicians who publicly espouse this same
sentiment. Former vice president and past presidential candidate Al
Gore lent his voice to teaching creationism alongside evolution, and
his running mate Joe Leiberman stated that belief in God was essential to "secure the moral future of our nation, and raise the quality of
life for all our people" (Paul 2007).

While Leiberman's quote does not directly address the teaching
of either evolution or creationism, it does assert that the moral future
and quality of life for Americans is dependent upon a belief in God.
This lends credence to the notion that teaching of evolution (if that
leads us from a belief in God, and it often does) might be a bad thing.
This is problematic as it is a baseless assertion that our quality of life
is enhanced by belief in God. Not only is there is no evidence at all
that morality and quality of life are enhanced by belief in God, as was
demonstrated earlier in this chapter as well as chapters 3 and 4, the
opposite may well be the case.

This sentiment is not limited to our politicians. Religious influence has long retarded science education in the United States. From
Jerry Coyne's *Why Evolution Is True*, "In the famous 'Monkey Trial'
of 1925, high school teacher John Scopes went on trial in Dayton,

Tennessee—and was convicted—for violating Tennessee's Butler Act. Tellingly, this law didn't proscribe the teaching of evolution in general, but only the idea that humans had evolved" (Coyne 2009). The desire by some to introduce creationism into public school science class curricula has more recently taken a turn that is either creative or sinister depending on your perspective. After creation science was ruled to represent a particular religion's view in the case of *Edwards v. Aguillard* in 1987, the term "intelligent design," or ID, started to take its place. The ruling in the previously mentioned *Tammy Kitzmiller, et al. v. Dover Area School District, et al.* case found that ID is clearly nothing more than repackaged creationism and as such is a religious position, not science and not appropriate for inclusion into the science curriculum in public schools. In both cases, of creation science and intelligent design, there was an intentional desire to have biblical creationism surreptitiously smuggled into our schools by misrepresenting it as science and by dishonestly pretending it is not religiously motivated.

In the Kitzmiller case, the idea that intelligent design is a viable scientific alternative theory to Darwin's idea of evolution through natural selection was decided in federal court. This case, covered in the Nova program *Judgment Day: Intelligent Design on Trial* (2007) covered many of the issues in the ongoing debate between the intelligent design movement and science education. Fortunately "intelligent design" was revealed for what it really is, a poorly veiled attempt to illegally introduce creationism into the science class.

There were very influential proponents of ID weighing in on the case, and they are still very active. The Thomas Moore Law Center, which calls itself "the sword and shield for people of faith," has been a driving force behind the ID movement from the beginning. Senator Rick Santorum was once on the board of governors of the Thomas Moore Law Center and was a leading proponent of ID and was responsible for getting it into the Santorum Amendment (no child left behind). The Discovery Institute, also active on behalf of ID in the Dover case, is still pursuing the teaching of ID in public schools through the use of such tactics as falsely portraying evolution as "a theory in crisis" and creating a fake controversy over the validity of evolution.

This was not just a local small-town issue. Had Judge John E. Jones III not ruled against the teaching of intelligent design in this case, it might have opened the door to the teaching of the biblical creation myth as an "alternative theory" to evolution in science classrooms across the country. This was already happening when the decidedly unscientific idea of creationism, in the guise of intelligent design, was being taught in a public school science class until a federal court stopped it. It is important to remember the primary motivation for introducing intelligent design was not the weight of scientific evidence but religiously motivated beliefs. This is fine in church but not in public school science class.

The fact that the Dover case was decided in favor of legitimate science is not as reassuring as it might seem on the surface. Those who were on the side of the Dover Area School District are still fighting to get creation science taught in biology classrooms. About the presiding judge, John Jones, Jerry Coyne noted he was "a devoted churchgoer and a conservative Republican—not exactly pro-Darwinian credentials. Everyone held their breath and waited nervously" (Coyne, *Why Evolution Is True*, 2009). Even though the science is clear, the outcome of the case was not necessarily assured. Judge Jones was appointed by President Bush and recommended for the appointment by then Pennsylvania Senator Rick Santorum. Both Bush and Santorum supported the teaching of intelligent design alongside evolution, Santorum saying that intelligent design is a "legitimate scientific theory that should be taught in science classes" (Easton 2005). For Santorum to state that intelligent design is a legitimate scientific theory requires a tremendously deep level of willful ignorance, or of dishonesty—or both.

In our increasingly competitive global society, the ability of the United States to continue its lead in science and technology depends on solid science education and a broad societal understanding of the scientific method. It is a bit unsettling then to realize that the United States ranks near the bottom in a survey of nations that asked about belief in Darwin's theory of evolution through natural selection. A theory, by the way, that is among the most widely accepted in all of science, by scientists, and has been corroborated by fields of science such as genetics that did not even exist during Darwin's lifetime.

The geneticist and evolutionary biologist Theodosius Dobzhansky observed, "Nothing in biology makes sense except in the light of evolution," and Dobzhansky is far from alone in this position. In *The Language of God*, the deeply religious Francis Collins wrote, "Virtually all working biologists agree that Darwin's framework of variation and natural selection is unquestionably correct." Collins even goes on to one-up Dobzhansky's above assertion by stating, "Truly it can be said that not only biology but medicine would be impossible to understand without the theory of evolution."

Collins expresses a sense of dismay at many in the religious community who refuse to accept Darwin's ideas, saying that "believers would be well advised to look carefully, at the overwhelming weight of the scientific data supporting this view of the relatedness of all living things, including ourselves. Given the strength of the evidence, it is perplexing that so little progress in public acceptance has occurred in the United States." While I respect Dr. Collins's work as a scientist and he truly does seem to be a very kind and decent person, I am obligated to point out that while he does support evolutionary theory, he is also very religious. He is, in fact, one of the few notable scientifically literate Christians who also vocally support evolution over creation. I offer this caveat because it is clear that the only real impediment to near-universal acceptance of evolution is religious belief. There simply is no other reason to deny evolution. Certainly, there is no evidence at all against evolution and an unbelievable amount of evidence in favor of it. In fact, in every single instance where there is evidence worthy of consideration on this matter, it comes down in favor of evolution. Collins is one of the relatively few religious scientists, and fortunately, he does not let his religion cloud his judgment on evolution.

The blinders of religion is the only thing that I know of that can allow otherwise intelligent and rational people to arrive at the irrational conclusion that evolution is not true or at the dishonest position that scientific evidence is inconclusive on the matter. This situation would be bad enough if all that matters was the intrinsic value of truth and there were no repercussions of belief other than a personal feeling. This is not the case, however. Collins tells a story about presenting the evidence for evolution at a national gathering of Christian physicians. At what had been a warm environment of open sharing of ideas, things changed when he dared to talk about evolution. When he talked of the evidence for evolution and his view that it was perhaps "God's elegant plan for creating humankind," the warmth and literally some of the participants left the room. That a group of intelligent, educated people would literally leave the room because well-established and consistently verified scientific facts offend their religious sensibilities speaks volumes about the challenge faced by rational thinkers in our society.

While I attempt to be polite in most of my comments about friends of religion with whom I disagree on a great many issues, for the evolution denier, I am unable to express honestly how I feel about their beliefs without being sometimes offensive, unintentionally as it may be. To deny evolution requires that you either be willfully ignorant, breathtakingly unintelligent, or intellectually dishonest, at least on this one issue. If, for example, you claim that no transitional fossils exist, this is an uninformed lie of almost unimaginable stupidity. (Did you see what I did there? Yes, I captured all three of the categories.) To either accept evolution or reject it is not simply a matter of differing opinions, each of equal merit and equally deserving of respect. To reject evolution, especially when evolution deniers so often fight the teaching of evolution in public schools, is to deny a central pillar of our understanding of biology and medicine. To deny evolution could literally cost lives. A great many advances in modern medicine rely on an understanding of evolution.

Evolution is true and scientific on every characteristic one can look to in order to judge something as "scientific." Evolution is falsifiable; it makes testable predictions, and it has explanatory power about what it describes, specifically the diversity of life. While evolution is not refuted by a single scientific discipline, it is corroborated by scientific disciplines such as bacteriology, biology, botany, genetics, medicine, paleontology, pathology, physiology, zoology, and others. All offer mutually supporting evidence for the fact of evolution, and not a single one offers evidence against. Again, from *Why Evolution Is True* by Jerry Coyne: "We've looked at evidence from many areas—the fossil record, biogeography, embryology, vestigial structures, suboptimal design, and so on—all of that evidence showing, without a scintilla of doubt, that organisms have evolved" (Coyne, *Why Evolution Is True*, 2009). On the other side of the argument, we have the creation myth of the Bible, a religious view without a bit of scientific corroboration, that is directly contradicted by almost every field of science that offers a position on the matter.

The Lie: Hitler Was a Result of Darwin's Ideas

One of the greatest victims of liars for truth is the memory of Charles Darwin and his great contribution to our understanding of the interconnectedness of all life on Earth—what some people consider the greatest idea anyone ever had (Dennett D. C., Darwin's Dangerous Idea, 1995), the theory of evolution. Evolution is certainly one of the great intellectual accomplishments of our species and one of the most robustly supported, reliable theories in all of science. Yet in a series of egregious insults to human intellect, there are many who, for religious reasons alone, attack not only Darwin's theory but the man himself with allegations of racism and charges that his theory is responsible for such atrocities as the Nazi holocaust. This should be a red flag for the reader. It is a hyperbolic "Hail Mary" argument often offered by those who actually have no argument.

As it turns out, this attempted defamation holds up to scrutiny no better than most other religious claims. A familiar pattern emerges when we unpack the charges against Darwin. We see a known cast of characters and organizations using the tried and true tactics of ad hominem attacks, quote mining, selective reporting, and intellectual dishonesty. A textbook example of this is seen in the book *From Darwin to Hitler: Evolutionary Ethics, Eugenics, and Racism in Germany*. In this book, Richard Weikart (a senior fellow at the Discovery Institute) attempts to argue that without Charles

Darwin's ideas, the Holocaust would likely have not occurred and even blamed Darwinism for "turning morality on its head" (Weikart, 2004, p. 233).

This is not only widely panned by most historians; it displays a disregard for the nature of science with respect to morality—namely that science is morally neutral and focuses on what *is*, not what *should be* or what we might want. Science seeks the truth, not what is moral or immoral. Scientists may be morally upstanding, and most are, but Darwin's theory itself takes no position with respect to morality. It only describes a very specific subset of what happens in nature.

Very tenuous connections are drawn between evolutionary theory, as introduced by Charles Darwin, and a straw man mischaracterization that Weikart and some others term Darwinism. While occasional concessions are made that this Darwinism may not perfectly align with what Darwin actually proposed, the intent is to link Darwin's theory of evolution to the Nazi atrocities. The motivation for this is clear. It is part of a broader campaign designed to discredit evolution by any and all means. The hope then is that if evolution can't be discredited, then creationism may be seen as an alternative theory and introduced into the American public school system. This is a central goal of the Discovery Institute, which is why Weikart's affiliation with this group is relevant enough to point and reinforce.

While I do disagree strongly with his conclusions, I do wish to thank Dr. Weikart for taking the time to correspond on his views. Just as when I had a similar difference of opinion with Dr. Gary Habermas from Liberty University, Dr. Weikart seems a kind and decent man—both men I could easily call friends if given the chance to know them better, no matter how vociferously we may disagree on certain issues. While I have not altered my position with respect to Dr. Weikart or his book, his candor in corresponding with me on these points did cause me to temper the way I articulated that disagreement here. I will revisit this point in my conclusion of this book.

Another Christian apologist and creationist, Ray Comfort, went so far as to pay for the production of a "special edition" of Darwin's *Origin of Species* with a fifty-four-page introduction written by Comfort that attempts (very badly) to refute evolution. In this deceptively packaged edition of Darwin's book as well as in many other public pronouncements, Comfort claims it is *sheer chance* that drives evolution. This is not true and is not claimed to be true either in Darwin's writings or in subsequent refinements of his theory. Evolution is a process guided by natural selection. Factors such as random mutation, genetic drift, sexual selection, migration, and geographic isolation all contribute to evolution. It is far from sheer chance.

In his misleading introduction to this copy of Darwin's book, Ray Comfort alleges there are no transitional fossils (there are many), attempts to link Hitler to Darwin (there is no link), and even indicates that you can't be a good Christian if you accept evolution (in spite of the fact that many Christians accept evolution). Fortunately, the good folks at the National Center for Science Education offers a blow-by-blow refutation of Comforts attempted assassination of the truth that can be viewed at http://www.dontdissdarwin.com/analysis.php should you care to investigate this further.

As for Comfort's claim that there are no transitional fossils, it is hard to understand how he can make such a statement in the face of such overwhelming evidence to the contrary. I have beaten the transitional fossil dead horse thoroughly and repeatedly already. All I will add at this point is that not only are there a great many transitional fossils, but some are so clearly "transitional" that they are hard to classify because they are so close to either its ancestor or descendant species. If you only consider the line to modern humans from when we broke with our common ancestor with chimpanzees, there are a number of very clearly transitional species for which we have very good fossil remains. Consider just a few: *Ardipithecus ramidus* (4.4 million years ago), *Australopithecus afarensis* (3.6 million years ago); *Australopithecus africanus* (3 million years ago), *Homo habilis* (2 million years ago), *Homo erectus* (1 million years ago), *Homo heidelbergensis* (500,000 years ago). Keep in mind that the examples of transitional fossils given here are only for the lineage of one species (us), and we are a latecomer. These examples only go back 4.4 million years. Life has been evolving on earth for about 3.6 billion years.

Comfort displays an appalling and dishonest view of what a transitional fossil actually is, saying we should expect to find a "half-monkey, half-man" if humans and chimps have a common ancestor. This is simply not how evolution works, and Comfort has been told this on many occasions. These are not simple honest mistakes or differences of opinion. These are truth claims about easily verifiable empirical facts. This is not like a skeptic having a difference of opinion with a believer on exegetical interpretation; it is like a skeptic claiming all extant copies of the Bible are only written in Mandarin Chinese. I am free to believe that (or claim to believe it) if I wish, but I should never expect to be taken seriously with such beliefs.

Contrary to another claim made by Comfort, the DNA evidence is among the most compelling evidence for evolution. DNA evidence not only strongly supports evolution, it confirms interesting facts about evolution. For example, DNA analysis shows that humans and chimpanzees diverged from a common ancestor somewhere around 7 million years ago (Smithsonian National Museum of Natural History). Not only does DNA support evolution, it is amazing that Darwin made his great discovery without the benefit of DNA evidence. Surely, if Darwin's theory were false, the discovery of DNA evidence would not have so clearly and convincingly supported it.

Comfort used other less-than-honest tactics in the publication of this "special edition." Apparently, there were a couple of editions of this book published. In one, Comfort saw fit to just delete a number of chapters. According to Eugenie Scott, director for the National Center for Science Education, "Two of the omitted chapters, Chapters 11 and 12, showcase biogeography, some of Darwin's strongest evidence for evolution. Which is a better explanation for the distribution of plants and animals around the planet: common ancestry or special creation? Which better explains why island species are more similar to species on the mainland closest to them, rather than to more distant species that share a similar environment? The answer clearly is common ancestry" (Gilgoff, "How Creationist 'Origin' Distorts Darwin," 2009).

In another printing, Comfort event went so far as to manipulate font size, apparently in an attempt to influence which parts of this special edition gets read, the intro or the book itself. According to Chris Mooney, "Comfort's introduction is in big font and nicely spaced. You can breeze through those fifty pages, almost like reading *Harry Potter*. By contrast, Darwin's text at the back is in tiny, cramped font, a real trial to get through. Gee, what part of the book do you think students are intended to read?" (Mooney, 2009).

Christians are not alone in these unjust attacks on the reputation of Charles Darwin. Another writer often-quick to blame racism on Darwin is Adnan Oktar, who writes books under the name Harun Yahya (which is how I will refer to him here as it is how he is best known). Yahya, an Islamic creationist and longtime propagandist against Darwin, alleges not only that Darwin was a racist, but the end result of Darwin's ideas was the rise of racism in the twentieth century and ultimately the carnage of twentieth-century warfare. In an article titled "Darwin's Racism" (Yahya 2003), Yahya explicitly states, "Darwin's theory's denying the existence of God had been the cause of peoples' not seeing that man was something created by God and that all men were created equal. This was one of the factors behind the rise of racism, the acceleration of its acceptance in the world and the 20th century saw massacres carried out for reasons of racism...!" Again, the detractors of Charles Darwin seem to focus only on their desired end state without concern for the truth. While one may believe (and some have claimed) that the fact of evolution may make it possible to not believe in a god, there are absolutely no God claims inherent in Darwin's theory.

The simple fact is that Darwin did more than perhaps any human being in the history of our species to add to the sum of our understanding of ourselves, where we came from and how. Have some used his explanations of human origins as excuses to harm others? Maybe. Maybe not. But there is nothing inherent in Darwin's ideas that naturally lead to a Hitler; and Hitler himself, while often invoking the Christian god, never cited Darwin as his motivation or inspiration.

It is interesting to note that while Hitler never mentioned Darwin as his motivation, he did very frequently refer to his Lord and Savior, Almighty Creator, and other specifically religious allusions. It is also worth noting that while Weikart, Comfort, and other Christians try mightily to show that Darwin's ideas resulted in the Nazi atrocities, they seemed unwilling to give equal time to the possibility that anti-Semitism of the sort championed by such church leaders as Martin Luther might have much more to do with Hitler's motivations. A simple reading of the commendations made by Luther in "On the Jews and Their Lies" might cause one to wonder if the Nazis had pulled liberally from this source for their final solution playbook.

Among the "advice" offered by Martin Luther to address the Jewish problem are such actions as:

1. to set fire to their synagogues or schools and to bury and cover with dirt whatever will not burn
2. that their houses also be razed and destroyed
3. that all their prayer books and Talmudic writings, in which such idolatry, lies, cursing, and blasphemy are taught, be taken from them
4. that their rabbis be forbidden to teach henceforth on pain of loss of life and limb
5. that safe conduct on the highways be abolished completely for the Jews
6. that usury be prohibited to them and that all cash and treasure of silver and gold be taken from them, that they be forbidden to utter the name of God without our hearing
7. putting a flail, an ax, a hoe, a spade, a distaff, or a spindle into the hands of young, strong Jews and Jewesses and letting then earn their bread in the sweat of their brow, as was imposed on the children of Adam (Luther 2014)

While Martin Luther may be among the most famous of Church leaders to spread such venomous litanies against the Jews, he was far from the first (or the last). Fourteen or so centuries earlier, Melito of

Sardis was perhaps the first Christian leader to explicitly attack the Jews for their role in deicide, or killing of God. In a vitriolic sermon on this subject, Melito offered in part:

> It was necessary for him to suffer, yes, but not by you; it was necessary for him to be dishonored, but not by you; it was necessary for him to be judged, but not by you; it was necessary for him to be crucified, but not by you, not by your right hand, O Israel! (chs. 75–76)
>
> Therefore, hear and tremble because of him for whom the earth trembled. The one who hung the earth in space is himself hanged; the one who fixed the heavens in place, is himself impaled; the one who firmly fixed all things, is himself firmly fixed to the tree. The Lord is insulted, God has been murdered, the king of Israel has been destroyed, by the hand of Israel. (Ehrman B., "Melito and Early Christian Anti-Judaism," 2012)

How can any truly honest commentator see the spurious and often-creative connections drawn poorly between Darwin's teachings compared with the explicit, blatant, and irrefutable sanctions from Martin Luther and still arrive at the conclusion that Darwin was a significant influence on the Nazi final solution?

It is not my assertion here that the WWII Nazi atrocities can be traced entirely back to religious teachings. If, however, I wrote a book entitled *From Jesus to Hitler*, I would rightly be criticized if I could not make that very solid case. No, there were a great many very complex issues that contributed to the attempted genocide against the Jews under Hitler's leadership. The point I hope is well-made here is that attempting to lay blame at the feet of Charles Darwin is seriously misguided and motivated by preconceived religious notions and desires.

I mentioned already that Dr. Richard Weikart did respond to my request for comment, and his correspondence was greatly appreciated. Ray Comfort and Harun Yahya were also given the opportunity to comment on any or all what I have written above. That offer was declined outright by Harun Yahya, and Ray Comfort did not respond.

The Lie: There Is a War on Christmas (and Other Christian Holidays)

I should be careful to not overstate my case here, and I am not completely sure what to make of this situation. The word *holiday* does come from "holy day" after all, but holidays like Christmas and Easter can properly be said to be "Christian holidays" only within a certain historical context, and there is much more to the story. Even among true believers, these holidays are so secular and commercialized that the original meaning (as defined by Christians) is all but lost. Most importantly, it seems that any time there is talk of a "war on Christmas," it is coming from right-wing pundits like Bill O'Reilly or other friends of the more fundamentalist religious set and not atheists or liberal Christians. Of course, we should observe the separation of Church and State and keep explicitly religious displays off public spaces, but beyond that, I am not aware of any nonreligious people taking issue with the celebration of Christmas.

Most of us know that Christmas, or Christ's Mass, is the annual celebration of the birth of Christ and is celebrated on December 25. This is in spite of the fact that we do not know what date, even what year, Jesus may have been born. Many of the customs, as well as the date of the celebration most likely came, at least in part, from non-Christian sources such as the pagan holidays Dies Natalis Solis Invicti (the birthday celebration for Sol Invictus, or invincible Sun god), the birthday of Mithras (Metzger and Coogan 1993), Saturnalia (ancient Roman festival in honor of Saturn) (Salusbury 2009), and Yule (winter solstice celebration of the Germanic peoples later incorporated into Christmas). Many ancient civilizations celebrated the winter solstice, and there are many practices from antiquity around this time of year. This, it seems, was a very common time of year to celebrate a great many things, some religious in nature and some not so much.

It is interesting to note that some early Christian writers such as Origen of Alexandria challenged the wisdom of celebrating the birth of Christ. According to Origen, celebrating birthdays is something sinners do, and others have questioned the logic of celebrating the birth of an eternal being "of all the holy people in the Scriptures, no one is recorded to have kept a feast or held a great banquet on his birthday. It is only sinners (like Pharaoh and Herod) who make great rejoicings over the day on which they were born into this world below" (Thurston 1911).

According to Stephen Nissenbaum, author of *The Battle for Christmas* (Vintage 1997), one reason for the adoption of the Christmas tradition was to reinforce the idea that Jesus actually had been a real person and, like all real people, had been born. Apparently, among the many early Christian heresies was an idea that Jesus was never actually a real earthly being but rather had only existed as a spiritual entity.

Not only the origins of our most popular holiday are surprising to many; the things we do during the Christmas season often have non-Christian roots. As Christianity spread throughout Europe, with the corresponding conversion of Pagans, many traditions that had been important to the Pagan converts were incorporated into Christian practices. The Christmas tree and the practice of bringing greenery into the home during the winter months, for example, have roots in German paganism. The yule log and decorating with holly and mistletoe likewise had non-Christian origins.

If one were really interested in an all-out war on Christmas, just look back to our nation's early years. From Nissenbaum's *The Battle for Christmas*: "In fact, the holiday was systematically suppressed by Puritans during the colonial period and largely ignored by their descendants. It was actually illegal to celebrate Christmas in Massachusetts between 1659 and 1681 (the fine was five shillings)" (Nissenbaum, 1996). Nissenbaum goes on to point out that Christmas did not gain legal recognition as a public holiday in New England until the middle of the nineteenth century. Historically speaking, it seems that even the most stridently anti-religious atheist has a very tame view toward Christmas celebrations when compared to the Puritans.

Easter, the holiday which celebrates the supposed resurrection of Jesus on the third day following his crucifixion, is grounded in just as much confusion as is Christmas. At the risk of appearing doctrinaire, the date of this celebration can't always (if ever) fall on the right day even if Jesus really did exist, was crucified, and was resurrected bodily on the third day. This difficulty is owed to the fact that, unlike Christmas, which is on December 25 every year, Easter falls sometime between March 22 and April 25. The First Council of Nicaea decided that Easter should fall on the first Sunday after the first full moon after the vernal equinox (timeanddate.com).

Like Christmas, Easter has non-Christian elements with respect to origin, practices, and etymology. The name Easter derives from the Anglo-Saxon pagan goddess Eastre. Christmas and Easter are, to be sure, important religious holidays, but they are also more than that. They are not purely religious, and even the religious aspects are not purely Christian. None of these facts in any way dimish the cultural significance of Christmas and Easter nor take away from the degree to which I personally enjoy the holidays, but it is interesting that most Christians are not aware of these aspects of their most revered celebrations.

So what of this alleged atheist war on Christmas and by extension other Christian holidays? I have been asked by friends who know I am an atheist if it bothers me to hear "Merry Christmas," and this always surprises me. I personally say, "Merry Christmas," and I love the holiday season. I can see a certain logic in saying, "Happy holidays," because that pretty much works from Halloween through to New Years, but I just feel more comfortable personally with "Merry Christmas." No, I don't believe Jesus is the son of God, born on December 25, and I am well aware of all the non-Christian influences on the customs and traditions associated with the holiday; but it is still a great time of year, and everyone is free to celebrate it to their heart's content. I suspect that much of this war on Christmas talk is the result of some members of the Christian super-majority in the United States playing the "hurt feelings" card because they are expected to actually respect the feelings of others while exercising their near-monopoly on influence in America.

While I initially contacted him about other issues relating to this book, I took the opportunity to ask Dr. Richard Carrier about his take on this war on Christmas talk. He admitted that this is somewhat out of his area of expertise but did offer the following:

> All I can say is that it does fit a pattern of many reactionary attitudes now, whereby conservative Christians feel persecuted because they are no longer in charge and they are now being forced to consider the rights of non-Christians (and more liberal Christians) and respect a national model that accepts all religions and nonreligious equally. We see this with the gay rights issue: progress there is a redress of a longstanding injustice, we are creating a more just and fair world, but what they see is infringement on their desire to be bigoted and prejudiced and abuse power in their own interests, and they translate this in their minds as losing religious freedom, as persecution. The racists of the Jim Crowe era reacted the same way: having to treat blacks equally they saw as a restriction on their freedom, as a loss of liberty, as a persecution of white people.

I support, as I believe do most nonbelievers, the right of religious people to celebrate their religious holidays, as they deem appropriate. These religious celebrations should not, however, trespass upon our secular public spaces, especially our government or taxpayer-supported spaces. Nativity scenes are just fine on private property or on church grounds. They are not fine at a courthouse or city hall.

In the final analysis, one thing that should matter to all of us, religious or irreligious, is an honest understanding of the historical context and origins of our holidays. This is not a battle tactic in a war on Christmas or Easter; it is simply the honest pursuit of a historically accurate understanding of where these holidays came from, when, and why.

The Lie: You Can't Be Good without God

It should be abundantly clear from the previous discussions of both questionable biblical morality and the apologetic argument from morality that we simply need not resort to religion for what it means to be good. Not only can we be good without God, we can be better than what any dogmatic religious text would sanction. Secular morality is so clearly superior to morality based on religious scripture that even religious people defer to secular morality when ignoring the "bad parts" of the various religious foundational documents. If you doubt this, just consider this simple math: All the moral issues the Bible got exactly wrong (slavery, genocide, human sacrifice, etc.) plus all the people (virtually everyone) who choose secular morality over biblical morality on these issues equals the truth that good people are good in spite of the Bible, not because of it.

Not only does all available evidence point to evolutionary explanations of morality; the very source of universal, eternal, objective morality that is claimed by Christians, namely God's word in the Bible, is so replete with examples of getting morality exactly wrong that no truly moral person can honestly claim it as a source of morality. Lest one be tempted to ask why I am being so hard on the Bible, remember that it is the only rule book we have for the Christian religion. If morality is to be found in the Christian religion and not borrowed from secular civilization, then it must by definition come from the Bible. Biblical morality, however, has been shown inferior in many ways. In spite of lip service to the contrary, we do not turn to the Bible for morality, and it is good that we do not.

The Lie: If You Don't Believe in God, You Have No Wonder or Mystery in Your Life

> I know that I am mortal by nature and ephemeral
> but when I trace at my pleasure the windings to
> and fro of the heavenly bodies I no longer touch
> earth with my feet but I stand in the presence of
> Zeus himself and take my fill of ambrosia.
> —Claudius Ptolemy, CE 150

A frequent challenge to unbelievers is that there must be something missing in our lives, that we have no place for wonder, mystery, and the numinous. This argument falls far short of its intended mark. There is wonder in the universe that does not require an appeal to the divine. In fact, part of the appeal of religion lies in an ignorance of the true beauty and wonder of nature. There is no need at all to resort to the supernatural for a sense of the wonderful.

It is a mistake to think there is no sense of wonder for the unbeliever. The only difference for the unbeliever is that our mystery and wonder is grounded in what is real. Religious wonder, on the other hand, is limited to belief in things based on faith. Consider the definition of faith offered in Hebrews 11:1: "Now faith is the substance of things hoped for, the evidence of things not seen." Reality is so much more amazing than this! One of the most awe-inspiring things I know of is that we do understand so much about how the universe works and how we actually know it to be true. Yet for all the things we understand, often with exquisite detail and extraordinary confidence, that which we do not yet understand still provides an inexhaustible source of mystery and wonder. This mystery and wonder is often about things we only recently came to know exists and we are yet to understand. These are things undreamt of in religion. Imagine if you could go back to any time in human history, before about three hundred years ago, and share what we now know about biology, cosmology, physics, etc. Is it hard to imagine truth beating out the Genesis creation myth or the burning bush from Exodus?

Consider what we have come to know of nature's wonders, from very small to very large. At the smallest level (we currently understand), quarks of different "flavors" are held together by the strong force, moderated by gluons, to form protons and neutrons. Protons and neutrons are bound together (except in the case of hydrogen atoms, which have a single proton) by binding nuclear energy to form atomic nuclei, around which electrons orbit, in corresponding number to the protons in its nucleus (if it is a neutral atom), held in place by the electromagnetic force. These quarks, neutrons, protons, and electrons make up atoms in which almost all (99.999999 percent) the mass is found in the relatively very small nucleus. Almost all the physical space of an atom, conversely, is emptiness between the nucleus and the electron cloud.

By way of simple analogy, envisioning this mass, size, distance ratio is like imagining a football stadium in which at the fifty-yard line is a grape seed which represents the atomic nucleus (and nearly 100 percent of the mass) and the last rows of seating represent the electron cloud (most of the "area" of an atom and virtually none of the mass). Everything between the nucleus and electrons is empty space; the upshot of which is truly mysterious and awe-inspiring! What this means is that everything you perceive as solid—the book you are reading, the chair upon which you sit as you read, even *you*— is essentially empty space. To put this into mind-blowing perspective, if you could remove all the empty space between atomic nuclei and electrons and tightly pack these all up against each other and did this for all seven billion humans alive today, we would all occupy about as much space as a golf ball!

But wait, there's more! We know that everything in the current observable universe was "created" in the big bang about 13.8 billion years ago but not the way we currently observe it. Initially, the only atoms that existed were of the most rudimentary nature. We know that now atoms in different combinations of protons, neutrons, and electrons work in synchronicity to form some 118 distinct elements, but most of these were not formed in the initial beginning of the universe. Elements like helium, lithium, and deuterium existed very soon after the big bang; but heavier elements came later, forged in the crucibles of stars in a process known as stellar neucleosynthesis.

Most of the elements of which you and I are made came from this process of stellar neucleosynthesis and the natural life cycle of stars. Collapsing nebulae heat up, nuclear fusion of hydrogen into helium begins, and a star is born. When this star is in a state of equilibrium, it is known as a main sequence star, but eventually, it consumes most of its nuclear fuel, and its core begins to collapse. In so doing, it throws off its outer shell, enriching the cosmos with heavier elements that formed as a result of it simply doing what stars do. I will resist the urge to get into more detail about the life cycles of stars. As fascinating a story as it is, this is not the purpose of this book. The important thing to understand is that generations of stars had to die in order that we might be here today. To quote Lawrence Krauss:

> The amazing thing is that every atom in your body came from a star that exploded. And, the atoms in your left hand probably came from a different star than your right hand. It really is the most poetic thing I know about physics: You are all stardust. You couldn't be here if stars hadn't exploded, because the elements—the carbon, nitrogen, oxygen, iron, all the things that matter for evolution—weren't created at the beginning of time. They were created in the nuclear furnaces of stars, and the only way they could get into your body is if those stars were kind enough to explode. So, forget Jesus. The stars died so that you could be here today. (Krauss 2009)

Thus far, I've focused my sense of wonder at the very small, speaking of the very large, only with respect to how the very large creates the very small—stars creating elemental atoms—but what of the very large for its own sake? Why would I need to resort to the idea of biblical miracles when I can simply peer, vicariously as it is, at the Hubble Deep Field image? An image of a very small (approximately one 24 millionth) section of the sky that appeared to contain nothing actually revealed over three thousand individual galaxies. In addition to reaffirming just how vast our universe really is, the Hubble Deep Field observation provided further confirmation that we occupy a spot in the universe that is in no way unique and that the universe is ever expanding in all directions with the further objects moving away the fastest.

Consider this grand scale of the universe for a moment. If you could travel at the speed of light, which you can't, you would be able to make more than seven trips around the earth in less than one second. Remember that the speed of light is 186,242 miles per second, and most interestingly, you may remember from the discussion on the speed of light, this is a constant speed regardless of your inertial frame of reference. If you could travel at this speed, however, it would still take a little over eight minutes to reach our own sun, about thirty-five minutes to reach Jupiter, over four years to reach the nearest star to us other than our own sun, about twenty-five thousand years to the star field near the center of our own galaxy; 2 million years to reach Andromeda (the nearest galaxy to our own), 2 billion years to the nearest cluster of galaxies outside our own, and between 6 billion and 12 billion years to reach the galaxies in the previously mentioned Hubble Deep Field image. Yes, we can actually use the tools we created to view light from galaxies that have been traveling toward us for three times the age of our own planet! When we view these distant objects (many of which have not existed for hundreds, thousands, even millions of years), we really are peering back into the distant past.

These are not superstitious attempts to explain things that go bump in the night or other things for which human understanding is limited. This is not just colorful metaphor in some interesting myth. It is hard-earned knowledge that is amazing not only because of what it describes but especially because it is true. We understand these things quite well, and we believe these things for very good reasons. When compared with religion, which once claimed to explain everything, science explains little (when compared to everything); but all the answers we actually do have that are testable, verifiable, which make reliable predictions about our cosmos, come from science. From the birth of our universe almost 14 thousand, thousand, thousand years ago until now, in almost the entirety of the history of the universe, our species only arrived at the very latest moment in cosmological time. In that brief moment, however, our knowledge has been ever expanding. We are constantly filling in the great many gaps in our knowledge, and not one single time have we ever filled any of these gaps (reliably) by turning to supernatural explanations—not once.

That we are made up of atoms, which are almost completely empty space made to seem solid only because of the forces of nature, that those atoms make up elements formed in the crucibles of stars, that this all started so long ago, that we even know now where we really came from—all these things are wonderful and astonishing, uplifting, and beautiful to me. It is amazing and wonderful that only through the miraculous laws of nature that the conditions exist which allow that wondrous accident of creation, destruction, and recreation that we call life to occur. Life without which by the way the universe would never have known it even existed. We are the way that the universe is aware of itself. This is true wonder, and it is even more wondrous for the fact that we know it is true, how we know it is true, and for the realization that through our own collective and cumulative efforts alone may we further understand all that is. Carl Sagan observed that all we see around us, including us, are "some things that hydrogen atoms do, given 15 billion years of cosmic evolution. It has the sound of epic myth, and rightly. But it is simply a description of cosmic evolution as revealed by the science of our time." That is mystery and wonder enough for me!

CHAPTER 6

"Harmless Beliefs" Aren't Necessarily Harmless

They can't be allowed to forget what they used to say when they were strong enough to get away with it., and that is that this is really true, in every detail, and if you don't believe it we will kill you.

—Christopher Hitchens

I'll tell you what you did with Atheists for about 1500 years. You outlawed them from the universities or any teaching careers, besmirched their reputations, banned or burned their books or their writings of any kind, drove them into exile, humiliated them, seized their properties, arrested them for blasphemy. You dehumanised them with beatings and exquisite torture, gouged out their eyes, slit their tongues, stretched, crushed, or broke their limbs, tore off their breasts if they were women, crushed their scrotums if they were men, imprisoned them, stabbed them, disembowelled them, hanged them, burnt them alive.

And you have nerve enough to complain to me that I laugh at you.

—Madalyn Murray O'Hair

Does religion really poison everything as Christopher Hitchens pronounced in the subtitle to his book *God Is Not Great*? In a word, no, at least not in my opinion, but it isn't harmless either. While I concede that a great deal of good is done in the name of religion (though not for religious reasons as far as I can tell), it bears keeping in mind that this does not mean that God is real, only that people who believe God is real sometimes do good things. It is also true, however, that a great deal of harm is done for specifically religious reasons, and the palpable harm is far easier to directly and specifically correlate to religion than is the good.

The question "Is Christianity [or Judaism, Islam, etc.] good for the world?" is not at all the forgone conclusion many friends of religion would have us believe. If the good so clearly outweighs the bad, then there would be no room for debate. If, on the other hand, religious believers honestly look at the available evidence we could most likely do away with such flowery presumptions and insistences as God is love, Jesus is peace, and the like. Just as when I looked at the evidence for religiosity's impact on human well-being in the previous chapter, I am not arguing that religion causes all the evils of the world or even most of them, only that it is not a net positive force for good and that often there are clear examples of harm done that would be hard to justify without religious motivations.

Not only are the results of religiously inspired activities not always good, much of the good that does result from titular religious activities is tangential to the true motivation of those doing the actions and not an end in itself. I call this "titular religious activities" because they are often not really religious in nature but simply secular community activities carried out by church members or in a church-owned facility and not unique to, or because of, belief in God. Also, the actions of religious devotees are often meant to propagate the religion first and foremost, and the good that results is secondary. Church run soup kitchens, for example, rarely serve the soup sans proselytization. The cost of a meal is all too often the willingness to submit to marketing efforts of the church. Often, the good that has resulted from religion has not been so much the result of altruism toward all of "God's creatures" so much as public relations infrastructure developed for the furthering of a particular religion or denomination.

I have been told this is just not so, that many religious adherents do good just for the sake of God's love, but this position is problematic. Secularists often do the exact same good deeds and without consideration given to what God may want, so this cannot be motivated by religious truths—it is just what good people do for goodness's sake. Even if there is not an overt sermon attached to a free meal, the fact is that the marketing opportunity is inherently part of the overall religious effort. This is no different than a commercial business sponsoring a picnic and forgoing the hard sales pitch but with the hope that product placement and advertising will plant the seeds in the minds of prospective customers. I have even been told by more than one church member about the wonderful charity work they are doing in Muslim countries only to find out that the charity work is the shipping of Christian Bibles to be distributed among the people. As someone who has personally spent quite a bit of time in several Muslim countries in the Middle East, I can assure you the help they need does not include Western Christians sending over crates of Bibles.

There has been, in fact, a great deal of harm done by religious people for explicitly religious reasons. The very idea that faith in God is somehow a solution to problems is just unhelpful at best and evil at worst if carried to its logical conclusion. There are many cases in which religious parents withheld proper medical care from their children, opting instead for prayer. While there are many examples of harm that results from religious beliefs, I feel this is one of the most acute. A parent's most important role in life—their single greatest moral imperative—is to care for and protect their children, and for any parent to allow an innocent child to die from an easily curable disease because they believe it is better to just trust in God speaks volumes on this topic.

Faith itself is not a harmless concept, and it is not a good thing. The very idea that faith trumps facts for so many, that it is somehow virtuous to believe in things for which there is no evidence, and that to do so will somehow make up for all the injustices of this life is maladaptive to our best interests. We live in an increasingly complex world with more information available to us than ever before; and our ability to make sensible, informed, and effective decisions is critical. To do this requires that we employ our ability to think rationally. The willing suspension of disbelief and readiness to accept things based on faith runs perfectly counter to this end. Make no mistake; human beings are not rational animals. We are highly irrational animals that have developed the capacity for reason, and when we allow faith to outmaneuver facts, we are short-circuiting that ability to reason.

Pascal Revisited

Recall that in chapter 3 I addressed Pascal's wager. At some length, I pointed out how this is a very bad argument for believing in a god. I also made brief reference to the distinct likelihood that it is also flawed in the assertion that even if it turns out God is not real, then at least there is no harm in believing. I would now like to dive just a bit deeper into this pool of fallacious reasoning.

Consider that science has just recently begun to understand the astounding potential of embryonic stem cell research, unquestionably one of the most promising fields of medical research available to humanity. However, because of the religious belief that a blastocyst is host to a human soul, attempts to tap into the incredible good that may come of this research has been blocked, and federal funding has been withheld for years. As I wrote these words, I was living in Seoul, South Korea. One of the top news stories at this time was that President Lee Myung Bak was taking measures to ensure his country would be a world leader in the field of embryonic stem cell research. Religious considerations during this same time in the United States were causing us to lose our lead in this fascinating and tremendously important area.

Another clear and more direct example of the harm that comes from a belief in God is seen in Oregon City, Oregon, and the Followers of Christ Church. Over the past few decades, the deaths of some twenty children of parishioners of this church were investigated by Dr. Larry Lewman, the former chief medical examiner of Clackamas County. According to Dr. Lewman, most of these deaths could have been avoided with proper medical treatment. Members of the Followers of Christ Church believe that modern medicine is not necessary. They place their trust instead in prayer and the anointing of the affected part of the body with common olive oil, often with tragic results.

Neil Jeffry Beagley died in 2008 when medical care was withheld by his parents, members of the Followers of Christ Church, because of their religious beliefs. His parents were later sent to prison for this blatant neglect. According to a CNN report by Dan Simon on Anderson Cooper 360, the parents of two other victims of faith-based medicine from the same congregation were also being charged for withholding medical care from their children. According to attorneys, for the parents this was a matter of religious freedom (CNN. com, "Transcripts," 2010) Can you imagine any other belief being used as a defense for allowing your children to die by withholding medical care? No, belief in God is not always harmless.

More recently, the Montana State Supreme Court became involved in a case in which a woman refused to have a lifesaving operation on religious grounds. The case involving a woman identified only as LK at the time of this writing was in the State Supreme Court as a result of a an emergency petition filed on LK's behalf by a public defender. This petition was filed to stop an involuntary hysterectomy that had been ordered by Judge Karen Townsend after LK had been deemed not mentally competent. According to a psychiatrist in the case, LK suffered from delusions that, among other things, God cured her cancer (Florio 2011).

LK is a deeply religious woman who wants to follow the biblical mandate to "be fruitful and multiply." Of course, even nonreligious people often desire to have children. But it is difficult to see how believing that bearing children is more important than your own life unless you believe God commanded you to do so. Clearly, this court case is complex and not something to be resolved here. It is interesting, however, to consider that LK is refusing a lifesaving medical procedure on religious grounds and may die as a result. Remember the central premise of Pascal's wager—if the atheist is wrong and God is real, he has everything to lose, but if the Christian believes and they are wrong, there is nothing to lose. If LK dies and there is no God, she has died for no reason when secular medical science could have easily saved her life. No, there is much harm done by belief on insufficient evidence.

Voting for God?

We live in a time when 78 percent of the American public believes the Bible is either the literal, or at least inspired, word of the creator of the universe. As pointed out previously, a huge percentage of Americans believe that life has existed in its current form since the earth was created about six thousand years ago even though this is, perhaps, the most completely refuted notion anyone can possibly hold. This figure is 65 percent for White Evangelicals, a very influential voting bloc. Only 26 percent of Americans believe in evolution through natural selection in spite of the fact that if evolution were not true then your next flu vaccine would be ineffective. When the reason most often given for not believing in evolution is religion, and it is religious proponents who most vocally argue against the veracity of one of the most scientifically sound ideas known to man (American Association for the Advancement of Science, 2010), these figures are a cause for concern. Compare this to the overwhelming support for both the theory and fact of evolution among the members of the National Academy of Sciences (National Academy of Sciences 2013), 93 percent of whom are nontheists.

If it is indeed true (and I think it is) that a well-informed electorate is indispensable to a healthy democracy, this scientific illiteracy is actually a cause for concern at the ballot box. A huge proportion of voters want to see a person elected who is a good Christian. This is in spite of the evidence pointed out in the previous chapter that the most atheistic societies on earth fair far better than we do in almost any conceivable measure of morality, societal well-being, and overall happiness. As disturbing as it may be to many of us, when asked which should have more influence on US laws, the will of the American people or the Bible, 60 percent of white evangelicals said the Bible (The Pew Research Center 2006). This in spite of what was shown about religious illiteracy in chapter 1 and about the Bible in chapter 3.

Also consider a political issue of increasing concern of late, the attitude toward homosexuality, and associated policies such as same-sex marriage and the military's policy until 2010 of "don't ask, don't tell" and all-out ban on homosexuality prior to "don't ask, don't tell." I have alluded to this a couple of times already, but let's take a closer look now. According to a recent poll ("Survey: Less than 1 in 5 Give America's Places of Worship High Marks on Handling Issue of Homosexuality," 2010) America's places of worship get low marks when dealing with the issue of homosexuality. This is not at all surprising when you remember that the Bible itself calls homosexuality an abomination and calls for the death of anyone acting on homosexual urges.

This is not simply an issue restricted to Bronze Age bigotry or passages in the Bible that we selectively ignore. The open legal discrimination against gays is almost exclusively (perhaps entirely) driven by religious prerogatives. This is not limited to the issue of same-sex marriage and could even be a source of increased suicide rates among homosexuals in America. On the possibility that negative messages from religious organizations might contribute to higher rates of suicide among homosexual youths in the above survey, 33 percent of respondents said the rates are a lot higher, and 32 percent said a little higher, with only 21 percent responding that there was no correlation.

Religious leaders can do profound harm domestically, for specifically religious reasons and using purely religious justifications. According to *Time Magazine* (Healy 2006), Ted Haggard was an advisor to former President George Bush on evangelical matters. For those unfamiliar with Ted Haggard, he was the pastor and founder of New Life Church in Colorado Springs, Colorado. As a spiritual advisor to President Bush, it seems that Pastor Ted was somewhat influential. Pastor Ted was not influential because he had any expertise in matters of foreign or domestic policy, economics, national security, health or human services, urban planning, or anything else of any real use to a national leader. He just claimed a direct line to God.

A common topic of the sermons at Pastor Ted's mega-church was the abomination of homosexuality. But there was a problem here. And not the obvious problem that he was preaching hate against a group of people who were simply living the way they were born (either because of evolution or God created them that way). No, the problem was much more sinister. It seems Pastor Ted was using church money to pay for a male prostitute and crystal methamphetamine during a several year homosexual relationship.

It would be interesting to find out if the rate of suicide among homosexual parishioners was higher in Haggard's congregation than the national average. Imagine if you will that you are a believer in the Christian religion, with all that that conviction carries with it. You believe the Bible is indeed the word of God. You also believe that God loved you so much that he subjected himself to a horrible prolonged torture and murder on a cross as a substitutional atonement for human sin. Consider also that you sit in church every week and routinely hear Pastor Ted talk of the abomination of homosexuality. Pastor Ted can't be wrong after all; the Bible itself says that your sexual orientation is an abomination, and Ted is God's man. Finally, consider that in spite of the biblical prohibitions against homosexuality, in spite of the frequent sermons from Pastor Ted (and a great many others) against the abomination of homosexuality, in spite of the belief that Jesus died for your sins, you still can't help that you are simply not attracted to members of the opposite sex. What are you to do? I believe it is clear what I would recommend you do—accept that this entire religious narrative is antiquated and wrong. Unfortunately, a great many others have taken two common courses to deal with the guilt, either suicide or to live a lie, often hiding in plain sight as a member of the clergy preaching against the sin of homosexuality.

A final thought on the hypocrisy of religious leaders persecuting those with sexual (or other) proclivities not in keeping with the religions leader's proclaimed beliefs. I recently read Christopher Hitchens's memoir, *Hitch 22*, and as Hitchens so often did, he brought this hypocrisy to light with clarity, wit, and biting social commentary. In the Hitchens example, he was talking about Jerry Falwell, not Ted Haggard, but his point was prescient all the same:

> Whenever I hear some bigmouth in Washington or the Christian heartland banging on about the evils of sodomy or whatever, I mentally enter his name in my notebook and contentedly set my watch. Sooner rather than later, he will be discovered down on his weary and well-worn old knees in some dreary motel or latrine, with an expired Visa card, having tried to pay well over the odds to be peed upon by some Apache transvestite.

Freedom from Religion

Remember that in the course of researching and writing this book, I have been asked one question more than any other—why? I am constantly asked why write such a book. Not an unfair question and one I am happy to answer. But I wonder how many times the authors of those thousands of books in support of theism were challenged with *why*. After all, if God is real, does he really need human assistance in getting his word out? Almost as often as my motives have been challenged, my character has been challenged. Ad hominem attacks seem to be a favorite tactic of those who have nothing of value to offer in an intellectual debate. It is actually, at certain times and places, difficult to avoid those challenges.

I addressed these ad hominem attacks already in chapter 4 and elsewhere, but to illustrate the point, I will offer an experience I had today, a typical day, near my home in Virginia. I am writing these words late in the evening on a Wednesday. At lunch, I had an informal debate with a Christian apologist, which was going well until I asked him about the gross discrepancies in the genealogies offered for the lineage of Jesus by Matthew and Luke, which were discussed in chapter 2. After several attempts to just wish away the discrepancies, he opined that if the two genealogies were perfectly identical, then I would simply argue the lists were too perfect and would allege collusion on the part of the two Gospel writers. I countered that if the lists were the same, I would not have even questioned the issue and would have accepted the consistency of at least that part of the New Testament. His reaction was to tell me, point-blank, "That's not true. I know you are saying that, but atheists always say that. You would not accept it." So without using the word *liar*, this good Christian person resorted to personal slander when his argument was found lacking. Not only did he resort to slander because of his religious proclivities, he didn't even realize how rude he was being.

Just a few hours later, as I was working on this manuscript at a local coffee shop, a gentleman who was curious what I was working on approached me. He was a very nice person, and we had a pleasant conversation. At one point, however, after learning that I don't believe in God, he asserted that atheists can't truly respect human life because they don't believe in God—a complete non sequitur, as we were not even talking about anything even remotely related to his observation. He simply went from a general conversation about religion (which he initiated) to an assertion that atheists can't respect life. I replied that my firm belief that we each get only one life, not to be followed by another, eternal one, only increases the value I place on human life.

If I may be forgiven a brief but relevant diversion, my feeling that life is more precious now than when I was a Christian—the belief the Christian told me I don't really have—can actually be supported using biblical scripture. According to Revelation 21:4, "And God shall wipe away all tears from their eyes, and there shall be no more death, neither sorrow, nor crying, neither shall there be any more pain: for the former things are passed away." If this is true, then from the perspective of a Christian who is killed, no great disservice has been done as this merely hastens the time when all their tears will be wiped away, and you will have no more sorrows. I do not believe this to be the case. Life is extraordinarily precious precisely because it is temporary.

His reaction was to tell me abruptly that I don't really believe what I had just said. This Christian, a complete stranger only minutes earlier, was telling me that I am lying about my personal beliefs even though I am telling him about personal beliefs that only I can know for sure. Also, like the incident at lunch, I was told, "I have heard other atheists say they believe that, but they don't really believe that." Let me be perfectly clear on this. Neither of these men said they disagree with my conclusion; they both insisted that I was lying about what I claim to believe. The fact that in mainstream American daily life this behavior is perceived as acceptable (and to some even obligatory) is reason enough for me to write this book. Just as religious people should be free to worship as they deem appropriate, without strangers approaching them to call them liars, so too should the nonreligious have the same right. We should be free from religion if that is what we choose.

These were just two examples of religiously motivated personal attacks on my integrity. There have been a great many such instances, and they are so pervasive that many of us don't even realize they are happening. We are routinely bombarded with messages on billboards, radio, and television programming, even street preachers, that warn of the eternity in hell if we do not believe as they believe. I was even accosted recently in a subway station in Seoul, South Korea,[36] by a man who informed me that I must believe in Jesus or I will go to hell. He not only informed me that I was going to suffer an eternity of torture, he blocked my way and would only stop talking to me when I challenged his knowledge of the Bible. The same thing happened even more recently when a woman approached me and made the same statement about me believing or going to hell. In this latter case, I was at first told by this woman that I "must" follow the Bible. When I asked why, she said so I won't go to hell. She said she wanted to teach me about the Bible. I quoted 1 Timothy 2:12, "But I suffer

---

[36] As I have mentioned several times, this book was written over a period of years and in many places. The two conversations I had with Christian men who questioned my integrity took place in 2011, and when I said *today*, well, that was today when I wrote that. The Seoul subway encounter took place in 2013.

not a woman to teach, nor to usurp authority over the man, but to be in silence," and I was told I was being rude. I said it could be worse and I could assume she's a witch and shared Exodus 22:18: "Thou shalt not suffer a witch to live." This ended the conversation. It seems that to tell someone they will go to hell for not believing what you believe is perfectly okay but to simply quote from the exact same book the person is advocating is too rude to be humored.

In light of the fact there is no evidence at all that this whole story about hell is even true, combined with very good reasons to believe that it is an immoral story even if it were true, why should I or anyone else be bothered in this way ever? We shouldn't. If you want to be religious, you are free to do so, and I respect and defend that freedom. I simply also respect and demand the right of nonbelievers to be free from it.

Religion Doesn't Make You Dumb (but Does Teach You to Fake It Well)

> People demand freedom of speech as a compensation for the freedom of thought which they seldom use.
>
> —Søren Kierkegaard

> The fact that some geniuses were laughed at does not imply that all who are laughed at are geniuses. They laughed at Columbus, they laughed at Fulton, they laughed at the Wright brothers. But they also laughed at Bozo the Clown.
>
> —Carl Sagan

It has never been my position that someone is unintelligent simply because they believe in a god or gods. In fact, I have said many times that some of the most intelligent people I know are deeply religious. I was once a true believer, and I do not think that I somehow got smarter when I stopped believing or that I was less intelligent when I did believe. No, being religious does not mean that you are unintelligent. What it does do, however, is not only allow but actually require otherwise intelligent people to *sometimes* believe things they would almost certainly never believe (and might actually ridicule) were it not that their religion required belief in such things. These beliefs required by religion are not only hard to justify without religious sanction, but the beliefs themselves (though not necessarily the believer) are very often patently absurd. Not only do religious adherents sometimes believe ridiculous things, the rest of us are chastened against pointing out the ridiculous nature of these beliefs. Owing to the taboo against critiquing religious beliefs in our society, we are all but forced to respect (or at least pretend to respect) religiously inspired nonsense; at the same time, we would not hesitate to deride nonsense of the same scope and scale were it not religious.

This last point is more important than it may seem on the surface. While the degree to which our social norms and mores might sometimes require us to show deference to bad ideas for the sake of civility, this deference–by–default is virtually always there for the religious believer. The strong motivation to defend even the worst ideas of one's own faith and the taboo against ridiculing those ideas often extend beyond one's own religion. Religious adherents often feel obliged to honor the bad ideas of other religions (at least publicly) because to challenge the indefensible in another religion would open up one's own religion to richly deserved criticism. This is troubling for a number of reasons, not least of which is that ridicule of bad ideas is one thing that helps to rid us of bad ideas. Where ridicule of bad ideas is missing, there is an implicit approval of those ideas and to defend bad ideas often requires that one resort to intellectual dishonesty.

There are many examples that could illustrate this point—some already alluded to, some to come. Ray Comfort's mistreatment of Darwin's work and arguing that if evolution is true, we should expect to see a "crocoduck." John Hagee's easily refuted pronouncements, about biblical prophecies. But when it comes to perfectly revealing the dumbing-down effects of religion, Kent and Eric Hovind are hard to beat.

Kent Hovind is an American evangelical science denier, young Earth creationist, usurper of scientific language (remember scientifical), theme park operator, and convicted felon (more on this in a bit). Hovind established creation science evangelism in 1989 and has long promoted claims so ridiculous that he is even criticized by other young Earth creationists such as Ken Ham of Answers in Genesis. If Hovind's ideas were his alone, this would be mostly harmless, if still annoying. Hovind, however, developed something of a following and frequently gave public lectures and promoted his ideas in a series of DVDs as well as in many television and radio appearances. In recent years, Kent's son, Eric Hovind, has taken up his cause.

What sort of ideas have the Hovinds been espousing in spite of clear scientific evidence to the contrary? Among the cornerstones of the Hovind Theory are ideas such as:

- Noah, his family, and two of every "kind" of animal (and this includes dinosaurs) boarded the Ark.
- The "flood" was then caused by a giant ice meteor which broke up prior to impacting the Earth.
- Some of these meteor fragments formed Saturn's rings and craters on the moon.
- Most of the fragments that struck Earth were concentrated in the North and South Poles due to Earth's magnetic field.
- Because of all these polar ice fragments, mammoths were buried standing up in "super cold snow."
- There was a cracking of Earth's crust, resulting in a release of the "fountains of the deep."
- In only a few months of flooding, the animals and plants that were drowned became oil and coal.
- The Grand Canyon was formed in only a couple of weeks due to severe erosion.

Okay, this list could go on, and clearly not all these ideas are unique to the Hovinds, but I hope the point is sufficiently made. Kent Hovind went far beyond just a faith-based belief in the Bible, even a literal interpretation, and added a list of unsupported (and unsupportable) additional claims.

For an example of this intellectual dishonesty in action—one that paints the picture magnificently—just go watch the debate between "Dr." Kent Hovind and Dr. Michael Shermer that took place on April 29, 2004 (easily found with a quick Google search). Yes, I had to reach back a few years for this gem, but I will explain why shortly. In this debate, Hovind repeatedly insists that evolution is a religion, not science; that he loves and supports real science; and that anyone who supports evolution and most of the claims associated with it is either ignorant or a liar. All this in spite of his repeated ignorant and/or dishonest claims about science and evolution.

So why go back so far for this example of intellectual dishonesty? Four reasons really. First, it was the best example I could find to illuminate my intended point. Second, "Dr." Hovind (and his son Eric, who has taken up his cause and ministry), in spite of the breathtakingly stupid things he does and says, is clearly not an unintelligent man. He is, at least in my opinion, most certainly not stupid, but his beliefs are without question amazingly uninformed. Third, "Dr." Hovind was given a ten-year prison sentence (and three-year probation) after being convicted of fifty-eight federal counts. Relevant especially because Hovind, like so many other religious propagandists, claim a moral clarity unavailable to we unbelievers. Fourth, because of why I put the title "Dr." in quotes. Hovind was awarded his "doctoral degree" from an unaccredited distance-learning diploma-mill Patriot University, an all-too-common practice among religious apologists. Only someone who is accustomed to being allowed to freely do and say such patently absurd things unchallenged would travel the country making videotaped appearances in which such things are recorded for posterity. In spite of all this, Kent Hovind and many others were and still are treated as praiseworthy subject matter experts (on many subjects) for the sole reason that he claims a direct line to God. Such is the unjustified, unequal protection given to religious ideas and individuals in our society.

This problem of otherwise intelligent people doing and saying verifiably ridiculous things has become much more acute for friends of religion since the scientific revolution. One could have forgiven an apologist in centuries past for trying to explain how God created the universe or intervened in human affairs when we really didn't know about such things. There is a whole new level of cognitive self-deception required, however, to argue for religious explanations where scientific explanations not only work just fine, they've been proven to be true.

Religious Critiques of the Scientific Method

> Only two things are infinite, the universe and human stupidity, and I'm not sure about the former.
>
> —Albert Einstein

During a recent discussion with a friend who is a Christian apologist, I was challenged with the idea that science arbitrarily and unfairly presupposes that there is no God. I advised my friend that science can be said to be agnostic on the god hypothesis but not arbitrarily or unfairly so. Science doesn't rule God out necessarily, but in the absence of any evidence that supports the existence of God or even any explanatory power of the god hypothesis or of an actual theory of God, there simply is no reason to insert God into any inability of science to explain something.

It is doubly wrong to insert God where we already have perfectly good naturalistic explanations. Barbara Forrest, professor of philosophy at Southeastern Louisiana University, clearly articulates in four simple steps why there is no rational reason to insert the god hypothesis into legitimate scientific inquiry: "(1) the demonstrated success of methodological naturalism, combined with (2) the massive amount of knowledge gained by it, (3) the lack of a method or epistemology for knowing the supernatural, and (4) the subsequent lack of evidence for the supernatural. The above factors together provide solid grounding for philosophical naturalism, while supernaturalism remains little more than a logical possibility" (Forrest 2000).

I have touched upon the challenges faced by the true believer when placing greater confidence in religious faith than in empirical knowledge, even undermining science in the process, and here I would like to bring this concept full circle. While not a comprehensive treatment of this idea, I hope I will have sufficiently framed the discussion at least. In chapter 3, I addressed the inherent conflict between scientific and biblical beliefs. In chapter 4, I discussed the innate logical flaw in proceeding from preconceived notions and seeking only confirming evidence (even if you have to make it up) while discounting any contrary evidence (which is often stacked heavily against the theist). In chapter 5, I discussed the lie that Darwin's ideas led logically to the Nazi holocaust. Now I would like to address very briefly just some of the other ways theists often try to distort reality by attempting to discredit science. They often do this not so much to argue for their theistic beliefs but rather against what we know about reality, and they do this because they find reality threatens their preconceived religious notions. It seems that trying to disprove science or to coopt it and lie about scientific conclusions serves as a proxy for arguments in favor of religion. The intent of these actions, the attendant palpable harm, and the flaws in this approach should be clear. Remember always that even if these challenges to science were valid, they would still say nothing in favor of religion. Proving that one explanation is not valid does not prove another one is, especially if that other one has even less (usually no) evidence to bolster it.

In addition to the already mentioned court cases where creationists try to use the legal system to insert religion into science classes, we see religionists using the media to introduce religion as "news" into the popular discourse. An example of this is seen in a quasi-documentary film with Ben Stein as its front man. In case you were not aware, Ben Stein made a movie in 2008 entitled *Expelled: No Intelligence Allowed* in which he argued for the teaching of intelligent design, the idea that evolution is a theory in crisis, that creationists are a persecuted group in the United States, and other unsupported ideas. Stein attempted to present this movie as a sort of serious scholarly documentary in spite of the fact that Stein clearly either had no idea at all what the theory of evolution proposes or he was dishonest about his knowledge of it.

Stein repeatedly argued that among the weaknesses of evolutionary theory is that it does not explain where the universe came from or how life got started in the first place. This is problematic for two very simple reasons. First, these explanations lie in the realms of cosmology and abiogenesis, not biological evolution. Second, not only do religious arguments also fail to explain where the universe came from or how life got started in the first place, they also fail to explain the diversity of life on Earth, something that evolutionary theory does extraordinarily well.

Remember that I said religion might not make you stupid but it does allow you to fake it well? Ben Stein is a Columbia educated economist and graduate of Yale Law School. Not bad credentials, and for the record, I believe Ben Stein to be a very intelligent man, which in light of the stupidity of some of his religiously motivated proclamations only goes to prove the point of this part of this book. It may be a minor annoyance when woefully uneducated people demonstrate their lack of access to reliable information, but often this is not their fault. For someone of Stein's background to repeatedly issue such ill-informed challenges to one of the most trusted and thoroughly verified scientific theories known to man requires a willful ignorance that is beyond a minor annoyance.

Dogmatic Inertia—Religion Causes Persistent Confusion

Remember back to the chapter 2 discussion of epistemology and the way of knowing called tenacity and the difficulty we sometimes face in overcoming persistent beliefs even if all available evidence indicates we should jettison such beliefs. Among the problems with accepting ideas without evidence, especially dogmatic religious ideas, is that they come with a certain inertia that causes them to linger on long after they have ceased to be useful (if they ever were truly useful). Religious ideas, all superstitions for that matter, are not part of the real world and as such are not easily subjected to skeptical inquiry.

They are, however, acted upon by powerful emotions that keep them moving along in spite of a lack of any evidence at all to support them. This, again, might seem harmless, but it is not. Dogmatic inertia gets in the way of rational thinking and is largely what allows for immense wastes of time, effort, and resources (remember Rick Perry's proclamation that Texas undertakes three days of prayer for rain discussed in chapter 1).

From www.randi.org referencing, a collection of essays by Carl Sagan, James Randi wrote: "One thing that stands out in them is how skepticism was for Carl Sagan a deeply ethical enterprise, not just a debunking hobby, or a way to show how smart we are compared to the numbskulls who believe nonsense. For Sagan, as for so many other leaders in skepticism—though it is not often framed like this—his skepticism came out of a kind of deep moral imperative. Because undue credulity causes so much measurable harm, it follows that there is an ethical obligation to work to mitigate it through speaking out and educating our neighbors. Whether you believe that space aliens are coming to Earth to solve all our problems so we don't have to do any work to fix them ourselves, or you believe that going to a faith healer or New Age huckster rather than relying on medical science to heal you is the right course of medical care, believing in things uncritically can be bad for you and bad for society. Sagan felt that it was the right thing—the morally conscientious thing—to work against those trends."

This is a sound moral imperative. The reasons available to us for the belief in God, any god or gods, are irrational and often have a dumbing-down effect. Are there better, more rational reasons available that might be persuasive enough to convince even a skeptic? Perhaps, but I've not yet been exposed to them, and if there are, I would be among the first to welcome these persuasive arguments. But thus far, such explanations are not forthcoming. If the only result of these beliefs and arguments were a benign belief in God that brought joy and solace to your life, I would take no issue with religious belief, but this is not the case. The liberties taken with logic, truth, and reason that are so often a necessary prerequisite to belief have a spillover effect into other areas of life. And this spillover all too often not only affects the believer but others who do not share those beliefs. If I have in any way been ambiguous on this point and my opinion of it, let me here clarify that I fully understand the appeal of religion to many. If your reason for belief is pure faith and it makes you feel peace and comfort, while recognizing there is no proof or evidence, I am not really talking to, or about, you. If, however, you believe the earth is less than ten thousand years old, then I am talking to you and about you, especially if you support teaching this in science classes. This is a belief only made possible by the dumbing-down effect of religion on the human psyche and is perpetuated by dogmatic inertia.

First Corinthians 14:33 says, "For God is not the author of confusion, but of peace, as in all churches of the saints," but can you possibly imagine any source of greater confusion in the history of mankind than religion? There are around ten thousand distinct religions today each with mutually exclusive teachings, many of which say that you will be tortured for not believing that particular religion's teachings. In Christianity alone, there are major branches such as Catholicism, Protestantism, Orthodox Christianity of more than one flavor. Remember also there are the often many denominations within these major branches of Christianity. There are approximately 33,830 different denominations according to research by David B. Barrett in the *World Christian Encyclopedia* (Barrett 2001). To put that into perspective, there are only about 31,101 verses in the Bible. It is hard to conceive of something that causes more confusion when there are over 2,700 more Christian denominations than there are verses in the Bible.

Compare this with science, which provides us with a single theory for the diversity of life on earth (evolution) that is accepted almost universally by virtually all practicing scientists regardless of ethnicity, national origin, where they went to school, or gender. Also consider that cosmologists speak with virtually one voice about the origin of the current observable universe with the big bang some 13.8 billion years ago. On other issues such as gravitational theory, planetary motion, genetics, and the list goes on, rational people weigh the available evidence, form hypotheses, develop theories, then determine what is most likely true based upon that available evidence.

There are not 33,830 conflicting theories about any of these complex ideas, but one (or sometimes a very few) for each.

Penn Jillette put this into perspective quite well, saying, "If every trace of any single religion were wiped out and nothing were passed on, it would never be created exactly that way again. There might be some other nonsense in its place, but not that exact nonsense. If all of science were wiped out, it would still be true and someone would find a way to figure it all out again." The significance of this is hard to overstate. Truly, if all human knowledge were to be somehow wiped from every civilization simultaneously, all religion, science, literature, music, and every form of learning were to be gone tomorrow, what would happen? Eventually, we would probably have other religions, but it is a certainty they would not be the same religions. Some aspects of some religious would surely resurface as many religions seek, quite poorly, to explain what science ultimately does explain; but they would not be the same religions. The same dogmas would not resurface. They would be unrecognizable to us today. There would also eventually be myriad disparate and competing denominations of these emergent religions, just like today. In all likelihood, some of these new religions would carry threats of extreme punishment for a lack of belief or for believing in the wrong way, just like religions do today. On the other hand, someday, somewhere, the periodic table of elements, infinitesimal calculus, perturbation theory, the electromagnetic spectrum would all be rediscovered in exactly their current form.

CHAPTER 7

Conclusion: Significance Redux

No testimony is sufficient to establish a miracle, unless the testimony be of such a kind, that its falsehood would be more miraculous, than the fact, which it endeavors to establish.

—David Hume

People should reject god defiantly in order to pour out all their loving solicitude upon mankind.

—Albert Camus

A s I close this book, I would ask the reader, if only temporarily, to suspend disbelief, no matter your position with respect to theism in general and Christianity specifically. If you are deeply religious, try your best to consider the preceding pages, not as an atheist necessarily but simply from the perspective of "What if I am wrong?" I am asked by nearly every Christian I meet, "What if you are wrong?" Well, what if *you* are wrong? I suppose if God is real and he actually did see fit to command Abraham to sacrifice Isaac (or Ishmael if you happen to be a Muslim), then maybe, somehow that was okay since God created us all anyway, and perhaps he also decides what is moral, right, and just. I don't actually agree, but I am conceding the point for the sake of discussion. After all, if God is real, maybe he created morality and can define it. At least that seems to be the party line I am told by apologists.

What if God is not real? Or perhaps, what if God is real but imperfect men have misinterpreted the will of God or have made errors in recording the historical accounts? Then the Abraham story is possibly an egregious case of psychological abuse and intended murder of a child, an act of unadulterated evil? Or what of Jephthah's murder of his daughter as a sacrifice to God? How can this possibly be defended? What of the myriad sanctions for slavery, genocide, misogyny, or of infinite torture for finite crimes or for simply living in accordance with the nature some believe God created us? I am not asking you to even pretend to not believe in God, just imagine to the best of your abilities if the things you believe in carry the same implications if God happens to not be real or if your understanding of him may be in error. Are the things you believe to be good, moral, and just truly good, moral, and just if God happens to either not be real, if he didn't actually command those things, or if somehow something was lost in translation?

The personal experiences outlined in the introduction and the nature of epistemology discussed in chapter 2 and a few other places led me to have personal doubts on many god claims fairly early in life. This, combined with the failings of the Bible in chapter 3 and the unconvincing nature of arguments in favor of God in chapter 4, has built upon my early reservations and has had a cumulative effect of instilling very strong doubts about God's existence. In chapters 5 and 6, I explained why I believe it is very important to share these ideas with others. Your acceptance or rejection of my ideas and how you conduct your life is, of course, up to you alone. At the very least, allow yourself the dignity of weighing the evidence and make these assessments and decisions for yourself. Never allow anyone else to make this sort of decision for you—not your friends, not me, and certainly not someone with a vested interest in convincing you of it because his or her livelihood depends on it.

We have seen the dilemmas of Christianity (which apply equally to many other religions), how the Bible is fatally flawed as a source of literal truth or morality and of the failings of all arguments presented for God. We have seen that we don't need God to be good and also that many of the things so many believe about God are not supported by the evidence (even religious evidence such as the Bible). We have even seen that being more religious not only doesn't increase human well-being, it often correlates with decreased human well-being.

If I am right or even if I am wrong, this discussion is import-ant. I don't believe God is real, and I believe the evidence supports this view. Decide where you stand on my propositions, and even if you disagree with me, still ask yourself, "What if I am wrong about God?" Isn't it possible we are causing unnecessary suffering or at least retarding the greater good as a result? Also, isn't there a great many things in life that might increase your happiness, at least in small ways, that you don't do because of the misguided notion that God wouldn't like it?

When we begin any pursuit from the preconceived notion that we have an answer and then seek to prove that answer correct by any and all means, then we are not only failing to truly seek the truth, we are actively deceiving ourselves and others. I am of the opinion that, so far as we know, modern human civilization is the greatest feat yet accomplished in the entire universe and we did not come this far in such a short time by not seeking the truth. To illustrate the point of how far we've come in so short a time, consider just the three examples of transportation speed, height of man-made structures, and life expectancy.

From the domestication of the horse between 2,000 and 3,500 BCE until the invention of the steam locomotive (all of recorded human history to that point), the fastest we could hope to travel was only as fast as a horse could run, or approximately thirty miles per hour. Today humans routinely travel faster than the speed of sound, and the fastest man-made objects, the Helios space probes, travel in excess of forty-three miles per second.

As for tallest manmade structures, the Great Pyramid held this record from about 2560 BCE until approximately 1300 CE. Even then the record only increased by about twenty feet and went from about 481 feet tall to just barely over 500 feet tall for the next six hundred years plus. Then in just barely over the last century, that record has shot up to over 2,700 feet. This is due to rational, scientific thinking and our collective desire to achieve what until only very recently had seemed miraculous.

Life expectancy at birth (LEB) is now about three times what it was when the Bible was written. Of course, this is hard to quantify exactly as even today life expectancy varies greatly depending on a number of factors. At least one person, the previously mentioned

Jean Calment, has lived to be 122 years old. In Japan, LEB is about eighty-four years, and at the other end of the spectrum, in Sierra Leone, LEB is only fifty years. In any case or by any measure, life expectancy is far greater than the approximate LEB of twenty-six years during the Bronze Age. Most of this increase has taken place very recently, by the way, increasing from only about thirty-one as recently as 1900.

Sure, tomorrow we might be visited by a far more advanced civilization with even greater accomplishments in science, technology, architecture, and medicine (maybe even poetry, art, literature, and music) than anything yet dreamed in our experience. Until that time, however, what we have accomplished with our modern understanding of the power of science, rational thinking, and critical discourse is truly the most miraculous set of achievements consciously undertaken.

Modern civilization is not attributable in any way to religious thinking or divine revelation. Not only that, it came against the best efforts of religion and at the cost of religious teachings. At almost every turn, when civilization advanced, religious dogma retreated. This happened because brilliant and brave men and women were willing to reject the notion that we should accept a god as some first principle with no supporting evidence but rather to seek real explanations for what we see in nature—explanations that actually work and provide useful answers.

Religion tells us to look up at the heavens and believe they were created with us in mind. Science inspires us to peer back from the outer solar system with the Cassini spacecraft to see a sun eclipsed by Saturn with its rings beautifully illuminated in a ghostly halo (NASA 2011). Also, in this hauntingly beautiful image from 3.7 thousand million miles away is a barely perceptible tiny pale blue dot.[37] This single pixel in a photo taken from so far away, this speck of apparent near-nothingness is our home. A home some religions insist is at the center of a cosmos created just so that we could be here to serve the greater glory of a particular god. Religious explanations may *some-*

---

[37] A homage to the description of the earth from distant space by Carl Sagan.

times be reassuring to *some* people. Religious explanations of our place in the cosmos may *sometimes* be poetically beautiful (even to me). Are the religious explanations true, however? The answer is an unambiguous no in any of the areas that are testable and open to verification or falsification. In the end, science seeks to believe what is actually true; religion seeks to prove true what is already believed.

This book is not intended to destroy religion, and I could never achieve that end even if I wanted to. I remain a defender of freedom of belief and conscience. If suddenly a law were passed that made all religion illegal and the doors of all the churches, mosques, and synagogues were chained shut, I would stand alongside my religious friends to protest such action. This book is, in the end, nothing more than an appeal to honesty in the terms of religious disquisition. I only ask people to honestly consider what they believe and why and also to be a bit more tolerant of others who do not share their beliefs. I also want us all to realize how much more we have in common than not in spite of what many religions may teach to the contrary. Believers and nonbelievers share virtually all the same values, goals, norms, and mores. Followers of Christ know exactly what it is like to be an atheist with respect to all the other gods of all the other religions; I just take the lack of belief one god further. Other than that, we are in agreement on most things. I mentioned earlier that I would revisit my feelings about some of my correspondents in writing this book. What I want to say here applies not only to the people I had correspondence with but a great many others I met in person. Isn't it great to be alive in a time and place where we can disagree so strongly on one conclusion while not wanting to kill each other for disagreeing and also recognizing that we actually do agree on so many other issues? I wish to offer my sincerest gratitude to all the family, friends, even casual acquaintances with whom I've discussed these topics, often to frustrating extremes. Your patience in humoring me is greatly appreciated.

In the end, I can never prove there is no God or gods. What I can prove is that we are real, here, today. I cannot prove there is no life after death, but it is certain there is life here before death. The fact that we are here and that we can rely on each other to make the world a better, or worse, place is a fact even if God happens to be real. The terrorist attacks of September 11, 2001, and many more in the intervening years may have been religiously motivated, but they were the attacks of human beings who were thinking irrationally. Adolf Hitler may have said he had Jesus Christ in mind when justifying acts of unspeakable evil, but a god did not cause these acts—twisted ideas of men did. It was also other human beings who risked (and in some cases sacrificed) their lives to help others in the aftermath of most of these evil acts. All situations are human situations. Let us think and act accordingly.

APPENDICES

Comparison of Gospel Accounts of the Trial, Crucifixion, and Resurrection Stories of Jesus

Comparison of Gospel Accounts of the Trial, Crucifixion and Resurrection of Jesus

Event	Account according to:			
	Mark 15-16	Matthew 27-28	Luke 23-24	John 19-21
Who judged Jesus?	Pontius Pilate	Pontius Pilate	Pontius Pilate and Herod	Pontius Pilate
How did Jesus reply when questioned by Pilate?	Jesus said "Thou sayest it" when asked "Art thou the King of the Jews?" by Pilate	He spoke not a word.	Jesus replied "Thou sayest it" when Pilate asked "Art thou the King of the Jews?"	When Pilate asked "Whence art thou?" Jesus gave no answer. But when Pilate asked Jesus if he knew that he (Pilate) had the power to either release or crucify him Jesus
What color robe was placed on Jesus?	Purple	Scarlet	A gorgeous robe	Purple
Who bore the cross?	Simon	Simon	Simon	Jesus
Did both me crucified with Jesus rebuke him?	Yes	Yes	No. One asked "Lord, remember me when thou commest into thy	No mention of this.
Was the veil in the Temple torn before or after Christ	After	After	Before	No mention of this.
Who found the empty tomb?	Mary Magdalene, Mary mother of James and Salome	Mary Magdalene and "the other Mary"	A number of women. Mary Magdalene, Joanna, Mary mother of James and "other women".	Mary Magdalene alone
What was discovered at the empty tomb?	One angel	An earthquake and an angel rolled back the stone and sat upon it.	Two men "in shining garments".	No angel
If there was an angel at the tomb, what did he direct and to whom?	The one angel told the two Marys and Salome to direct the disciples to Galilee where Jesus would meet them.	The one angel (not two, not zero) told the two women (both Marys) to go tell the disciples to go to Galilee where Jesus will be.	No message was given with respect to Galilee, nor any instructions for the disciples. Only a reminder that Jesus had said "The son of man must be delivered into the hands of sinful men, and be crucified, and the third	The angel who wasn't there spoke nothing in a voice as loud as ... well, as loud as a non-existent angel can be expected to proclaim things.
What did those who found the empty tomb do?	The three women said nothing for they were afraid.	As the angel told them. "And they departed quickly from the sepulchre with fear and great joy; and did run to bring his disciples	Went back and told the others what they had seen.	Mary (she alone went there) ran and told the disciples "they have taken away the Lord..."
To whom did Jesus first appear?	Mary Magdalene.	The two Marys: Mary Magdalene and the "other Mary".	Emmaus. "Jesus himself drew near, and went with them." They did not recognize Jesus.	mistook him for the gardener. That's not a joke, it says that in John 20:14-15.
Miscellaneous events that	Judas hanged himself for betraying Jesus. This is only told in Matthew. This is important because we often hear about the resurrected Christ	Dead saints rose from their graves	After eating together Jesus led the disciples out as far as Bethany where he blessed them and was carried away up into heaven.	on the shore: but the disciples knew that that it was Jesus." They only believed it was him when he told them where to cast their nets to

Comparison of Gospel Genealogies

According to Matthew 1:1-17	According to Luke 3:23-28
1 Abraham	1 Abraham
2 Isaac	2 Isaac
3 Jacob	3 Jacob
4 Judas	4 Juda
5 Pharas	5 Pharas
6 Esrom	6 Esrom
7 Aram	7 Aram
8 Aminadab	8 Aminadab
9 Naasson	9 Naasson
10 Salmon	10 Salmon
11 Booz	11 Booz
12 Obed	12 Obed
13 Jesse	13 Jesse
14 David	14 David
15 Solomon of her that had been the wife of Urias	15 Nathan
16 Roboam	16 Mattatha
17 Abia	17 Menon
18 Asa	18 Melea
19 Josephat	19 Eliazim
20 Joram	20 Jonan
21 Ozias	21 Joseph
22 Joatham	22 Juda
23 Achaz	23 Simeon
24 Ezekias	24 Levi
25 Manasses	25 Matthat
26 Amon	26 Jorim
27 Josias	27 Eliezer
28 Jechonias	28 Jose
29 Salathiel	29 Er
30 Zorobabel	30 Elmodam
31 Abiud	31 Cosam
32 Eliazim	32 Addi
33 Azor	33 Melchi
34 Sadoc	34 Neri
35 Achim	35 Salathiel
36 Eliud	36 Zorobabel
37 Eleazar	37 Rhesa
38 Matthan	38 Joanna
39 Jacob	39 Juda
40 Joseph the husband of Mary	40 Joseph
41 Jesus	41 Semei
	42 Mattathias
	43 Maath
	44 Nagge
	45 Esli
	46 Naum
	47 Amos
	48 Mattathias
	49 Joseph
	50 Jnna
	51 Melchi
	52 Levi
	53 Matthat
	54 Heli
	55 Josheph
	56 Jesus

While the genealogies from Matthew and Luke match nearly perfectly from Abraham to David, the portion that applies to the prophesy of Jesus being the messiah, born in the line of David is more problematic.

Whereas the two genealogies from Abraham to David vary by only a single letter, from David to Jesus the genealogies are terribly contradictory. Only three of the names match from each list after David and before Jesus. Two others are close, but not exact matches.

Apologists often argue that different names used for the same people account for this discrepancy. Other apologists argue that one list actually goes backward from Mary and the other forward from Joseph. Both explanations are unconvincing when Matthew lists 28 generations between David and Jesus and Luke lists 43. It is also curious that the genealogies match nearly perfectly before the "important portion" (after David) to the idea that Jesus is the messiah.

Data Comparing Religiosity
with Human Well-Being

TABLE 1   Degree of Religiosity Compared With Rates of HIV and Homocides

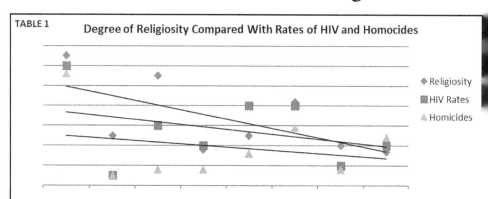

Note: Religiosity determined by Gallup polling data that determined the percentage of populations that felt "religion is very important to my daily life."

HIV and homocide rates were obtained from the United Nations Development Program's Human Development Index. In order to show a correlation on this comparison chart the numbers for HIV rates were mulitplied by 100, and homicide rates were multiplied by 10. Relative positions between nations are accurate; magnitude was changed.

Nations addressed: (1) USA, (2) Japan, (3) Austria, (4) Denmark, (5) France, (6) Switzerland, (7) Norway, (8) Sweden.

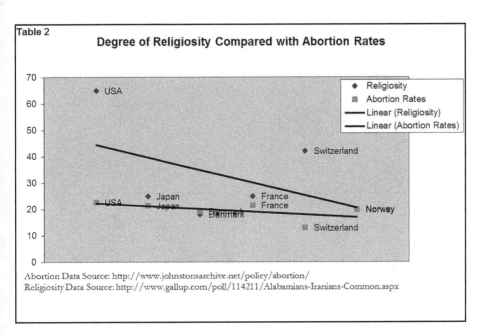

Table 2

Degree of Religiosity Compared with Abortion Rates

Abortion Data Source: http://www.johnstonsarchive.net/policy/abortion/
Religiosity Data Source: http://www.gallup.com/poll/114211/Alabamians-Iranians-Common.aspx

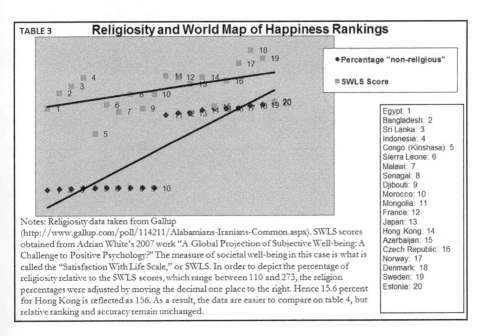

TABLE 3   **Religiosity and World Map of Happiness Rankings**

| Egypt: 1 |
| Bangladesh: 2 |
| Sri Lanka: 3 |
| Indonesia: 4 |
| Congo (Kinshasa): 5 |
| Sierra Leone: 6 |
| Malawi: 7 |
| Senagal: 8 |
| Djibouti: 9 |
| Morocco: 10 |
| Mongolia: 11 |
| France: 12 |
| Japan: 13 |
| Hong Kong: 14 |
| Azerbaijan: 15 |
| Czech Republic: 16 |
| Norway: 17 |
| Denmark: 18 |
| Sweden: 19 |
| Estonia: 20 |

Notes: Religiosity data taken from Gallup
(http://www.gallup.com/poll/114211/Alabamians-Iranians-Common.aspx). SWLS scores
obtained from Adrian White's 2007 work "A Global Projection of Subjective Well-being: A
Challenge to Positive Psychology?" The measure of societal well-being in this case is what is
called the "Satisfaction With Life Scale," or SWLS. In order to depict the percentage of
religiosity relative to the SWLS scores, which range between 110 and 273, the religion
percentages were adjusted by moving the decimal one place to the right. Hence 15.6 percent
for Hong Kong is reflected as 156. As a result, the data are easier to compare on table 4, but
relative ranking and accuracy remain unchanged.

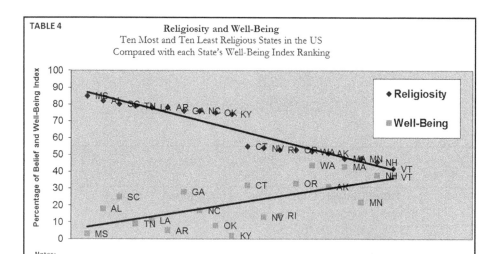

TABLE 4

Religiosity and Well-Being
Ten Most and Ten Least Religious States in the US
Compared with each State's Well-Being Index Ranking

Notes:
1. Religiosity data taken from Gallup: http://www.gallup.com/poll/114211/Alabamians-Iranians-Common.aspx.
2. Well-Being data taken from Gallup: http://www.ahiphiwire.org/WellBeing/Display.aspx?doc_code=RWBStateRanks
3. Well-Being Index based on an average of "six sub-indexes, which individually examine life evaluation, healthy behaviors, work environment, physical health, emotional health, and access to basic necessities."

REFERENCES

Abdullah, H. August 21, 2012. "Akin's 'legitimate rape' comments trouble for GOP." Retrieved September 15, 2012, from CNN.com: http://edition.cnn.com/2012/08/20/politics/akin-political-fallout/index.html.

Adams, D. 2002. *The Salmon of Doubt: Hitchhiking the Galaxy One Last Time.* New York: Ballantine Books.

Alsop, Z. December 10, 2009. "Uganda's Anti-Gay Bill: Inspired by the US." Retrieved March 27, 2010, from Time.com: http://www.time.com/time/world/article/0,8599,1946645,00.html.

American Association for the Advancement of Science. 2010. "AAAS Evolution Resources." Retrieved November 4, 2010, from AAAS.org: http://www.aaas.org/news/press_room/evolution/qanda.shtml.

Anselm. August 1998. *Internet History Sourcebooks.* Retrieved October 2, 2012, from Fordham University the Jesuit University of New York: http://www.fordham.edu/halsall/basis/anselm-proslogium.asp.

Aquinas, T. S. *Summa Theologica.* (F. O. Privince, trans.)

Armstrong, K. 1993. *A History of God: The 4,000 Year Quest of Judaism, Christinity and Islam.* New York: Ballentine Books.

Aslan, R. 2013. *Zealot: The Life and Times of Jesus of Nazareth.* New York: Random House.

Atkins, P., and Craig, W. L. October 26, 2011. Debate between William Lane Craig and Peter Atkins at the University of Manchester. Manchester, UK.

Barna Group, The. March 31, 2008. *New Marriage and Divorce Statistics Released.* Retrieved September 21, 2013, from Barna Group: https://www.barna.org/barna-update/article/15-familykids/42-new-marriage-and-divorce-statistics-released#.Uj0CUrzPGU0.

Barrett, D. B. 2001. *World Christian Encyclopedia: A Comparative Survey of Churches and Religions in the Modern World.* New York, New Yord, USA: Oxford University Press.

BBC News. May 7, 2002. "Don Quixote Gets Authors' Votes." Retrieved April 12, 2010, from BBC News: http://news.bbc.co.uk/2/hi/entertainment/1972609.stm.

Bennett-Smith, M. August 31, 2012. "Father Benedict Groeschel, American Friar, Claims Teens Seduce Priests in Some Sex Abuse Cases." Retrieved September 15, 2012, from *Huffington Post*: http://www.huffingtonpost.com/2012/08/29/father-benedict-groeschel-teens-seduce-priests_n_1840900.html.

Benson, H. April 2006. "Study of the Therapeutic Effects of Intercessory Prayer (STEP) in Cardiac Bypass Patients: A Multicenter Randomized Trial of Uncertainty and Certainty of Receiving Intercessory Prayer." Retrieved May 13, 2012, from National Center for Biotechnology Information: http://www.ncbi.nlm.nih.gov/pubmed/16569567.

Bidwell, A. July 3, 2013. "One Civil War Veteran's Pension Remains on Government's Payroll." Retrieved December 11, 2016, from *US News and World Report*: http://www.usnews.com/news/newsgram/articles/2013/07/03/one-civil-war-veterans-pension-remains-on-governments-payroll.

Brooks, M. August 2, 2008. "Is Our Universe Fine-Tuned for Life?" Retrieved October 1, 2012, from New Scientist: http://www.newscientist.com/article/mg19926673.900.

Carlston, C. E. 1994. Prologue. In B. Chilton, and C. A. Evans, *Studying the Historical Jesus: Evaluations of the State of Current Research* (pp. 1–8). Leiden: Brill.

Center for Inquiry. June 25, 2009. "John Shook v. William Lane Craig Debate: Does God Exist?" Retrieved October 1, 2012, from Youtube: http://www.youtube.com/watch?v=Wf9–vwnzqOo.

Central Intelligence Agency. 2008. "World Population." Retrieved February 10, 2010, from *The World Factbook*: https://www.cia.gov/library/publications/the-world-factbook/

Clarifying Christianity. n.d. "Science and the Bible." Retrieved September 10, 2011, from Clarifying Christianity: http://www.clarifyingchristianity.com/science.shtml.

CNN.com. "Transcripts." December 23, 2010. Retrieved September 27, 2012, from CNN.com: http://transcripts.cnn.com/TRANSCRIPTS/1012/23/acd.02.html.

Collins, F. S. 2006. *The Language of God: A Scientist Presents Evidence for Belief.* New York: Free Press.

Coyne, J. A. 2009. *Why Evolution Is True.* New York: Viking.

Crabtree, S. A. April 7, 2010. "More Religious Countries, More Perceived Ethnic Intolerance." Retrieved July 10, 2009, from Gallup: http://www.gallup.com/poll/117337/Religious-Countries-Perceived-Ethnic-Intolerance.aspx.

Crabtree, S. A. February 9, 2009. "What Alabamians and Iranians Have in Common." Retrieved July 11, 2009, from Gallup: http://www.gallup.com/poll/114211/Alabamians-Iranians-Common.aspx.

Craig, W. L. 2007. "Question 16 Slaughter of the Canaanites." Retrieved August 26, 2011, from Reasonable Faith: http://www.reasonablefaith.org/site/News2?page=NewsArticle&id=5767.

———— and Bart Ehrman. n.d. "Is There Historical Evidence for the Resurrection of Jesus?" Retrieved September 9, 2012, from http://www.philvaz.com/apologetics/: http://www.philvaz.com/apologetics/p96.htm.

————. November 8, 2015. "The Teleological Argument and the Anthropic Principle." Retrieved October 1, 2012, from Leadership U: http://www.leaderu.com/offices/billcraig/docs/teleo.html.

————. n.d. "Theistic Critiques of Atheism." Retrieved January 31, 2015, from Reasonable Faith: http://www.reasonablefaith.org/theistic-critiques-of-atheism.

————. 2007. "What Price Biblical Errancy?" Retrieved April 13, 2010, from Reasonable Faith: http://www.reasonablefaith.org/site/News2?page=NewsArticle&id=5717.

Dante. 2008 Compilation. *The Divine Comedy* (2008 ed.). (H. W. Longfellow, trans.) New York: Barnes & Noble, Inc.

Darwin, C. 2004. *The Origina of Species.* New York, New York, USA: Barnes & Noble Classics.

Davis, K. C. 1998. *Don't Know Much about the Bible: Everything You Need to Know About the Good Book but Never Learned.* New York: Perennial.

Dawkins, R. April 11, 2006. "Atheists for Jesus." Retrieved September 13, 2011, from the Richard Dawkins Foundation for Reason and Science: http://richarddawkins.net/articles/20.

———. n.d. "What If You're Wrong?" Retrieved September 27, 2012, from Youtube: http://www.youtube.com/watch?v=6mmskXXetcg.

———. 2008. *The God Delusion.* Boston: Mariner Books.

———. 2009. *The Greatest Show on Earth: The Evidence for Evolution.* New York: Free Press.

———. 1993. Viruses of the Mind. In B. Dahlbom, *Dennett and His Critics: Demystifying Mind (Philosophers and their Critics)* (pp. 13–27). Malden: Wiley-Blackwell.

Dennett, D. C. 2006. *Breaking the Spell: Religion as a Natural Phenomenon.* New York: Penguin Books.

———. 1995. *Darwin's Dangerous Idea.* New York: Touchstone.

———. October 3, 2010. "The Unbelievable Truth: Why America Has Become a Nation of Religious Know-Nothings." Retrieved December 26, 2014, from Daily News: http://www.nydailynews.com/opinions/2010/10/03/2010–10–03_the_unbelieveable_truth_why_america_has_become_a_nation_of_religious_knownothing.html.

Department of Systematic Biology, Entomology Section, National Museum of Natural History. n.d. "Numbers of Insects (Species and Individuals)." Retrieved September 11, 2011, from BUGINFO.com: http://www.si.edu/encyclopedia_si/nmnh/buginfo/bugnos.htm.

Early, J. J. 2008. *Readings in Baptist History: Four Centuries of Selected Documents.* B & H Academy.

Easton, N. J. December 25, 2005. "US Judge Rejects Intelligent Design." Retrieved July 18, 2009, from Boston.com: http://

www.boston.com/news/education/k_12/articles/2005/12/21/
us_judge_rejects_intelligent_design/.

Eckholm, E. May 4, 2011. "When David Barton Talks, Concervative
Candidates Listen." Retrieved October 28, 2012, from the *New
York Times*: http://www.nytimes.com/2011/05/05/us/poli-
tics/05barton.html?_r=0.

Edgell, P., Gerteis, J., and Hartmann, D. 2006. Atheists As "Other":
Moral Boundaries and Cultural Membership in American
Society. *American Sociological Review April*, 211–234.

Ehrman, B. April 22, 2008. Biblical Insights into the Problem of
Suffering (H. Kreisler, Interviewer).

———. 2009. *Jesus, Interrupted: Revealing the Hidden Contradictions
in the Bible (and Why We Don't Know About Them)*. New York:
HarperCollins.

———. December 2, 2012. "Melito and Early Christian Anti-
Judaism." Retrieved January 5, 2017, from the Bart Ehrman
Blog: The History and Literature of Early Christinity: https://
ehrmanblog.org/melito-and-arly-christian-anti-judaism/.

Encyclopædia Britannica. 2015. "Index Librorum Prohibitorum."
Retrieved June 10, 2015, from *Encyclopedia Britannica*:
http://global.britannica.com/EBchecked/topic/285220/
Index-Librorum-Prohibitorum.

Evans, C. A. 1994. Jesus in Non-Christian Sources. In B. Chilton
and C. A. Evans, *Studying the Historical Jesus: Evaluations of the
State of Current Research* (pp. 443–478). Leiden: Brill.

Florio, G. March 7, 2011. "State Supreme Court Halts Surgery to
Allow Appeal in Bysterectomy Ruling." Retrieved January 2,
2015, from Independent Record: http://helenair.com/news/
article_77a4e892–487f-11e0–a878–001cc4c002e0.html.

Forrest, B. 2000. Methodological Naturalism and Philosophical
Naturalism: Clarifying the Connection. *PhiloPhilo*, vol. 3, no.
2 (fall–winter), 7–29.

Fullwiley, D. May–June 2008. "Race in a Genetic World." Retrieved
January 30, 2015, from *Harvard Magazine*: http://harvardmag-
azine.com/2008/05/race-in-a-genetic-world-html.

Gilgoff, D. October 18, 2012. "Dinesh D'Souza Resigns as Christian College Chief in Face of Questions about Marriage." Retrieved October 24, 2012, from CNN Belief Blog: http://religion. blogs.cnn.com/2012/10/18/dinesh-dsouza-resigns-as-christian-college-chief-in-face-of-questions-about-marriage/.

———. October 30, 2009. "How Creationist 'Origin' Distorts Darwin." Retrieved February 20, 2015, from US News & World Report: http://www.usnews. com/news/blogs/god-and-country/2009/10/30/ how-creationist-origin-distorts-darwin.

Gould, S. J. 1999. *Rocks of Ages.* New York: Ballentine Books.

Grady, D. December 9, 2012. "In Girl's Last Hope, Altered Immune Cells Beat Leukemia." Retrieved May 23, 2014, from *New York Times*: http://www.nytimes.com/2012/12/10/ health/a-breakthrough-against-leukemia-using-altered-t-cells. html?pagewanted=all&_r=0.

Greene, R. A. July 6, 2009. "Oldest Known Bible Goes Online." Retrieved June 9, 2013, from CNN.com: http://edition.cnn. com/2009/WORLD/europe/07/06/ancient.bible.online/.

Habermas, G. September 11, 2008. "Audio Media Index." Retrieved March 1, 2010, from Dr. Gary R. Habermas Online: http:// www.garyhabermas.com/audio/audio.htm.

Ham, K. n.d. From Answers in Genesis: http://www.answersingenesis.org/.

Harris, S. 2008. *Letter to a Christian Nation.* New York: Vintage Books.

———. November 13, 2006. "The Case Against Faith." Retrieved January 2, 2015, from Sam Harris: http://www.samharris.org/ site/full_text/the-case-against-faith/.

———. 2004. *The End of Faith: Religion, Terro, and the Future of Reason.* New York: W. W. Norton and Company.

———. 2010. *The Moral Landscape: How Science Can Determine Human Values.* New York: Free Press.

———. 2014. *Waking Up: A Guide to Spirituality Without Religion.* New York: Simon & Schuster.

Harrison, G. P. 2008. *50 Reasons People Give for Believing in a God.* Amherst: Prometheus Books.

Haub, C. October 2011. "How Many People Have Ever Lived on Earth." Retrieved June 8, 2015, from Population Reference Bureau: http://www.prb.org/Articles/2002/HowManyPeopleHaveEverLivedonEarth.aspx.

Hawking, S. A. 2010. *The Grand Design.* New York: Bantam Books.

Healy, R. November 3, 2006. "A Mega-Scandal for a Mega-Church." Retrieved July 18, 2012, from TimeMagazine.com: http://www.time.com/time/nation/article/0,8599,1554388,00.html.

Hitchens, C. 2007. *God Is Not Great: How Religion Poisons Everything.* New York: Twelve.

———. 2007. *The Portable Atheist.* Philadephia: Da Capo Press.

Hitler, A. n.d. "Mein Kampf." Retrieved June 4, 2014, from Internet Archive: https://archive.org/stream/meinkampf035176mbp/meinkampf035176mbp_djvu.txt.

Hobbes, T. 1651. *Leviathan or the Matter, Forme, and Power of a Common Wealth Ecclesiasticall and Civil.*

Holmes, D. L. 2006. *The Faiths of the Founding Fathers.* New York: Oxford University Press.

Hu, E. August 9, 2012. "Publisher Pulls Controversial Thomas Jefferson Book, Citing Loss Of Confidence." Retrieved October 28, 2012, from National Public Radio: http://www.npr.org/blogs/thetwo-way/2012/08/09/158510648/publisher-pulls-controversial-thomas-jefferson-book-citing-loss-of-confidence.

Hume, D. January 2016. "An Enquiry Concerning Human Understanding." Retrieved May 18, 2014, from Project Gutenberg: http://www.gutenberg.org/files/9662/9662–h/9662–h.htm.

———. n.d. "Dialogues Concerning Natural Religion." Retrieved July 20, 2013, from Project Gutenberg: http://www.gutenberg.org/ebooks/4583.

Huntington, S. P. 1996. *The Clash of Civilizations and the Remaking of World Order.* New York: Simon and Schuster.

International Business Times. September 6, 2011. "Bastrop Country Fire Remains Uncontrolled, Could Continue for Days." Retrieved May 13, 2012, from *International Business Times*: http://www.ibtimes.com/articles/209263/20110906/bastrop-county-fire-texas-fire-fire-bastrop-county-fire-texas-bastrop-fire-deaths.htm.

Judgement Day: Intelligent Design on Trial. November 2007. *NOVA*.

Junger, S. 2016. *Tribe: On Homecoming and Belonging*. New York: Twelve.

Kantowitz, B. H., Roediger, H. L., and Elmes, D. G. 2001. *Experimental Psychology: Understanding Psychological Research*. Belmont: Wadsworth Group.

Knapp, A. February 6, 2012. "Chief Vatican Astronomer: Big Bang Is Compatible with Catholicism." Retrieved May 24, 2013, from Forbes.com: http://www.forbes.com/sites/alexknapp/2012/02/06/chief-vatican-astronomer-big-bang-is-compatible-with-catholicism/.

Krauss, L. October 21, 2009. "A Universe From Nothing." Retrieved June 4, 2014, from YouTube: http://www.youtube.com/watch?v=7ImvlS8PLIo#t=16m49s.

———. January 24, 2015. "No, Astrobiology Has Not Made the Case for God." Retrieved January 31, 2015, from the New Yorker: http://www.newyorker.com/tech/elements/astrobiology-made-case-god.

Kuhn, T. 1957. *The Copernican Revolution*. Cambridge: Harvard University Press.

Lewis, B. R. 2009. *A Dark History: The Popes Vice, Murder, and Corruption in the Vatican*. New York: Metro Books.

Lewis, C. S. 1952. *Mere Christianity*. New York: Harper One.

Lisle, J. March 13, 2008. "The Age of the Universe, Part 1." Retrieved December 17, 2016, from Answers in Genesis: https://answersingenesis.org/answers/books/taking-back-astronomy/the-age-of-the-universe-part-1/.

Loftus, J. W. March 20, 2009. "The Outsider Test for Faith." Retrieved August 25, 2013, from Debunking Christianity:

http://debunkingchristianity.blogspot.kr/2009/03/outsider-test-for-faith_20.html.

Lowance, M. I. 2003. *A House Divided: The Antebellum Slavery Debates in America, 1776–1865.* Princeton, NJ: Princeton University Press.

Luther, M. 2014. *On the Jews and Their Lies.* Eulenspiegel Press.

Malik, C. D. n.d. "The Universal Declaration of Human Rights." Retrieved August 30, 2011, from United Nations: http://www.un.org/en/documents/udhr/

Masci, D. May 16, 2007. "An Evolving Debate about Evolution." Retrieved September 10, 2011, from the Pew Forum on Religion and Public Life: http://pewforum.org/Politics-and-Elections/An-Evolving-Debate-about-Evolution.aspx.

Meacham, J. 2006. *American Gospel: God, the Founding Fathers, and the Making of a Nation.* New York: Random House.

Mendes, E. March 10, 2009. "Well-Being Rankings Reveal State Strengths and Weaknesses." Retrieved July 6, 2009, from Gallup: http://www.gallup.com/poll/116497/Rankings-Reveal-State-Strengths-Weaknesses.aspx.

Metaxas, E. December 25, 2014. "Science Increasingly Makes the Case for God." Retrieved January 31, 2015, from *Wall Street Journal:* http://www.wsj.com/articles/eric-metaxas-science-increasingly-makes-the-case-for-god-1419544568.

Metzger, B. M., and Coogan, M. D. (eds.). 1993. *The Oxford Guide to the Bible.* New York: Oxford University Press.

Miller, W. L. 1996. *Arguing About Slavery: The Great Battle in the United States Congress.* Alfred A. Knoph.

Mooney, C. November 20, 2009. "Ray Comfort's Anti-Darwinian Travesty." Retrieved May 17, 2012, from *Discover Magazine:* http://blogs.discovermagazine.com/intersection/2009/11/20/ray-comforts-anti-darwinian-travesty/

NASA. September 4, 2011. "Astronomy Picture of the Day." Retrieved January 12, 2015, from NASA.gov: http://apod.nasa.gov/apod/ap110904.html.

———. Septembr 26, 2012. "WMAP: Content of the Universe." Retrieved October 1, 2012, from National Aeronautics and

Space Administration: http://map.gsfc.nasa.gov/universe/uni_matter.html.

———. August 31, 2009. "NASA: Five Millenium Catalog of Solar Eclipses." Retrieved September 11, 2011, from NASA.gov: http://eclipse.gsfc.nasa.gov/SEcat5/SEcatalog.html.

Natioinal Institutes of Health. June 13, 2012. "NIH Human Microbiome Project Defines Normal Bacterial Makeup of the Body." Retrieved May 24, 2013, from NIH News: http://www.nih.gov/news/health/jun2012/nhgri-13.htm.

National Academy of Sciences. 2013. "Is Evolution a Theory or a Fact?" Retrieved February 22, 2015, from Evolution Resources from the National Academies: http://www.nas.edu/evolution/TheoryOrFact.html.

National Data Program for the Sciences, University of Chicago. July 2007. Retrieved July 9, 2009, from General Social Survey: http://www.norc.org/GSS+Website/.

Niose, D. March 30, 2011. "Misinformation and Facts about Secularism and Religion." Retrieved December 11, 2016, from *Psychology Today*: https://www.psychologytoday.com/blog/our-humanity-naturally/201103/misinformation-and-facts-about-secularism-and-religion.

Nissenbaum, S. 1996. *The Battle for Christmas.* New York: Vintage Books.

Onion, The. December 15, 2009. "Sumerians Look on in Confusion as God Creates World." Retrieved June 15, 2013, from *The Onion*: http://www.theonion.com/articles/sumerians-look-on-in-confusion-as-god-creates-worl,2879/.

Owen, J. August 10, 2006. "Evolution Less Accepted in the US than Other Western Countires, Study Finds." Retrieved June 25, 2009, from National Geographic: http://news.nationalgeographic.com/news/2006/08/060810–evolution.html.

Paine, T. 1796. *The Age of Reason.*

Paley, W. 1802. *Natural Theology, or Evidences fo the Existence and Attributes of the Deity Collected from the Apperances of Nature.*

Paul, G. 2007. "Cross-National Correlations of Quantifiable Societal Health with Popular Religiosity and Secularism in the Prosperous Democracies." Retrieved July 11, 2009, from

Journal of Religion and Society: http://moses.creighton.edu/ JRS/2005/2005–11.html.

Pelham, B. A. March 10, 2009. "Religiosity and Perceived Intolerance of Gays and Lesbians." Retrieved July 9, 2009, from Gallup: http://www.gallup.com/poll/116491/Religiosity-Perceived-Intolerance-Gays-Lesbians.aspx.

Perry, R. April 21, 2011. *Gov. Perry Issues Proclamation for Days of Prayer for Rain in Texas.* Retrieved May 13, 2012, from Office of the Governor Rick Perry: http://governor.state.tx.us/news/ proclamation/16038/.

Pew Research Center, The. August 24, 2006. *"Many Americans Uneasy with Mix of Religion and Politics."* Retrieved November 3, 2010, from the Pew Forum on Religion and American Life: http://pewforum.org/Politics-and-Elections/Many-Americans-Uneasy-with-Mix-of-Religion-and-Politics.aspx.

Pew Trust. 2008. *US Religious Landscapes Survey: Religious Beliefs and Practices, Diverse and Politically Relevant.* Retrieved June 7, 2009, from Pew Forum on Religion and Public Life: http://religions.pewforum.org/pdf/report2–religious-landscape-study-full.pdf.

Price, R. M. 2010. *The Case against the Case for Christ: A New Testament Scholar Refutes the Reverend Lee Strobel.* Cranford, NJ: American Athiest Press.

Prothero, S. 2007. *Religious Literacy: What Every American Needs to Know and Doesn't.* New York: Harper One.

Public Religion Institute. *Survey: Less than 1 in 5 Give America's Places of Worship High Marks on Handling Issue of Homosexuality.* October 21, 2010. Retrieved July 14, 2012, http://publicreligion.org/research/2010/10/less-than-1-in-5-give-americas-places-of-worship-high-marks-on-handling-issue-of-homosexuality/.

Rizzo, A. March 31, 2008. "Muslims 'Overtake' Catholics, Become Largest Religion." Retrieved February 21, 2015, from *National Geographic*: http://news.nationalgeographic.com/ news/2008/03/080331–AP-islam-largest.html.

Rowland, D. 1923. *Jefferson Davis, Constitutionalist: His Letters, Papers, and Speeches* (Vol. 1). Mississippi Department of Archives and History.

Russell, B. 1945. *A History of Western Philosophy.* London: George Allen & Unwin Ltd.

———. 1957. *Why I Am Not a Christian: and Other Essays on Religion and Related Subjects.* New York: Touchstone.

Salusbury, M. December 12, 2009. "Did the Romans Invent Christmas?" Retrieved June 9, 2015, from *History Today*: http://www.historytoday.com/matt-salusbury/did-romans-invent-christmas.

Science Daily. November 14, 2006. "Psychologist Produces The First-ever 'World Map Of Happiness.'" Retrieved July 12, 2009, from *Science Daily*: http://www.sciencedaily.com/releases/2006/11/061113093726.htm.

Segelstein, M. Winter 2008. "The Apologist." Retrieved May 8, 2012, from *Salvo Magazine*: http://www.salvomag.com/new/articles/salvo7/7segelstein.php.

Shermer, M. 1997. *Why People Believe Weird Things.* New York, New York, USA: W. H. Freeman / Henry Holt and Company.

Smithsonian National Museum of Natural History n.d. "What Does It Mean to be Human?" Retrieved February 15, 2015, from Smithsonian National Museum of Natural History: http://humanorigins.si.edu/evidence/genetics.

Specter, M. 2009. *Denialism: How Irrational Thinking Hinders Scientific Progress, Harms the Planet, and Threatens Our Lives.* New York: the Penguin Press.

Stenger, V. 2007. *God: The Failed Hypothesis.* Amherst: Prometheus.

———. 2003. *Has Science Found God?: The Latest Results in the Search for Purpose in the Universe.* Amherst, NY, USA: Prometheus Books.

Stringfellow, T. 1856. *Scriptural and Statistical Views in Favor of Slavery.* Richmond: J. W. Randolph.

Strobel, L. 2004. *The Case for a Creator: A Journalist Investigates Scientific Evidence That Points toward God.* Grand Rapids: Zondervan.

————. 2000. *The Case for Faith*. Grand Rapids: Zondervan.

Tashman, B. September 10, 2012. "Pat Robertson: Since 'We Don't Condone Wife-Beating These Days' Husband Should 'Move to Saudi Arabia' to Beat Her." Retrieved January 24, 2015, from *Right Wing Watch*: http://www.rightwingwatch.org/content/pat-robertson-condone-wife-beating-saudi-arabia.

Thurston, H. 1911. "Natal Day." Retrieved July 8, 2012, from *The Catholic Encyclopedia*: http://www.newadvent.org/cathen/10709a.htm.

timeanddate.com. n.d. "How the Easter Date Is Determined." Retrieved June 4, 2014, from timeanddate.com: http://www.timeanddate.com/calendar/determining-easter-date.html.

Twain, M. 1923. *Europe and Elsewhere*. New York: Harper and Brothers Publishers.

————. 2011. *What Is Man? And Other Mark Twain Essays*. CreateSpace Independent Publishing Platform.

Tyson, N. D. n.d. *"The Perimeter of Ignorance."* Retrieved September 22, 2012, from *Natural History Magazine*: http://www.natural-historymag.com/universe/211420/the-perimeter-of-ignorance.

United Nations Development Programme. 2007/2008. *United Nations Human Development Report*. New York: United Nations.

University of South Caroline at Chapel Hill. January 23, 2015. *Summary of Scriptural and Statistical Views in Favor of Slavery*. Retrieved January 24, 2015, from Documenting the American South: http://docsouth.unc.edu/church/string/summary.html.

USGS. July 22, 2011. *Earthquake Facts and Statistics*. Retrieved September 12, 2011, from US Geological Survey: http://earthquake.usgs.gov/earthquakes/eqarchives/year/eqstats.php.

Vilenkin, A. 2006. *Many Worlds in One: The Search for Other Universes*. New York: Hill and Wang.

Weikart, R. 2004. *From Darwin to Hitler: Evolutionary Ethics, Eugenics, and Racism in Germany*. Basingstoke, United Kingdom: Palgrave MacMillan.

Wells, S. October 23, 2009. "Contradictions in the Bible." Retrieved October 28, 2010, from Project Reason: http://www.project-reason.org/bibleContra_big.pdf.

WGBH Educational Foundation and Clear Blue Sky Productions. n.d. "Evolution: Library: Ken Ham: Bliblical Literalist." Retrieved July 9, 2009, from PBS: http://www.pbs.org/wgbh/evolution/library/08/1/l_081_04.html.

White, A. 2007. "A Global Projection of Subjective Well-Being: A Challenge to Positive Psychology." *Psychtalk*, pp. 17–20.

———. November 14, 2006. "Psychologist Produces the First-Ever 'World Map of Happiness.'" From www.sciencedaily.com: http://www.sciencedaily.com/releases/2006/11/061113093726.htm.

Whitney, C. R. August 5, 1997. *Jeanne Calment, World's Elder, Dies at 122*. Retrieved December 28, 2014, from the *New York Times*: http://query.nytimes.com/gst/fullpage.html?res=9C01E7D711 3DF936A3575BC0A961958260.

Word Vision Resources. 2010. *The Poverty and Justice Bible*. Retrieved May 8, 2011, from http://www.worldvisionresources.com/poverty-justice-bible-p-376.html.

World Without End. October 9, 2010. "Pastor John Hagee—Cornerstone Church Ministry, Heresy, Divorce & Dirty Deeds." Retrieved September 12, 2011, from World Without End: http://worldwithoutend.info/wwewp/?p=316.

Yahya, H. May 28, 2003. *Darwin's Racism*. Retrieved May 17, 2012, from Media Monitors Network: http://www.mediamonitors.net/harunyahya44.html.

Zaccaro, L. February 15, 2010. "Why Do Some People Live So Long? Researchers Study Centenarians' Genes, Lifestyle." Retrieved December 28, 2014, from ABC News: http://abcnews.go.com/GMA/OnCall/science-centenarians-live-100/story?id=9836752.

Zuckerman, P. 2005. "Atheism: Contemporary Rates and Patterns." In M. E. Martin, *The Cambridge Companion to Atheism* (pp. 47–65). Cambridge: Cambridge University Press.

ABOUT THE AUTHOR

Tony Davis is a retired Army officer, former county director for a congressionally chartered nonprofit organization in South Korea, and civil servant. He holds a bachelor's degree in political science and a master's degree in international relations. He is a graduate of both the US Army Command and General Staff College and the Joint Forces Staff College and is currently pursuing a second master's degree in professional writing from New York University.

In 1990, Tony began serving his country in the United States Army as a career military intelligence officer, retiring from Special Operations Command as a lieutenant colonel in 2011. In the interim, from commissioning to retirement, Tony served in a wide variety of staff and leadership positions globally, including combat operations in Iraq. Other overseas assignments and deployments include Germany, South Korea, Japan, Thailand, Egypt, Croatia, Spain, Qatar, Kuwait, Jordan, Bangladesh, and many others.

His hobbies include SCUBA diving, classical guitar, and traveling (forty-nine countries and forty-five states so far and counting).

Follow on Twitter and Instagram: @TonyOBDavis